AGN Kub
33327007688110
Kubert, Joe, 1926-
Jew Gangster [graphic novel]

JEW GANGSTER

JOE KUBERT

D1065761

LIBRARY DISCARD
NON RETURNABLE

DC COMICS
THE JOE KUBERT LIBRARY

MOOSE JAW PUBLIC LIBRARY

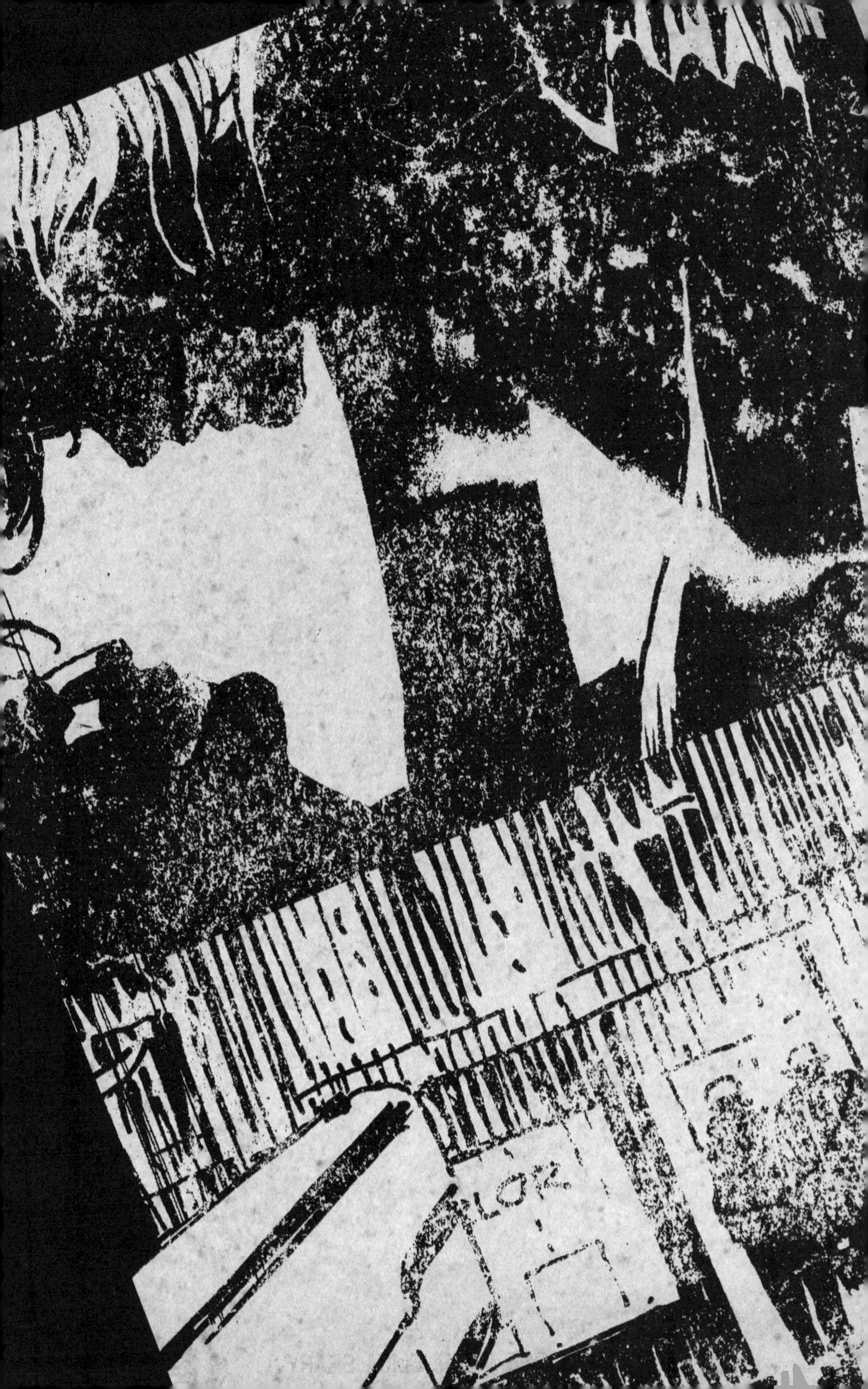

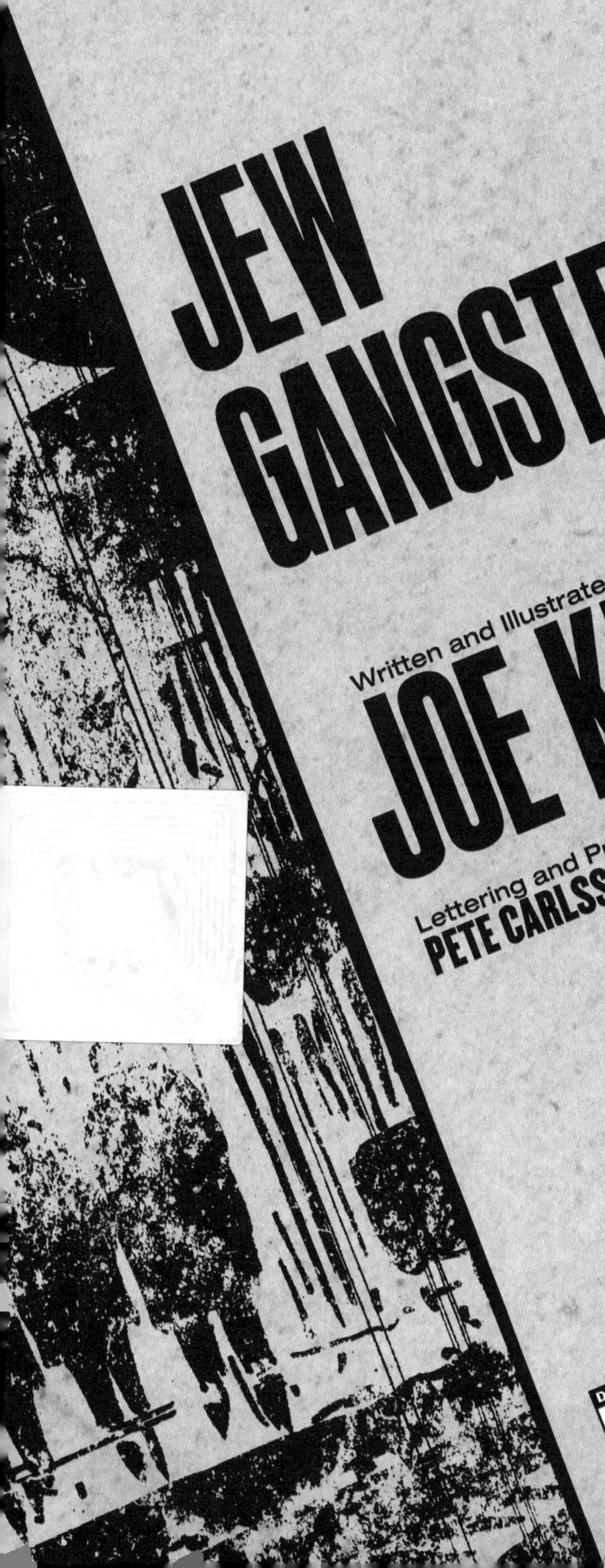

JEW GANGSTER

Written and Illustrated by

JOE KUBERT

Lettering and Production by

PETE CARLSSON

DC COMICS THE JOE KUBERT LIBRARY

Karen Berger SVP – Executive Editor
Will Dennis Editor
Robbin Brosterman Design Director – Books
Louis Prandi Art Director

DC COMICS
Diane Nelson President
Dan DiDio and Jim Lee Co-Publishers
Geoff Johns Chief Creative Officer
Patrick Caldon EVP – Finance and Administration
John Rood EVP – Sales, Marketing and Business Development
Amy Genkins SVP – Business and Legal Affairs
Steve Rotterdam SVP – Sales and Marketing
John Cunningham VP – Marketing
Terri Cunningham VP – Managing Editor
Alison Gill VP – Manufacturing
David Hyde VP – Publicity
Sue Pohja VP – Book Trade Sales
Alysse Soll VP – Advertising and Custom Publishing
Bob Wayne VP – Sales
Mark Chiarello Art Director

JEW GANGSTER
Published by DC Comics, 1700 Broadway, New York, NY 10019.
Copyright © 2005 by Joe Kubert. All rights reserved. All characters, the
distinctive likenesses thereof and all related elements are trademarks of
Joe Kubert. The stories, characters and incidents mentioned in this book
are entirely fictional. DC Comics does not read or accept unsolicited
submissions of ideas, stories or artwork. Printed in the USA.
First Printing. DC Comics, a Warner Bros. Entertainment Company.
ISBN: 978-1-4012-3179-8

SUSTAINABLE
FORESTRY
INITIATIVE
Certified Chain of Custody
Promoting Sustainable
Forest Management
www.sfiprogram.org
Fiber used in this product line meets the
sourcing requirements of the SFI program.
www.sfiprogram.org SGS-SFI/COC-US10/81072

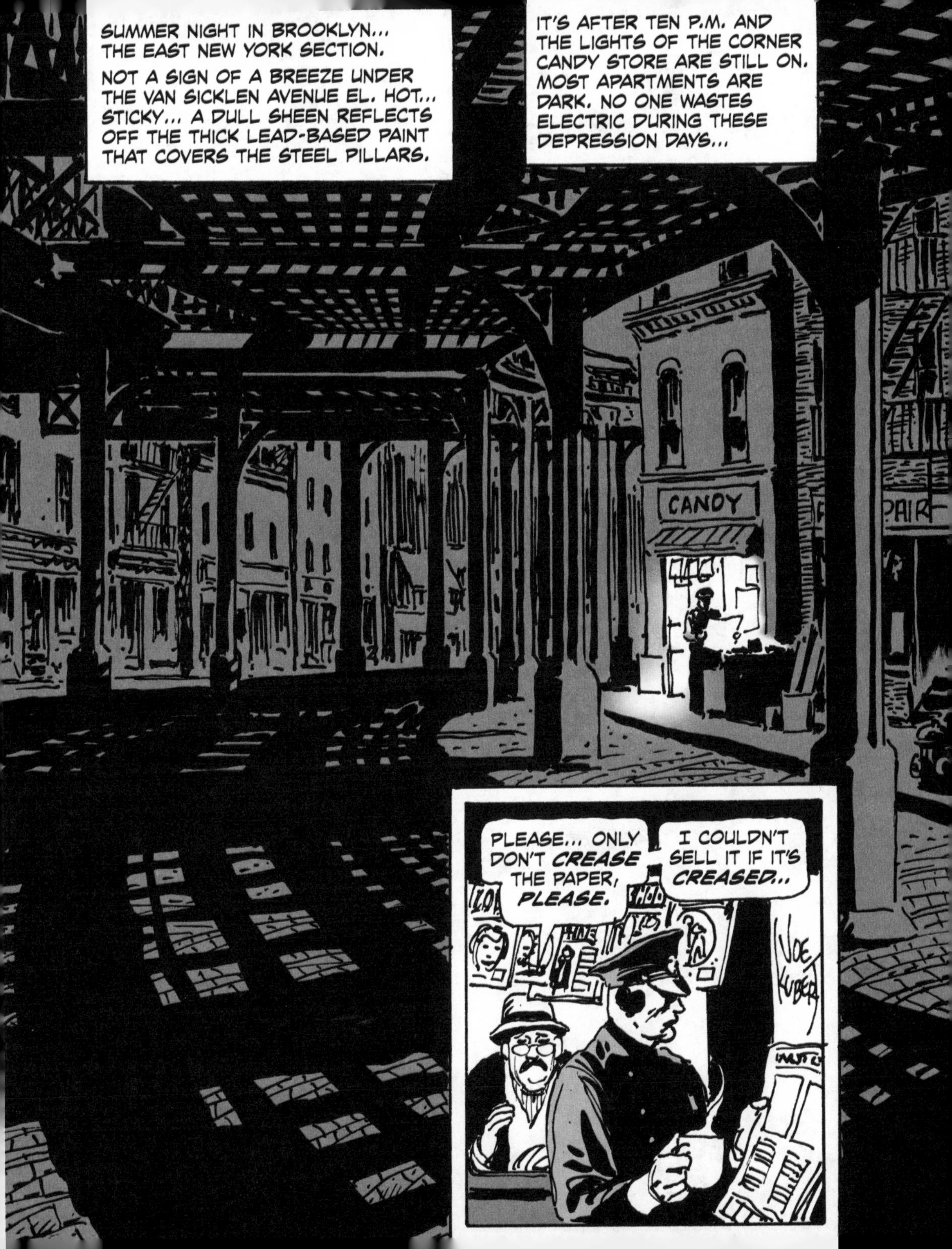
SUMMER NIGHT IN BROOKLYN... THE EAST NEW YORK SECTION.
NOT A SIGN OF A BREEZE UNDER THE VAN SICKLEN AVENUE EL. HOT... STICKY... A DULL SHEEN REFLECTS OFF THE THICK LEAD-BASED PAINT THAT COVERS THE STEEL PILLARS.
IT'S AFTER TEN P.M. AND THE LIGHTS OF THE CORNER CANDY STORE ARE STILL ON. MOST APARTMENTS ARE DARK. NO ONE WASTES ELECTRIC DURING THESE DEPRESSION DAYS...
CANDY
PLEASE... ONLY DON'T CREASE THE PAPER, PLEASE.
I COULDN'T SELL IT IF IT'S CREASED...
JOE KUBERT

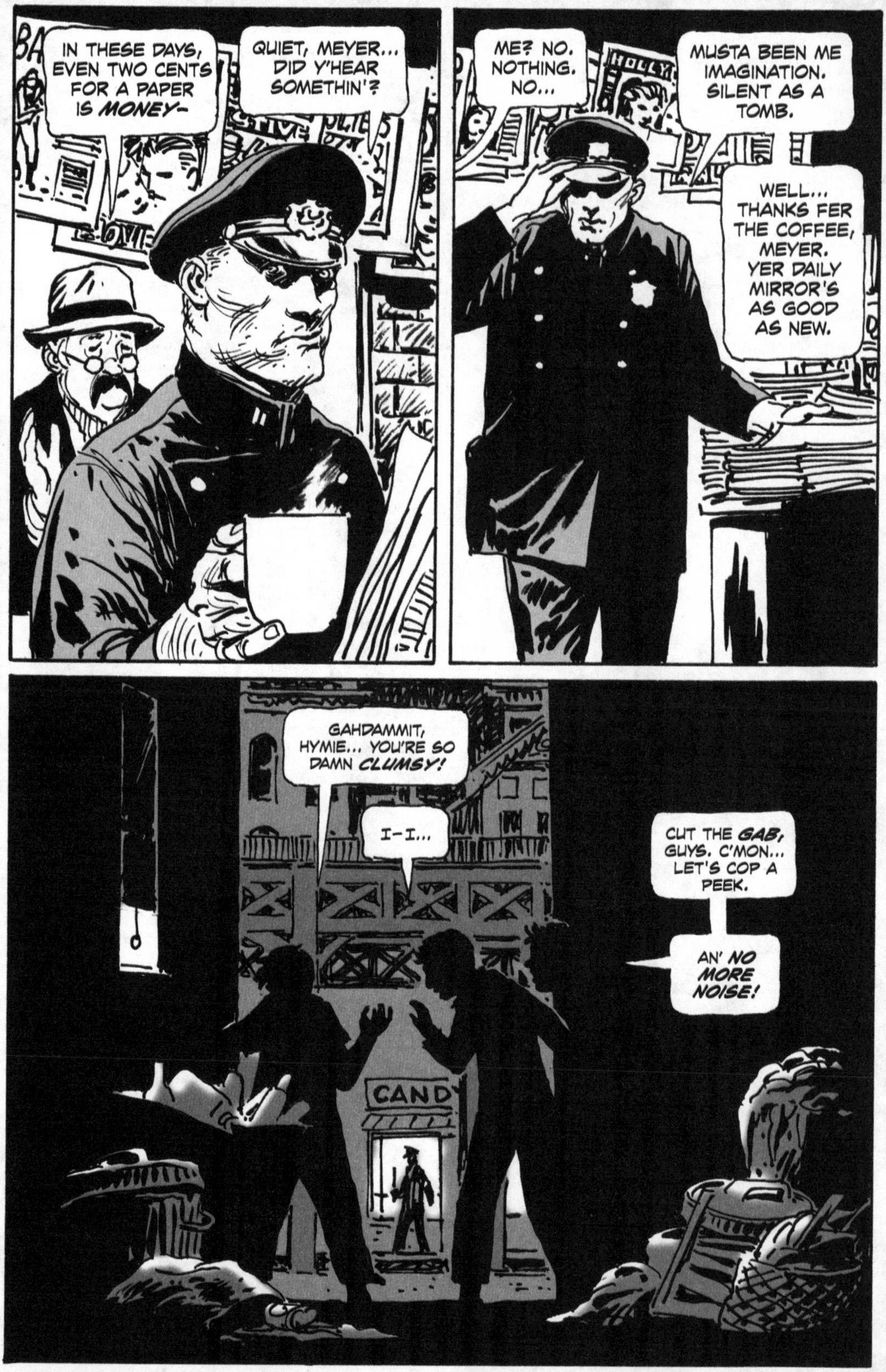
IN THESE DAYS, EVEN TWO CENTS FOR A PAPER IS *MONEY*-
QUIET, MEYER... DID Y'HEAR SOMETHIN'?
ME? NO. NOTHING. NO...
MUSTA BEEN ME IMAGINATION. SILENT AS A TOMB.
WELL... THANKS FER THE COFFEE, MEYER. YER DAILY MIRROR'S AS GOOD AS NEW.
GAHDAMMIT, HYMIE... YOU'RE SO DAMN *CLUMSY!*
I-I...
CUT THE *GAB*, GUYS. C'MON... LET'S COP A PEEK.
AN' *NO MORE NOISE!*
CAND

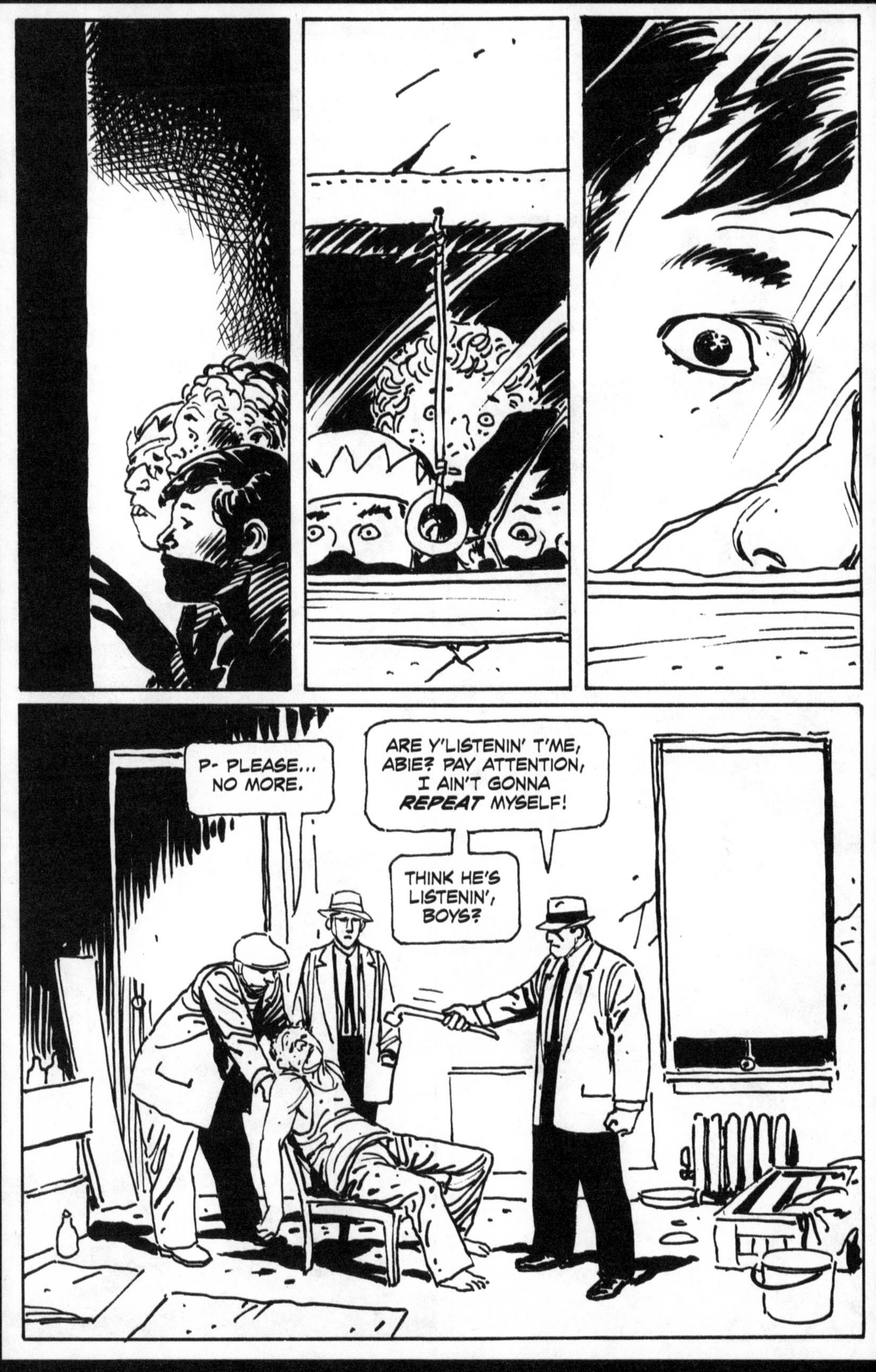
P- PLEASE... NO MORE.
ARE Y'LISTENIN' T'ME, ABIE? PAY ATTENTION, I AIN'T GONNA *REPEAT* MYSELF!
THINK HE'S LISTENIN', BOYS?

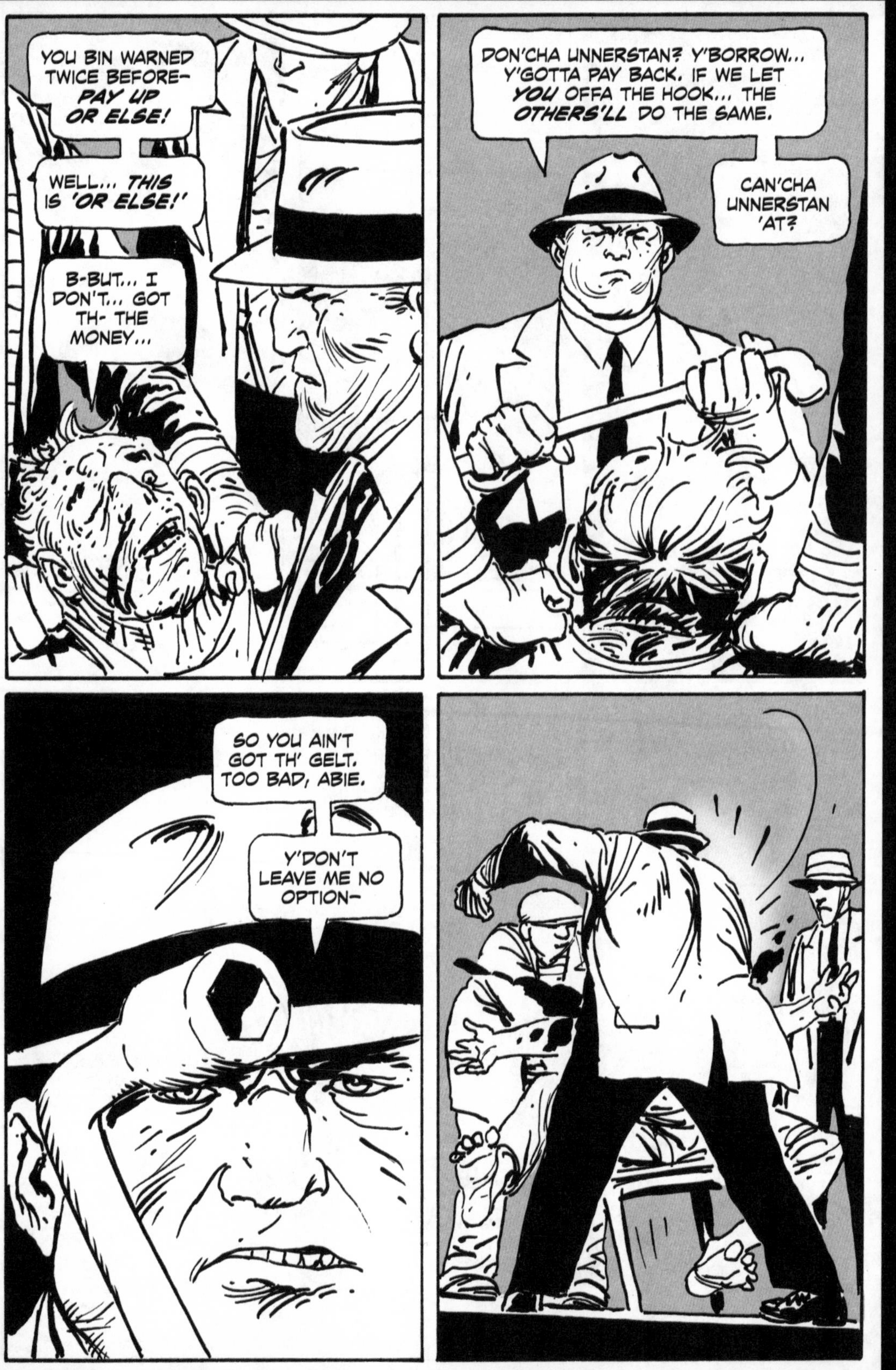
YOU BIN WARNED TWICE BEFORE- PAY UP OR ELSE!
WELL... THIS IS 'OR ELSE!'
B-BUT... I DON'T... GOT TH- THE MONEY...
DON'CHA UNNERSTAN? Y'BORROW... Y'GOTTA PAY BACK. IF WE LET YOU OFFA THE HOOK... THE OTHERS'LL DO THE SAME.
CAN'CHA UNNERSTAN 'AT?
SO YOU AIN'T GOT TH' GELT. TOO BAD, ABIE.
Y'DON'T LEAVE ME NO OPTION-

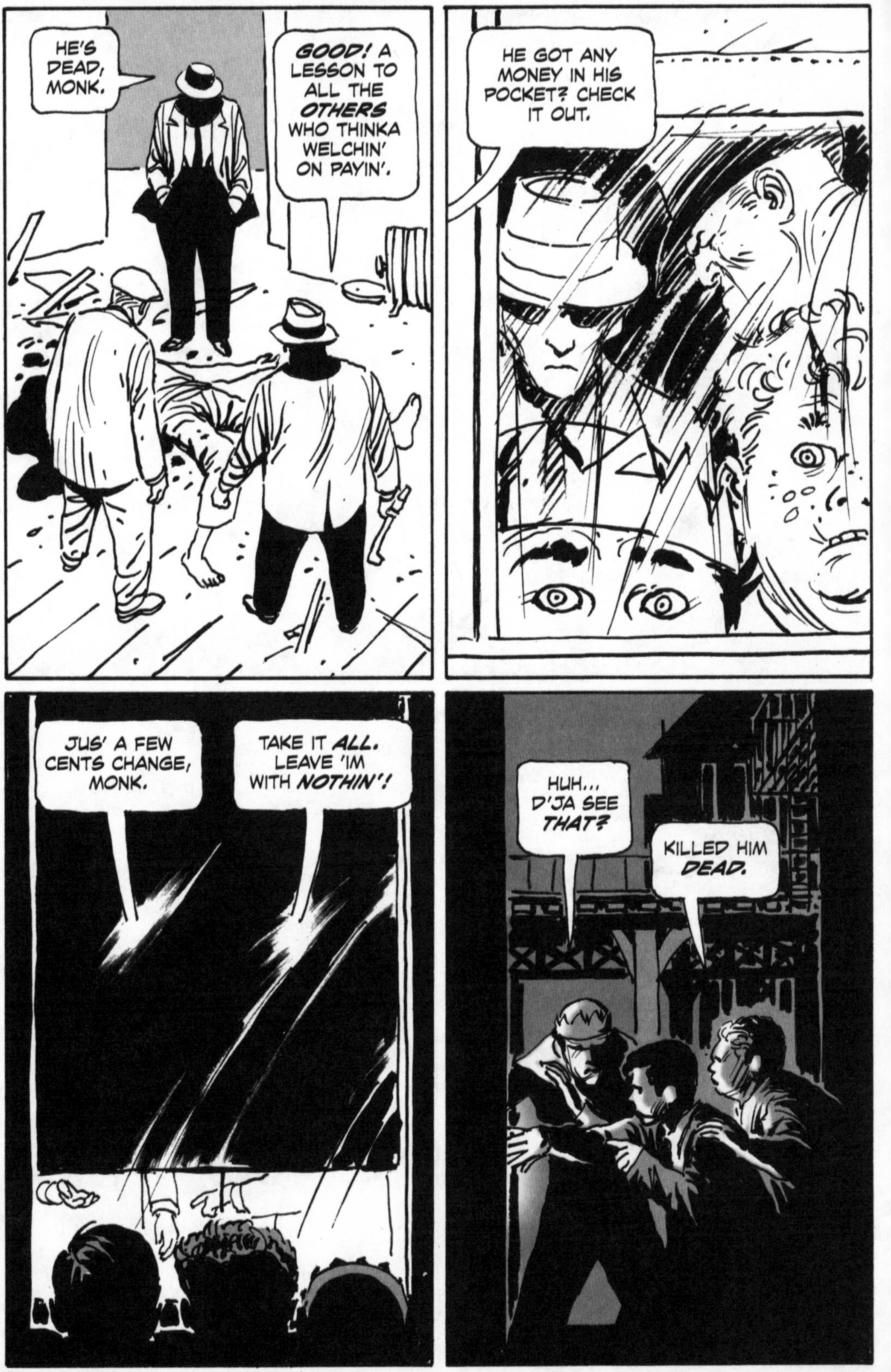
HE'S DEAD, MONK.
GOOD! A LESSON TO ALL THE OTHERS WHO THINKA WELCHIN' ON PAYIN'.
HE GOT ANY MONEY IN HIS POCKET? CHECK IT OUT.
JUS' A FEW CENTS CHANGE, MONK.
TAKE IT ALL. LEAVE 'IM WITH NOTHIN'!
HUH... D'JA SEE THAT?
KILLED HIM DEAD.

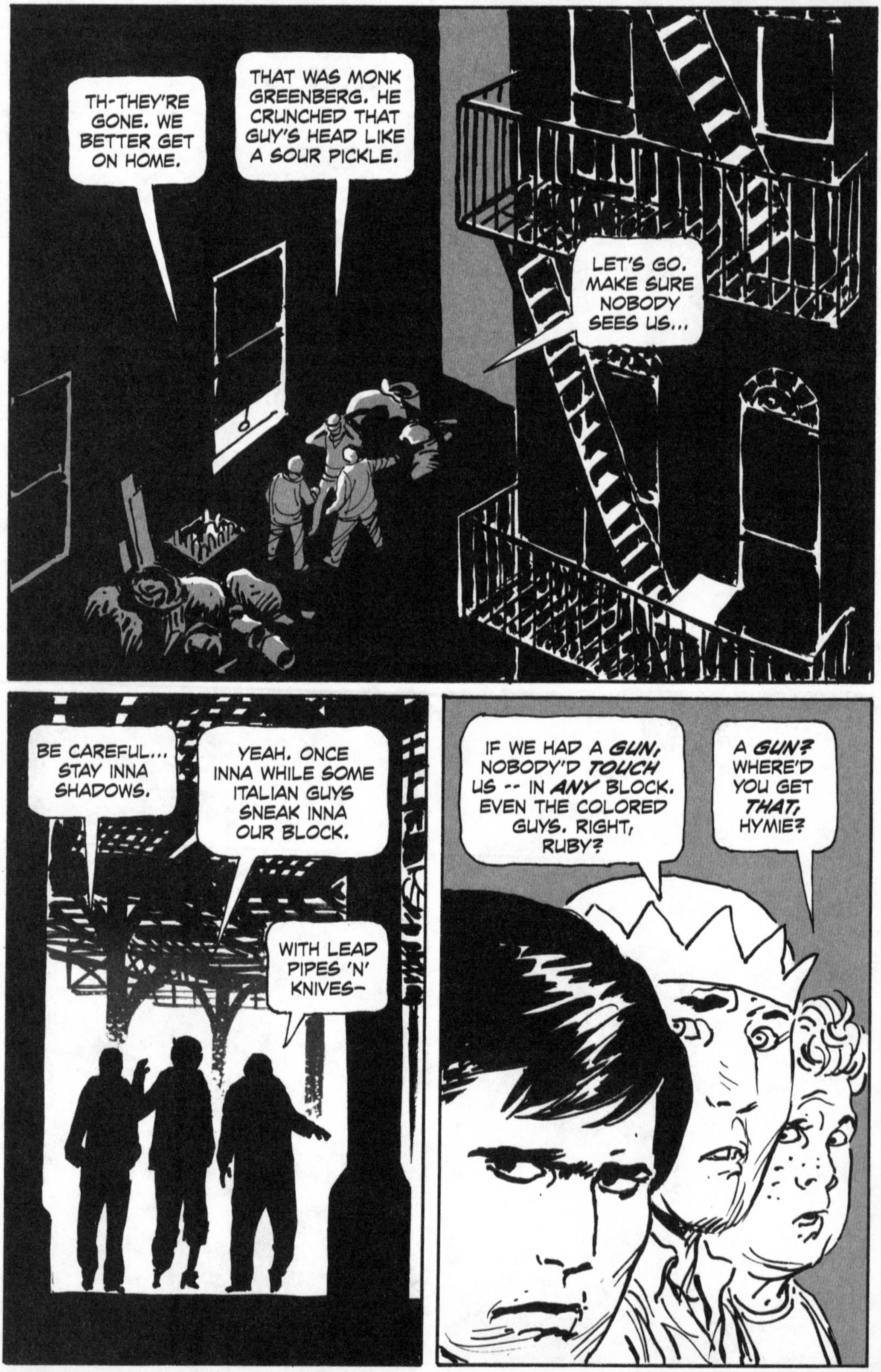
TH-THEY'RE GONE. WE BETTER GET ON HOME.
THAT WAS MONK GREENBERG. HE CRUNCHED THAT GUY'S HEAD LIKE A SOUR PICKLE.
LET'S GO. MAKE SURE NOBODY SEES US...
BE CAREFUL... STAY INNA SHADOWS.
YEAH. ONCE INNA WHILE SOME ITALIAN GUYS SNEAK INNA OUR BLOCK.
WITH LEAD PIPES 'N' KNIVES—
IF WE HAD A GUN, NOBODY'D TOUCH US -- IN ANY BLOCK. EVEN THE COLORED GUYS. RIGHT, RUBY?
A GUN? WHERE'D YOU GET THAT, HYMIE?

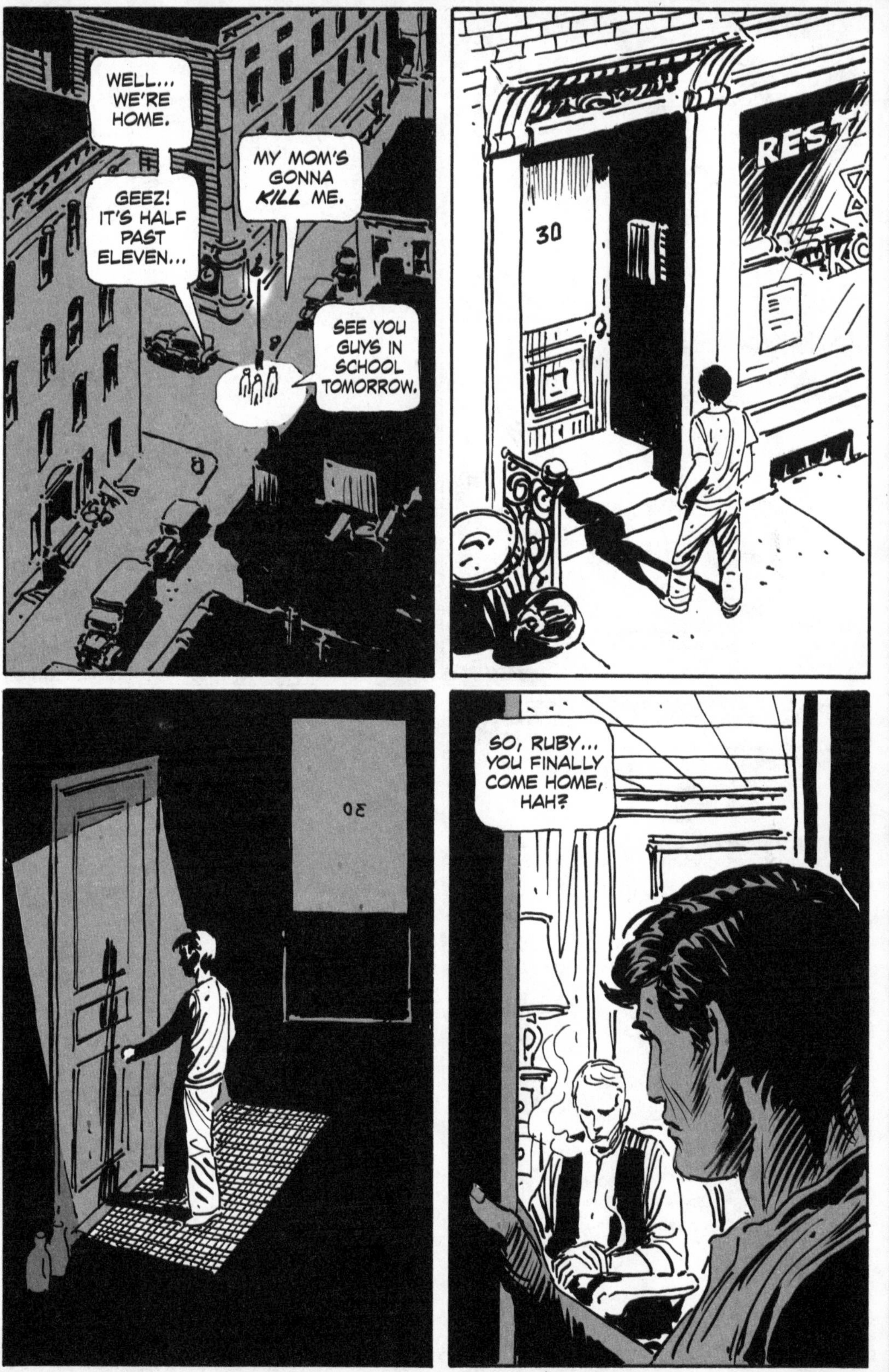
WELL... WE'RE HOME.
GEEZ! IT'S HALF PAST ELEVEN...
MY MOM'S GONNA *KILL* ME.
SEE YOU GUYS IN SCHOOL TOMORROW.
RES
30
30
SO, RUBY... YOU FINALLY COME HOME, HAH?

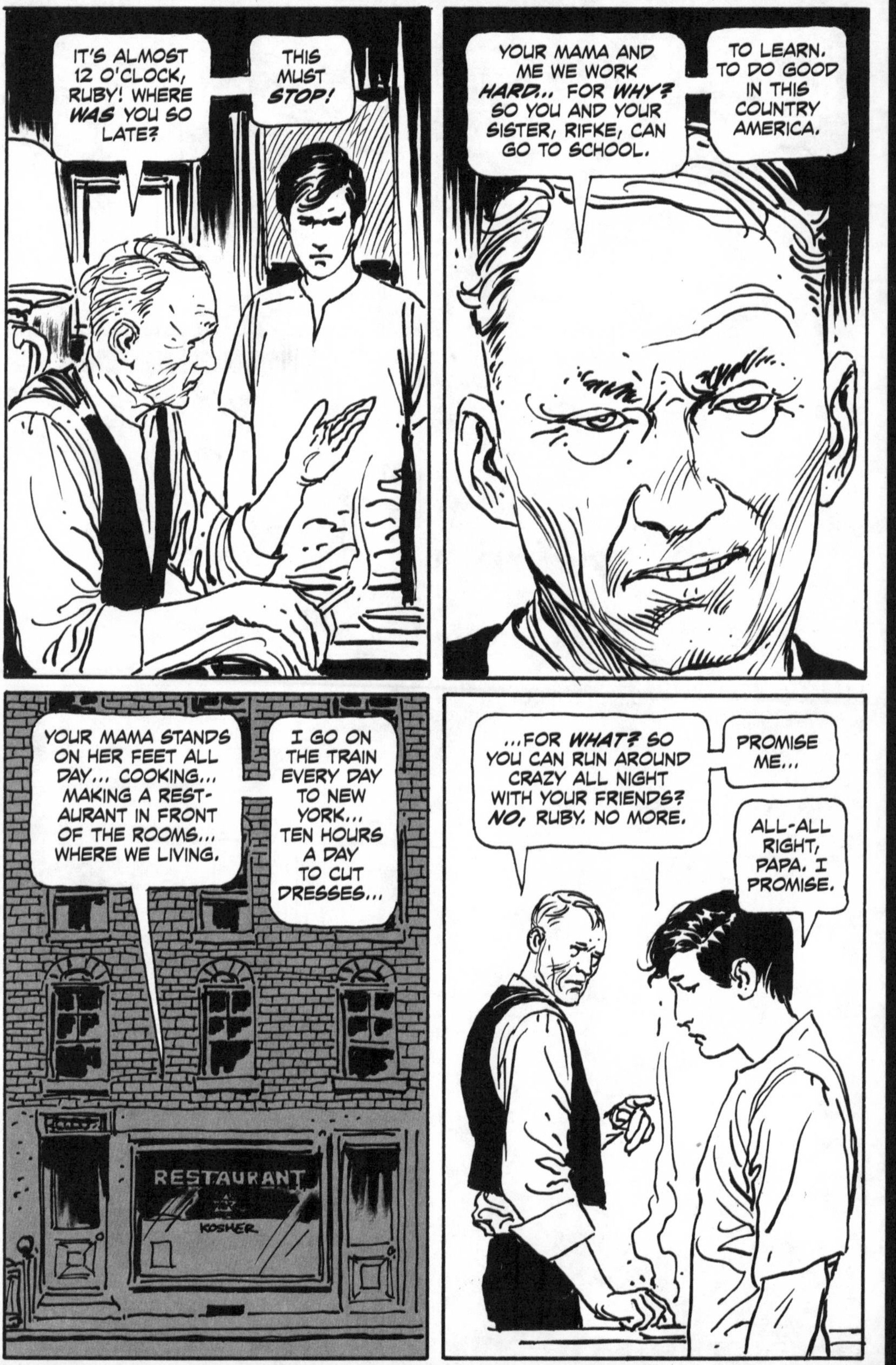
IT'S ALMOST 12 O'CLOCK, RUBY! WHERE WAS YOU SO LATE?
THIS MUST STOP!
YOUR MAMA AND ME WE WORK HARD... FOR WHY? SO YOU AND YOUR SISTER, RIFKE, CAN GO TO SCHOOL.
TO LEARN. TO DO GOOD IN THIS COUNTRY AMERICA.
YOUR MAMA STANDS ON HER FEET ALL DAY... COOKING... MAKING A REST-AURANT IN FRONT OF THE ROOMS... WHERE WE LIVING.
I GO ON THE TRAIN EVERY DAY TO NEW YORK... TEN HOURS A DAY TO CUT DRESSES...
RESTAURANT
KOSHER
...FOR WHAT? SO YOU CAN RUN AROUND CRAZY ALL NIGHT WITH YOUR FRIENDS? NO, RUBY. NO MORE.
PROMISE ME...
ALL-ALL RIGHT, PAPA. I PROMISE.

RIFKE'S FAST ASLEEP. EVEN THE *HEAT* DOESN'T BOTHER HER.

IT'S SO HOT. THERE'S NO *AIR.*

AM I GONNA BE LIKE PAPA? WORKING FOR PENNIES... MY LUNCH IN A PAPER BAG... TEN CENTS IN MY POCKET FOR CARFARE. EVERY DAY THE SAME...

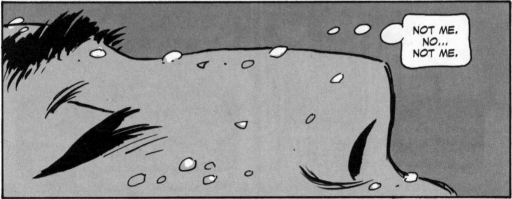

NOT ME. NO... NOT ME.

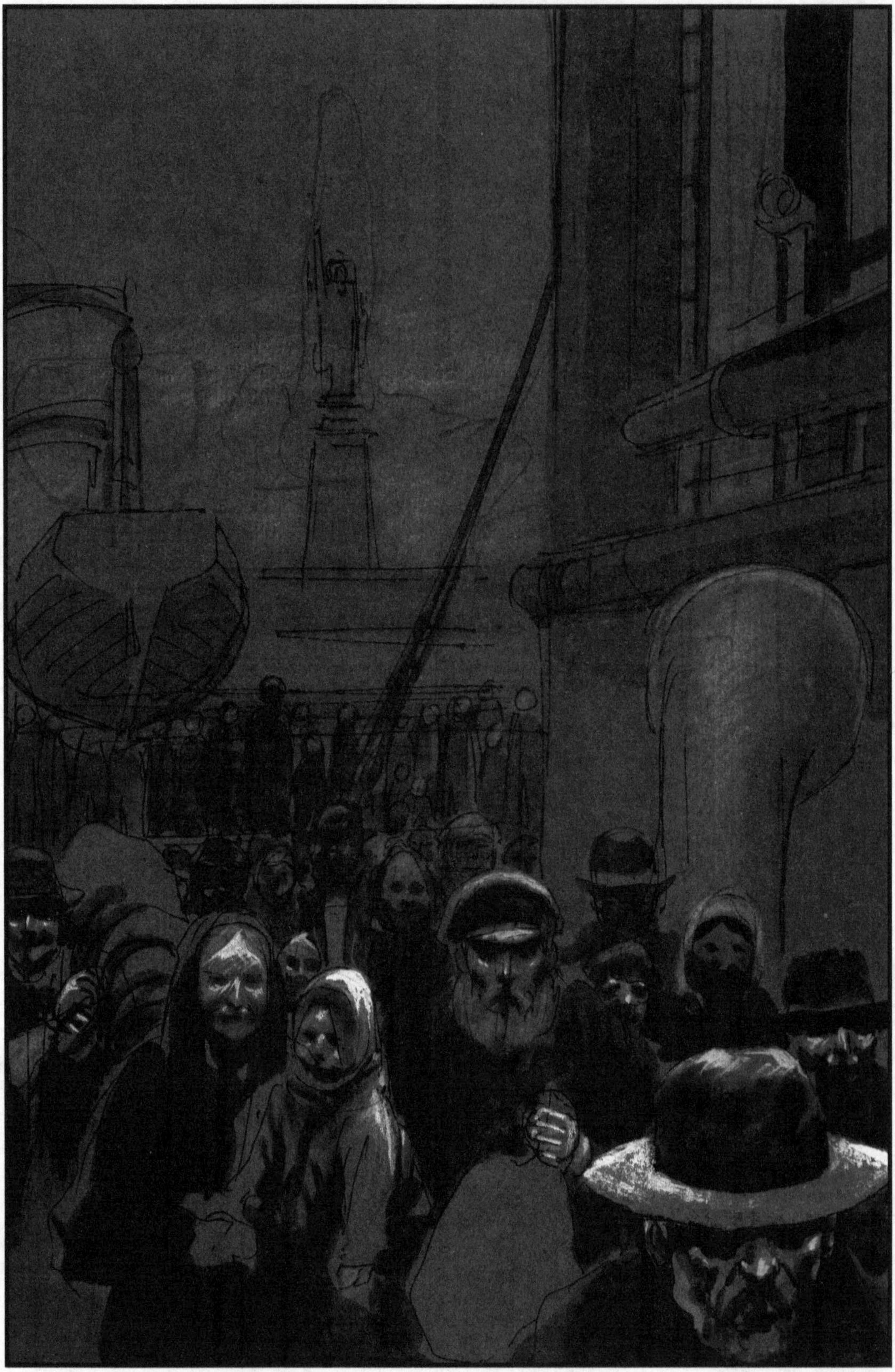

Arrival at Ellis Island

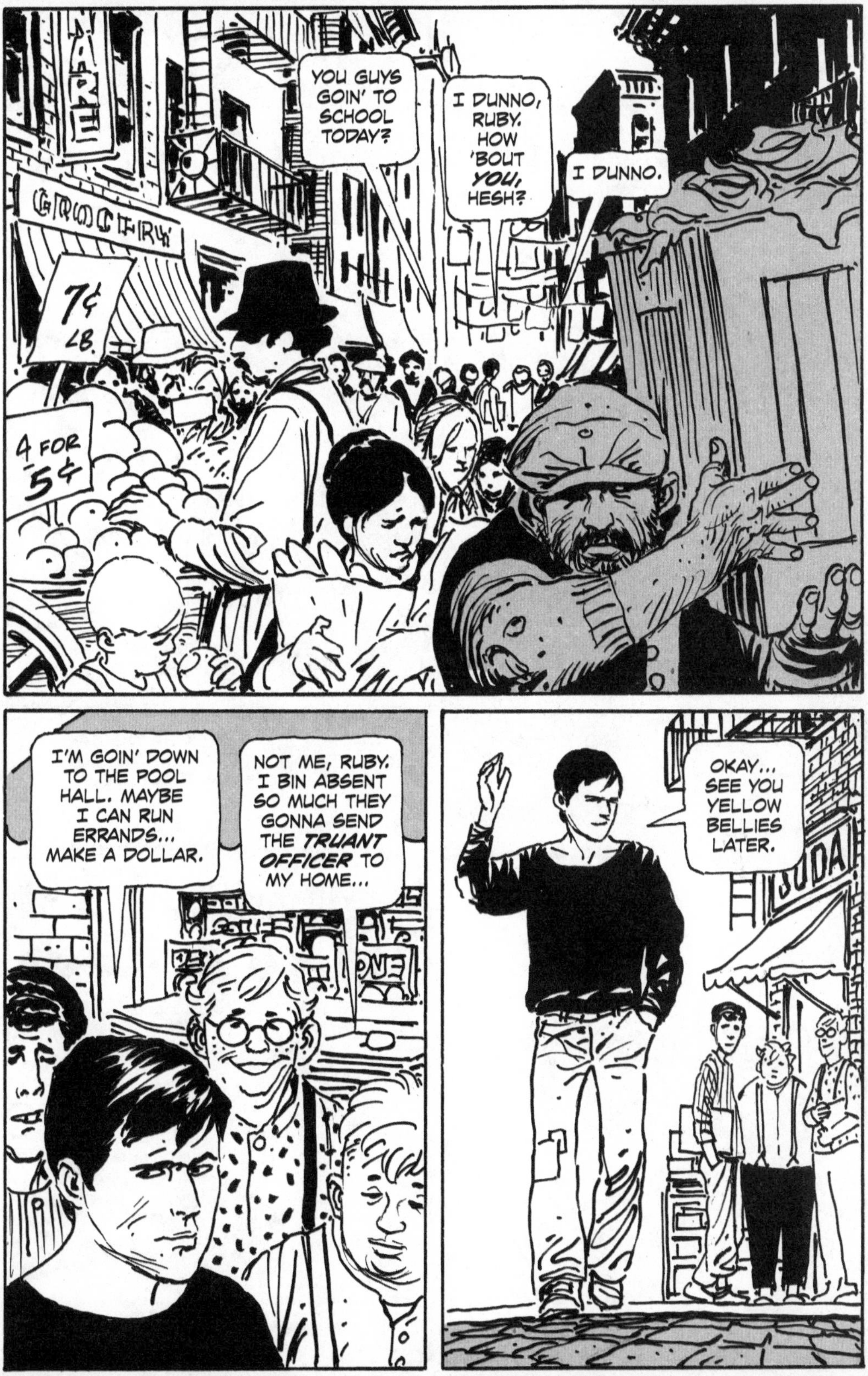
ARE
GROCERY
7¢ LB.
4 FOR 5¢
YOU GUYS GOIN' TO SCHOOL TODAY?
I DUNNO, RUBY. HOW 'BOUT YOU, HESH?
I DUNNO.
I'M GOIN' DOWN TO THE POOL HALL. MAYBE I CAN RUN ERRANDS... MAKE A DOLLAR.
NOT ME, RUBY. I BIN ABSENT SO MUCH THEY GONNA SEND THE TRUANT OFFICER TO MY HOME...
OKAY... SEE YOU YELLOW BELLIES LATER.
SODA

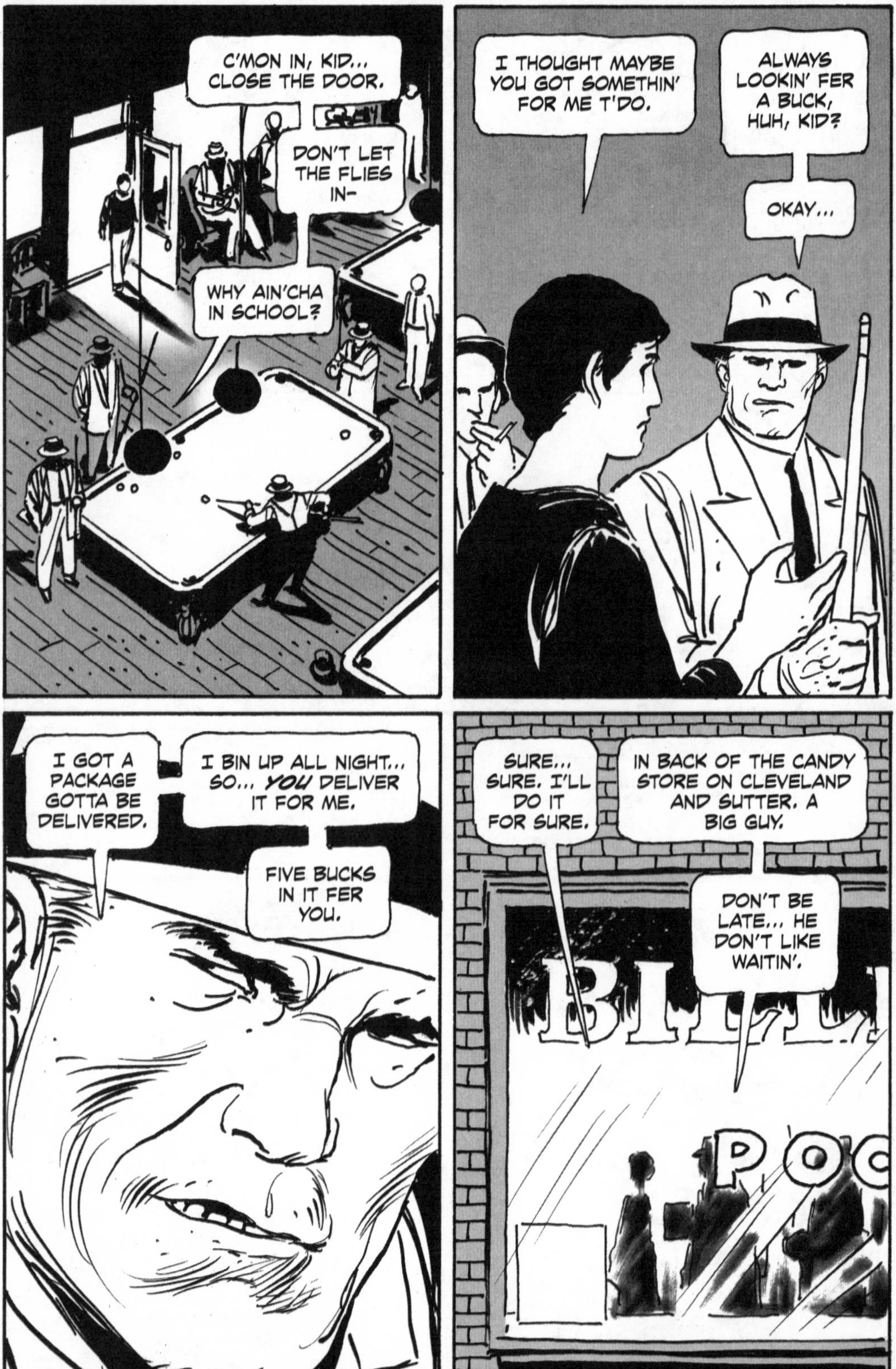
C'MON IN, KID... CLOSE THE DOOR.
DON'T LET THE FLIES IN–
WHY AIN'CHA IN SCHOOL?
I THOUGHT MAYBE YOU GOT SOMETHIN' FOR ME T'DO.
ALWAYS LOOKIN' FER A BUCK, HUH, KID?
OKAY...
I GOT A PACKAGE GOTTA BE DELIVERED.
I BIN UP ALL NIGHT... SO... *YOU* DELIVER IT FOR ME.
FIVE BUCKS IN IT FER YOU.
SURE... SURE. I'LL DO IT FOR SURE.
IN BACK OF THE CANDY STORE ON CLEVELAND AND SUTTER. A BIG GUY.
DON'T BE LATE... HE DON'T LIKE WAITIN'.
POO

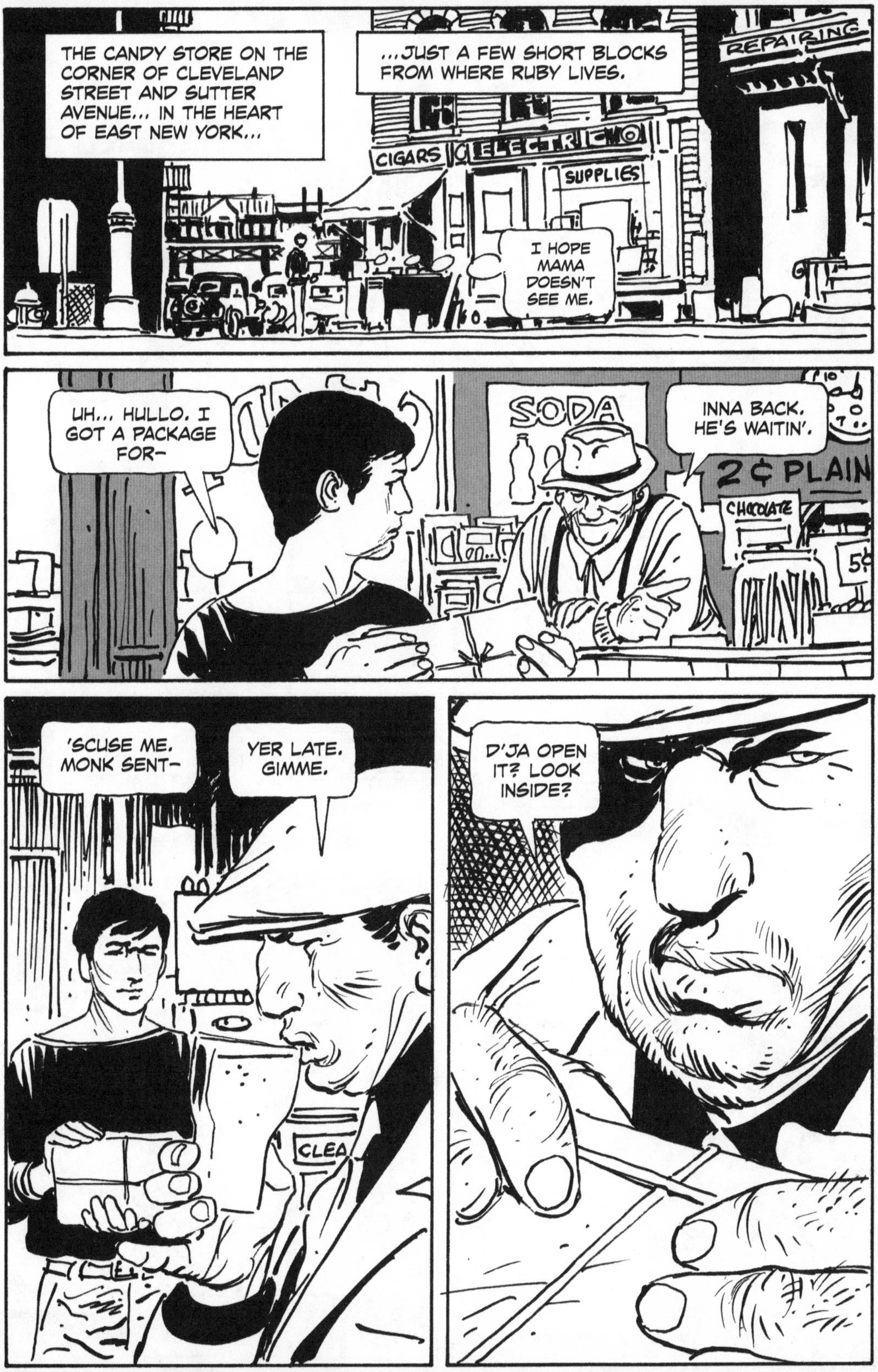
THE CANDY STORE ON THE CORNER OF CLEVELAND STREET AND SUTTER AVENUE... IN THE HEART OF EAST NEW YORK...
...JUST A FEW SHORT BLOCKS FROM WHERE RUBY LIVES.
REPAIRING
CIGARS
ELECTRIC
SUPPLIES
I HOPE MAMA DOESN'T SEE ME.
UH... HULLO. I GOT A PACKAGE FOR–
SODA
INNA BACK. HE'S WAITIN'.
2¢ PLAIN
CHOCOLATE
5¢
'SCUSE ME. MONK SENT–
YER LATE. GIMME.
CLEA
D'JA OPEN IT? LOOK INSIDE?

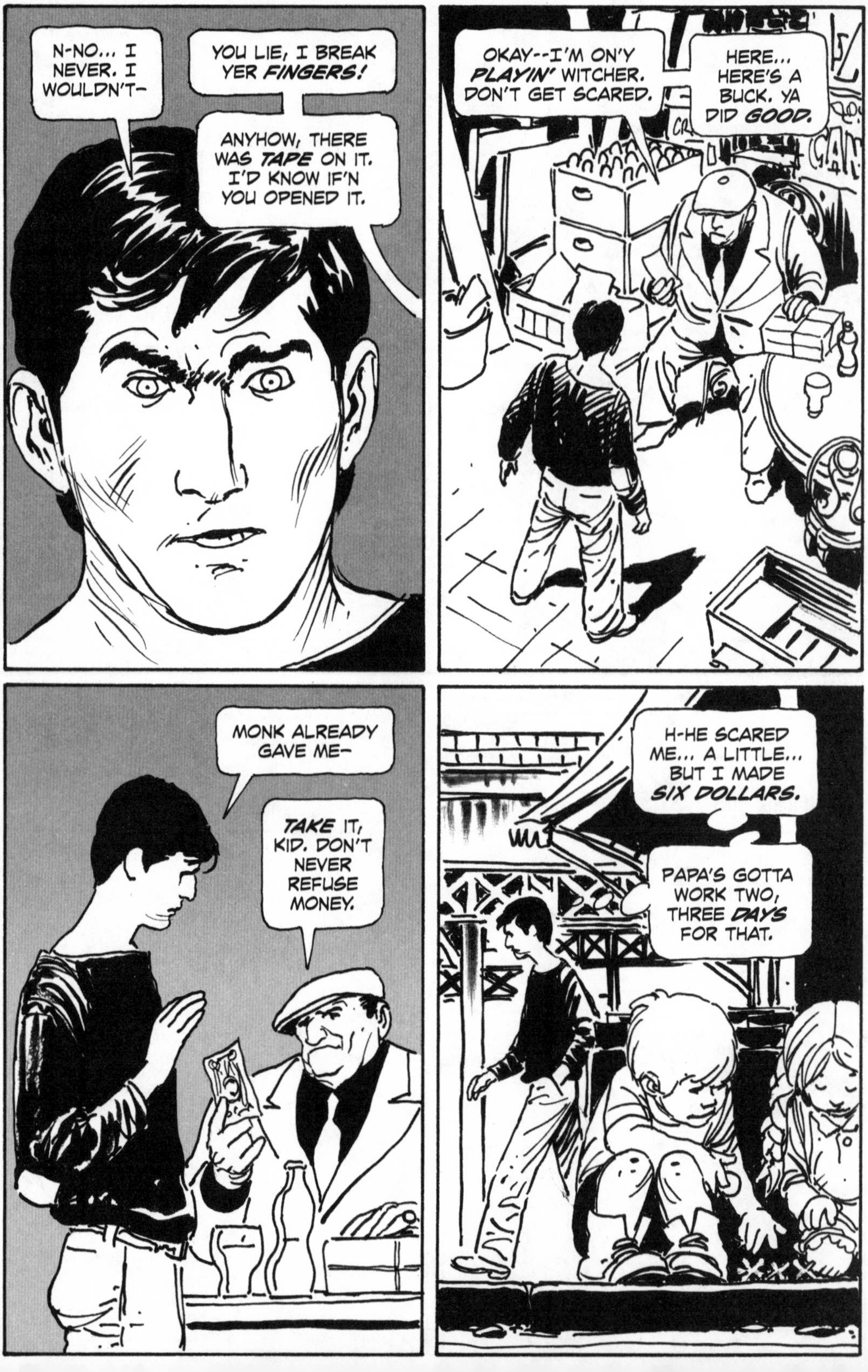
N-NO... I NEVER. I WOULDN'T-
YOU LIE, I BREAK YER FINGERS!
ANYHOW, THERE WAS TAPE ON IT. I'D KNOW IF'N YOU OPENED IT.
OKAY--I'M ON'Y PLAYIN' WITCHER. DON'T GET SCARED.
HERE... HERE'S A BUCK. YA DID GOOD.
MONK ALREADY GAVE ME-
TAKE IT, KID. DON'T NEVER REFUSE MONEY.
H-HE SCARED ME... A LITTLE... BUT I MADE SIX DOLLARS.
PAPA'S GOTTA WORK TWO, THREE DAYS FOR THAT.

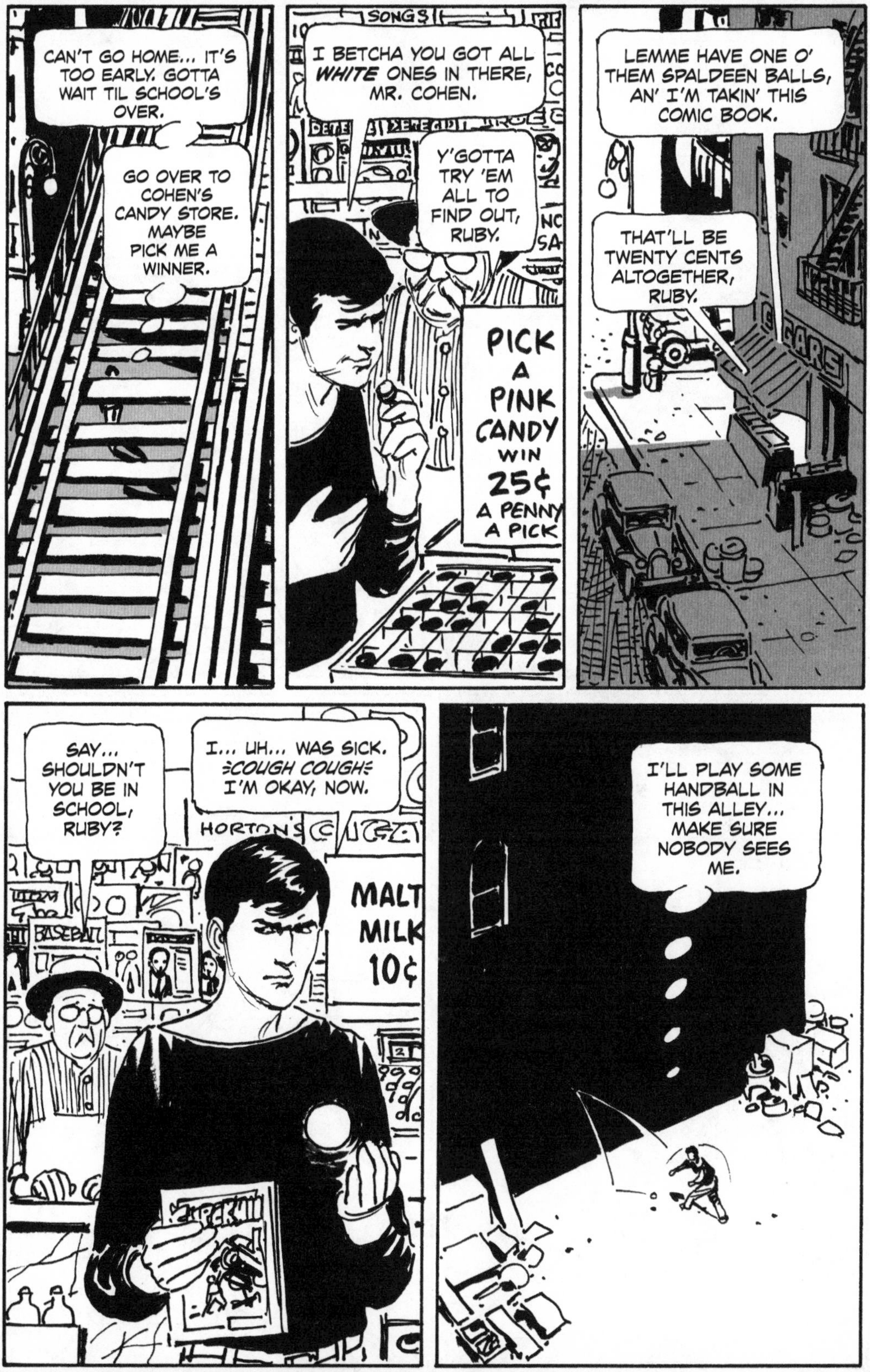
CAN'T GO HOME... IT'S TOO EARLY. GOTTA WAIT TIL SCHOOL'S OVER.
GO OVER TO COHEN'S CANDY STORE. MAYBE PICK ME A WINNER.
SONGS
I BETCHA YOU GOT ALL *WHITE* ONES IN THERE, MR. COHEN.
Y'GOTTA TRY 'EM ALL TO FIND OUT, RUBY.
PICK A PINK CANDY WIN 25¢ A PENNY A PICK
LEMME HAVE ONE O' THEM SPALDEEN BALLS, AN' I'M TAKIN' THIS COMIC BOOK.
THAT'LL BE TWENTY CENTS ALTOGETHER, RUBY.
CIGARS
SAY... SHOULDN'T YOU BE IN SCHOOL, RUBY?
I... UH... WAS SICK. *COUGH COUGH* I'M OKAY, NOW.
HORTON'S
BASEBALL
MALT MILK 10¢
I'LL PLAY SOME HANDBALL IN THIS ALLEY... MAKE SURE NOBODY SEES ME.

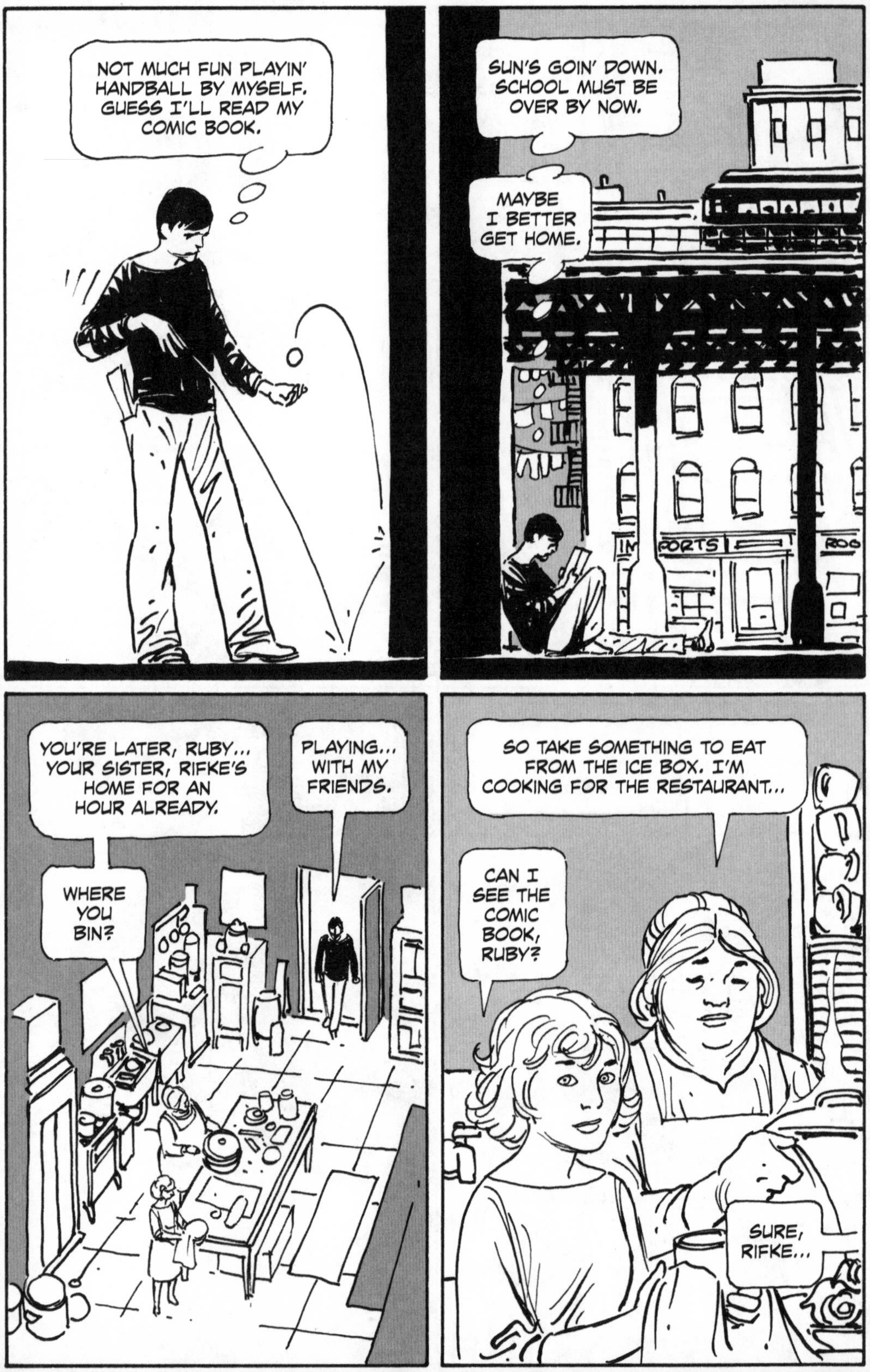
NOT MUCH FUN PLAYIN' HANDBALL BY MYSELF. GUESS I'LL READ MY COMIC BOOK.
SUN'S GOIN' DOWN. SCHOOL MUST BE OVER BY NOW.
MAYBE I BETTER GET HOME.
IMPORTS
YOU'RE LATER, RUBY... YOUR SISTER, RIFKE'S HOME FOR AN HOUR ALREADY.
WHERE YOU BIN?
PLAYING... WITH MY FRIENDS.
SO TAKE SOMETHING TO EAT FROM THE ICE BOX. I'M COOKING FOR THE RESTAURANT...
CAN I SEE THE COMIC BOOK, RUBY?
SURE, RIFKE...

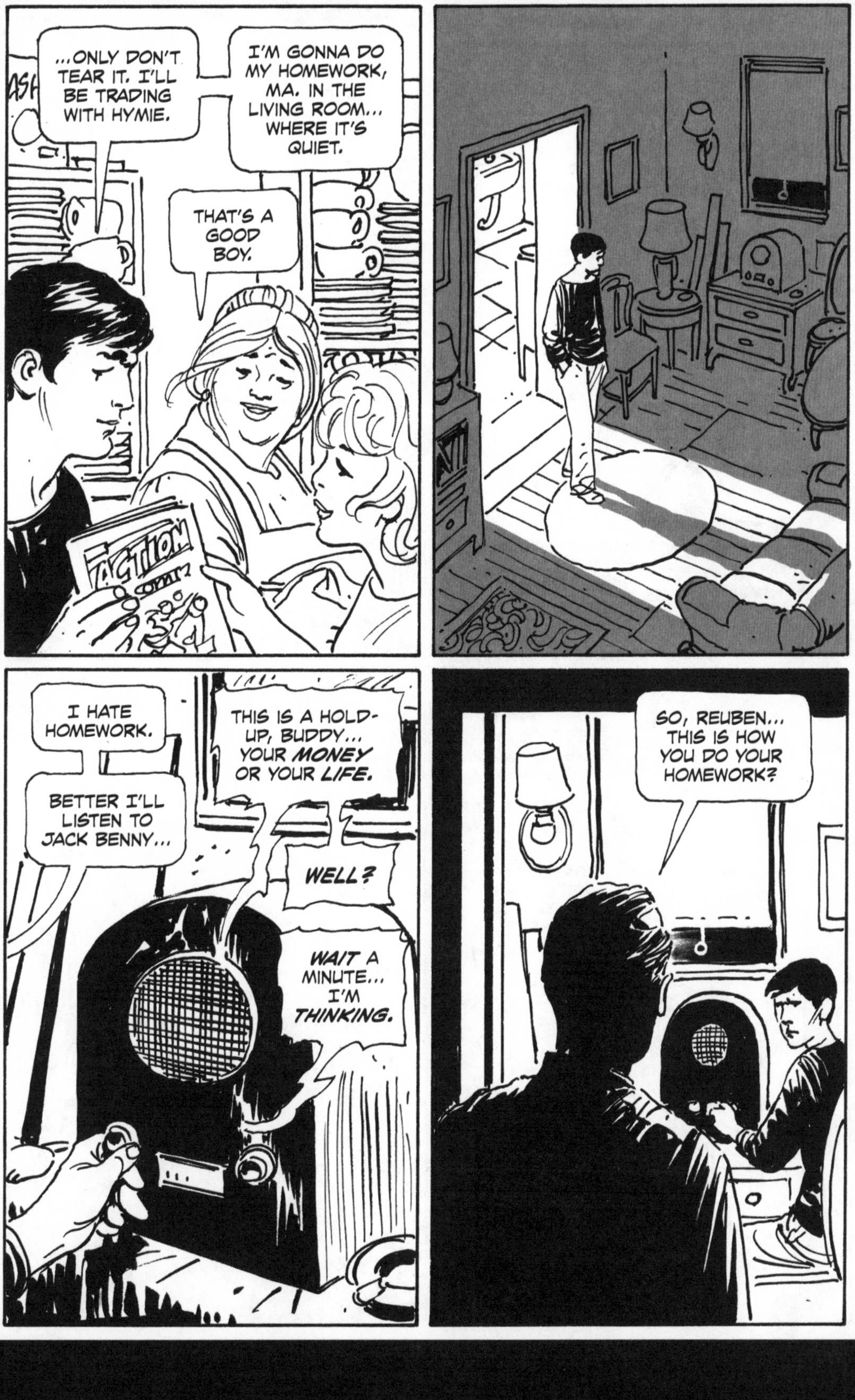
...ONLY DON'T TEAR IT. I'LL BE TRADING WITH HYMIE.
I'M GONNA DO MY HOMEWORK, MA. IN THE LIVING ROOM... WHERE IT'S QUIET.
THAT'S A GOOD BOY.
I HATE HOMEWORK.
BETTER I'LL LISTEN TO JACK BENNY...
THIS IS A HOLD-UP, BUDDY... YOUR *MONEY* OR YOUR *LIFE.*
WELL?
WAIT A MINUTE... I'M *THINKING.*
SO, REUBEN... THIS IS HOW YOU DO YOUR HOMEWORK?

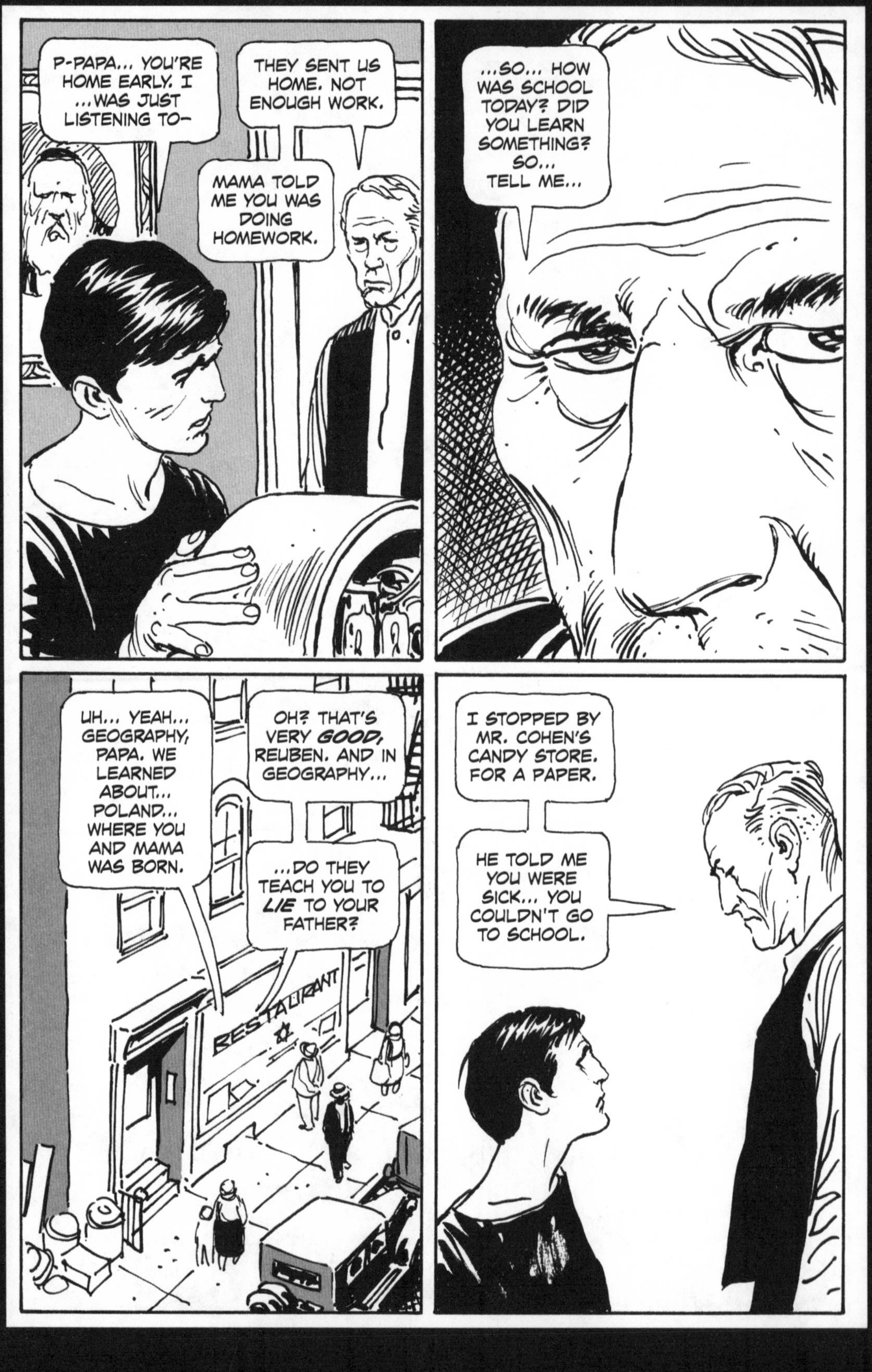
P-PAPA... YOU'RE HOME EARLY. I ...WAS JUST LISTENING TO—
THEY SENT US HOME. NOT ENOUGH WORK.
MAMA TOLD ME YOU WAS DOING HOMEWORK.
...SO... HOW WAS SCHOOL TODAY? DID YOU LEARN SOMETHING? SO... TELL ME...
UH... YEAH... GEOGRAPHY, PAPA. WE LEARNED ABOUT... POLAND... WHERE YOU AND MAMA WAS BORN.
OH? THAT'S VERY GOOD, REUBEN. AND IN GEOGRAPHY...
...DO THEY TEACH YOU TO LIE TO YOUR FATHER?
RESTAURANT
I STOPPED BY MR. COHEN'S CANDY STORE. FOR A PAPER.
HE TOLD ME YOU WERE SICK... YOU COULDN'T GO TO SCHOOL.

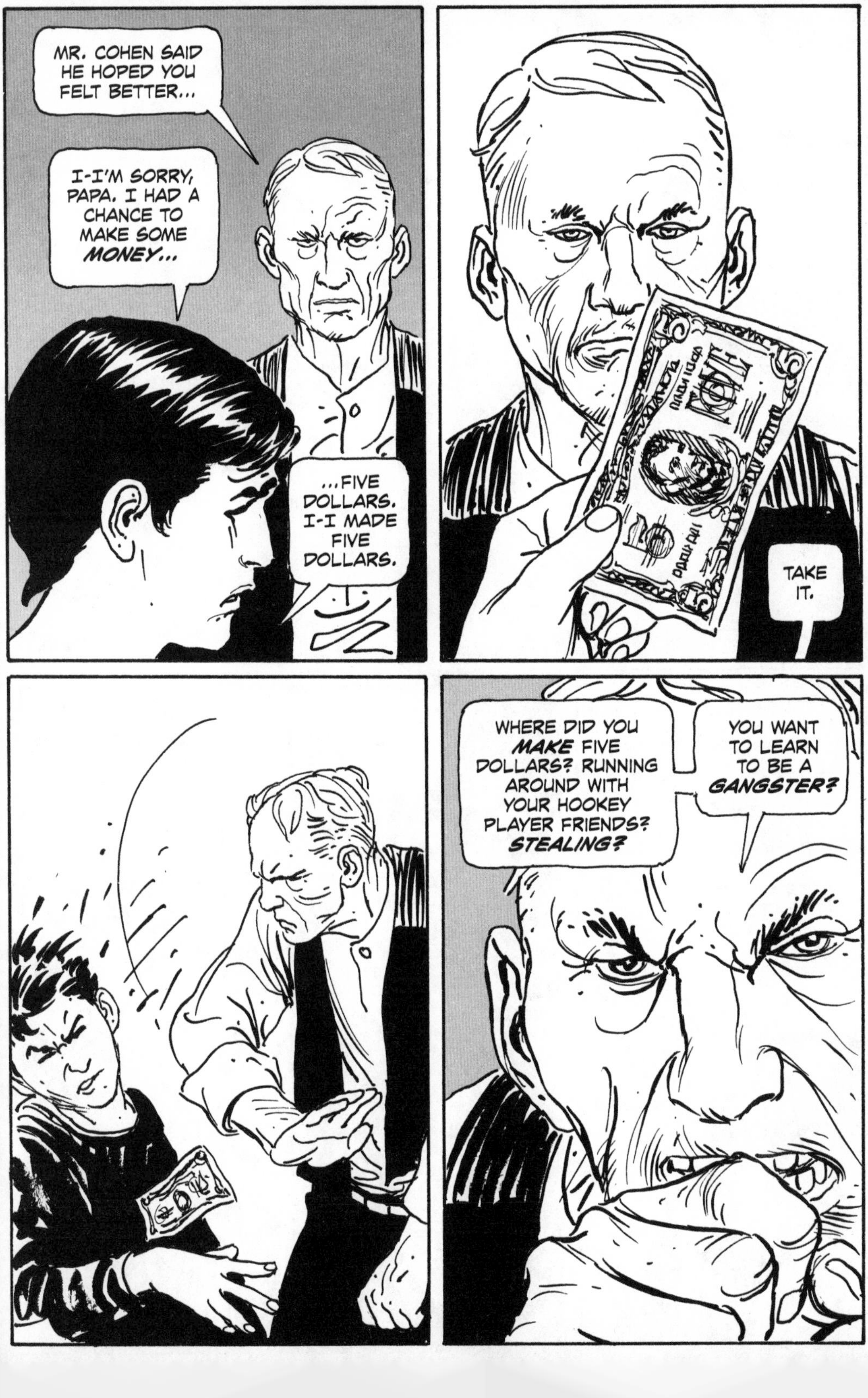
MR. COHEN SAID HE HOPED YOU FELT BETTER...
I-I'M SORRY, PAPA. I HAD A CHANCE TO MAKE SOME MONEY...
...FIVE DOLLARS. I-I MADE FIVE DOLLARS.
TAKE IT.
WHERE DID YOU MAKE FIVE DOLLARS? RUNNING AROUND WITH YOUR HOOKEY PLAYER FRIENDS? STEALING?
YOU WANT TO LEARN TO BE A GANGSTER?

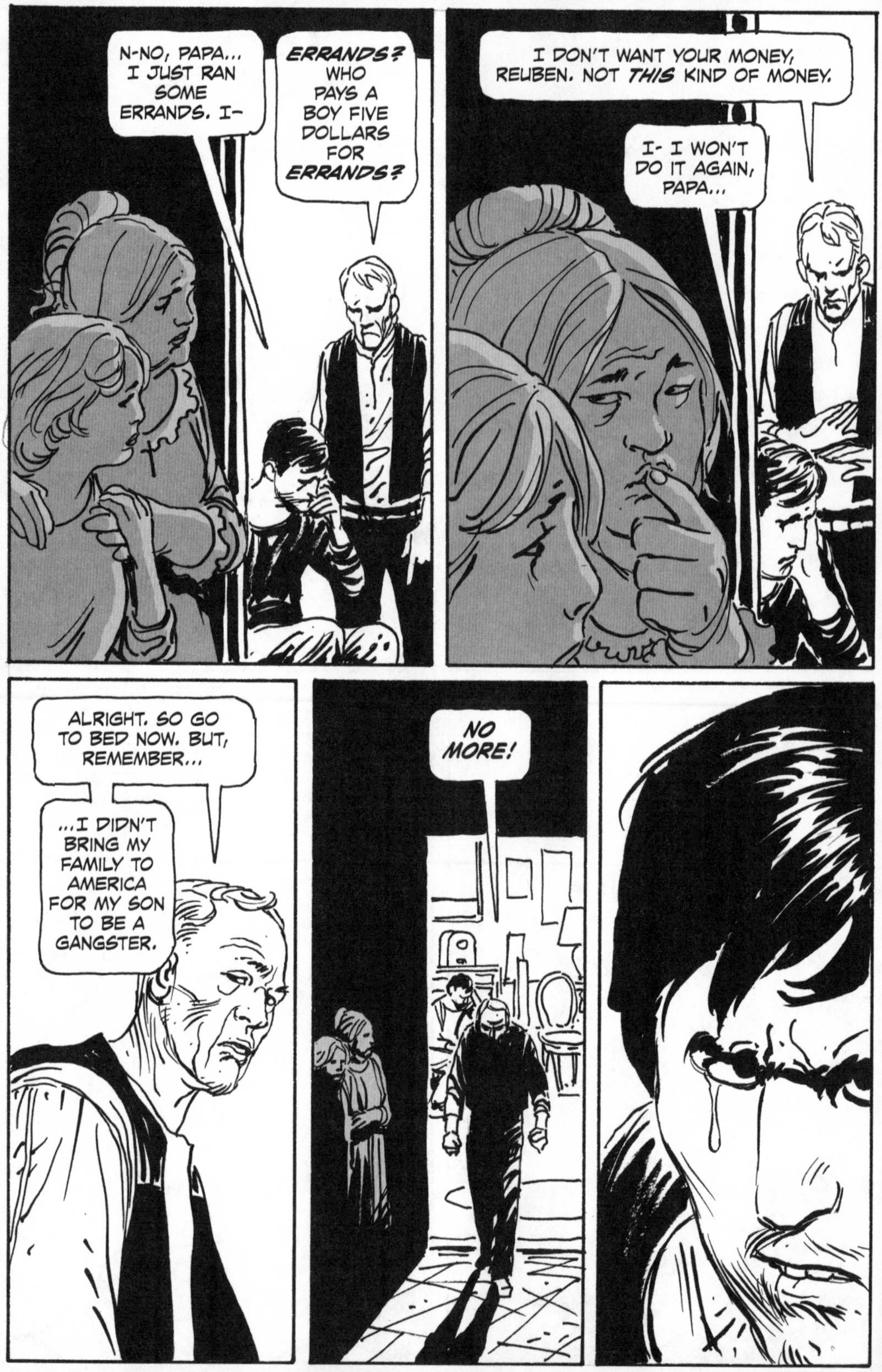
N-NO, PAPA... I JUST RAN SOME ERRANDS. I–
ERRANDS? WHO PAYS A BOY FIVE DOLLARS FOR ERRANDS?
I DON'T WANT YOUR MONEY, REUBEN. NOT THIS KIND OF MONEY.
I- I WON'T DO IT AGAIN, PAPA...
ALRIGHT. SO GO TO BED NOW. BUT, REMEMBER...
...I DIDN'T BRING MY FAMILY TO AMERICA FOR MY SON TO BE A GANGSTER.
NO MORE!

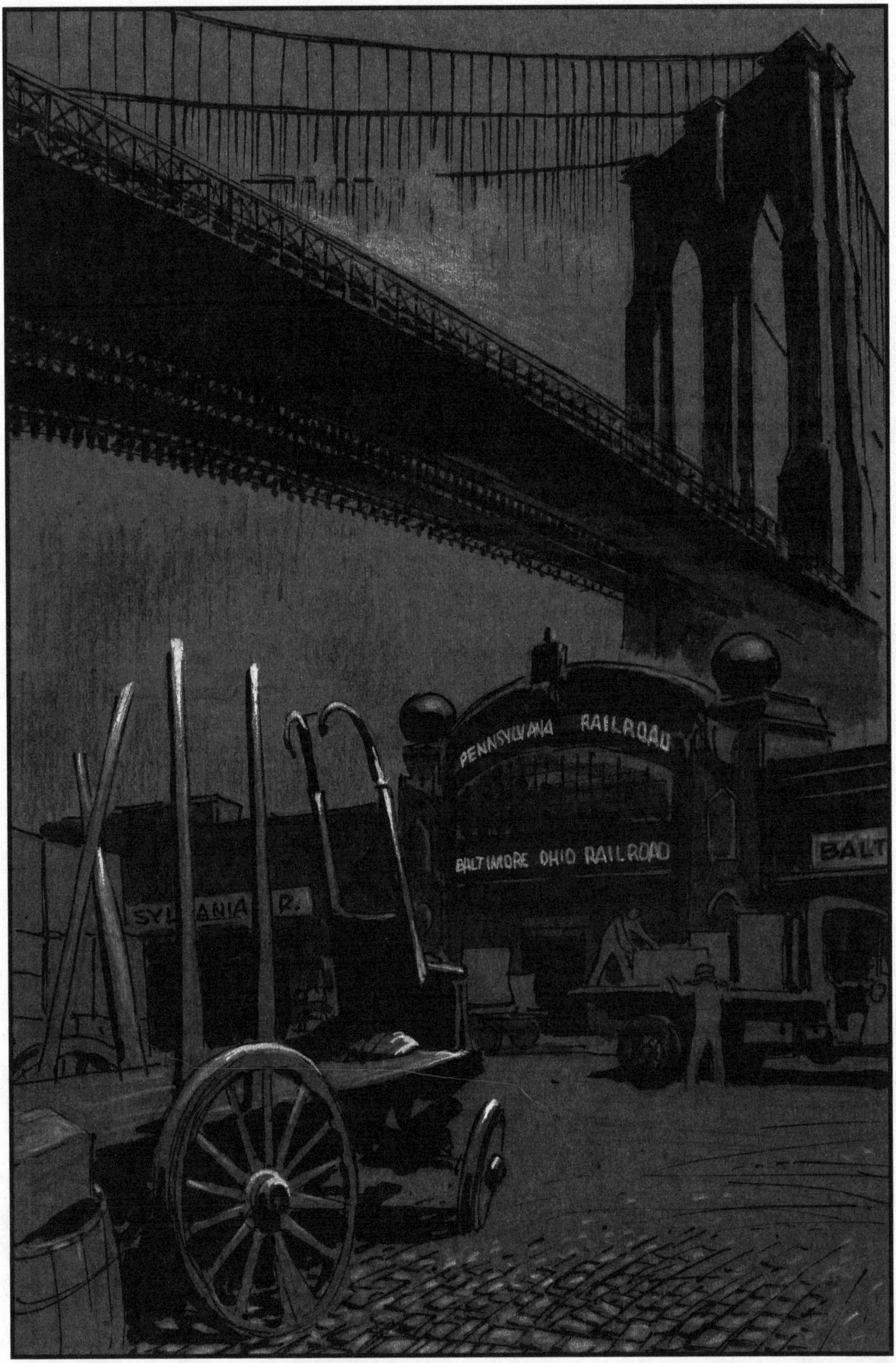
PENNSYLVANIA RAILROAD
BALTIMORE OHIO RAILROAD
BALT

Brooklyn Bridge

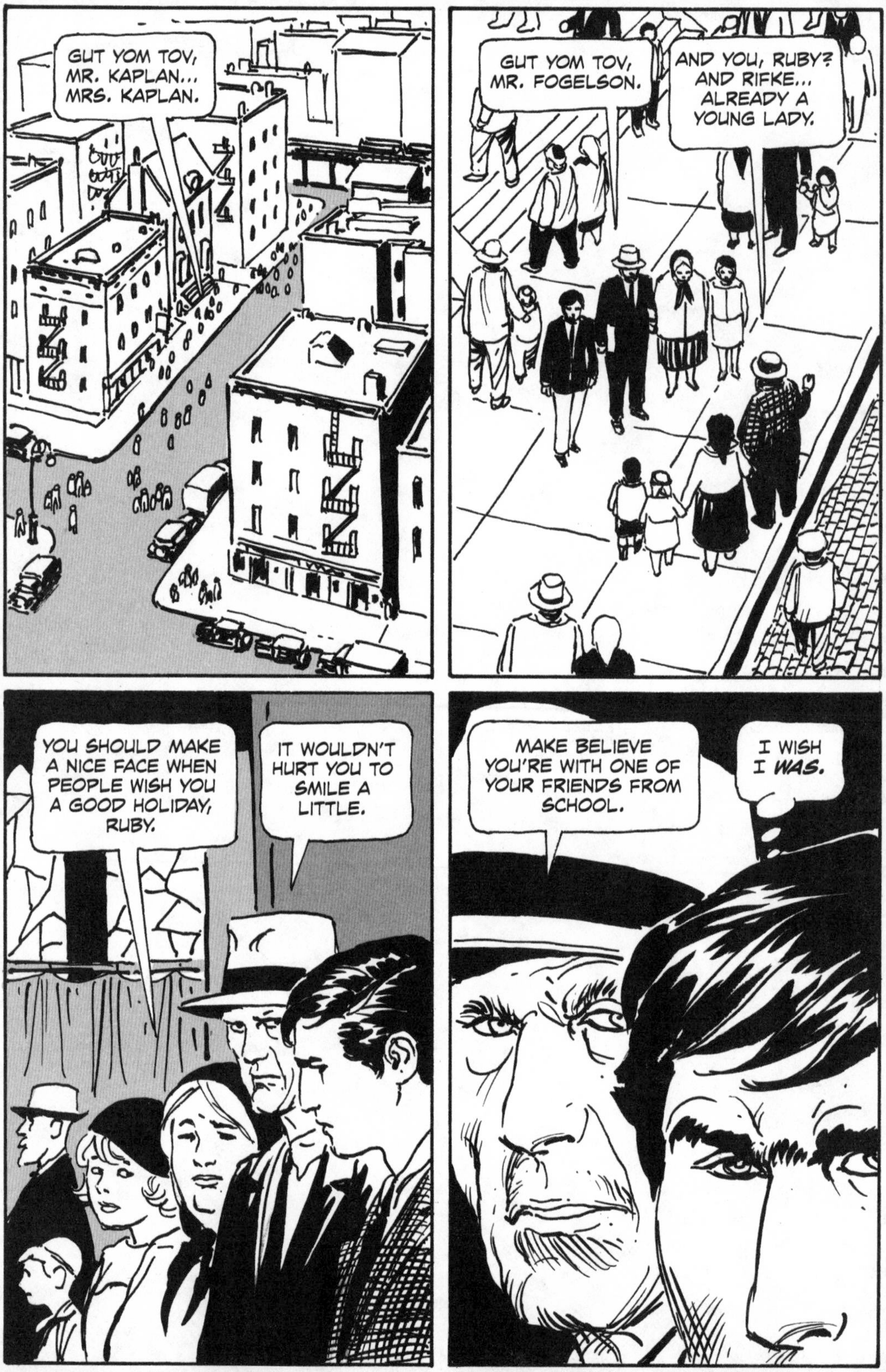
GUT YOM TOV, MR. KAPLAN... MRS. KAPLAN.
GUT YOM TOV, MR. FOGELSON.
AND YOU, RUBY? AND RIFKE... ALREADY A YOUNG LADY.
YOU SHOULD MAKE A NICE FACE WHEN PEOPLE WISH YOU A GOOD HOLIDAY, RUBY.
IT WOULDN'T HURT YOU TO SMILE A LITTLE.
MAKE BELIEVE YOU'RE WITH ONE OF YOUR FRIENDS FROM SCHOOL.
I WISH I *WAS.*

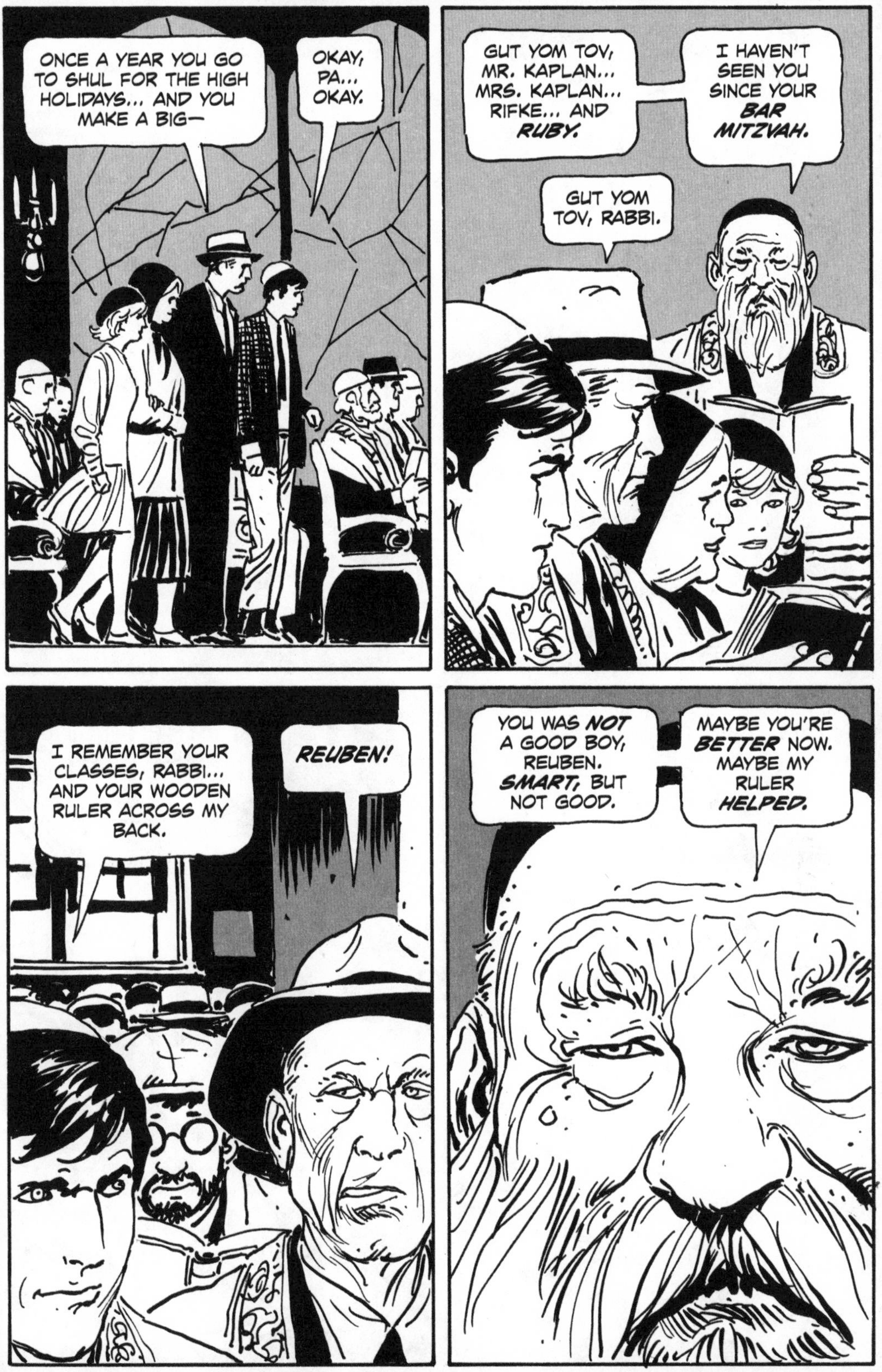
ONCE A YEAR YOU GO TO SHUL FOR THE HIGH HOLIDAYS... AND YOU MAKE A BIG—
OKAY, PA... OKAY.
GUT YOM TOV, MR. KAPLAN... MRS. KAPLAN... RIFKE... AND RUBY.
I HAVEN'T SEEN YOU SINCE YOUR BAR MITZVAH.
GUT YOM TOV, RABBI.
I REMEMBER YOUR CLASSES, RABBI... AND YOUR WOODEN RULER ACROSS MY BACK.
REUBEN!
YOU WAS NOT A GOOD BOY, REUBEN. SMART, BUT NOT GOOD.
MAYBE YOU'RE BETTER NOW. MAYBE MY RULER HELPED.

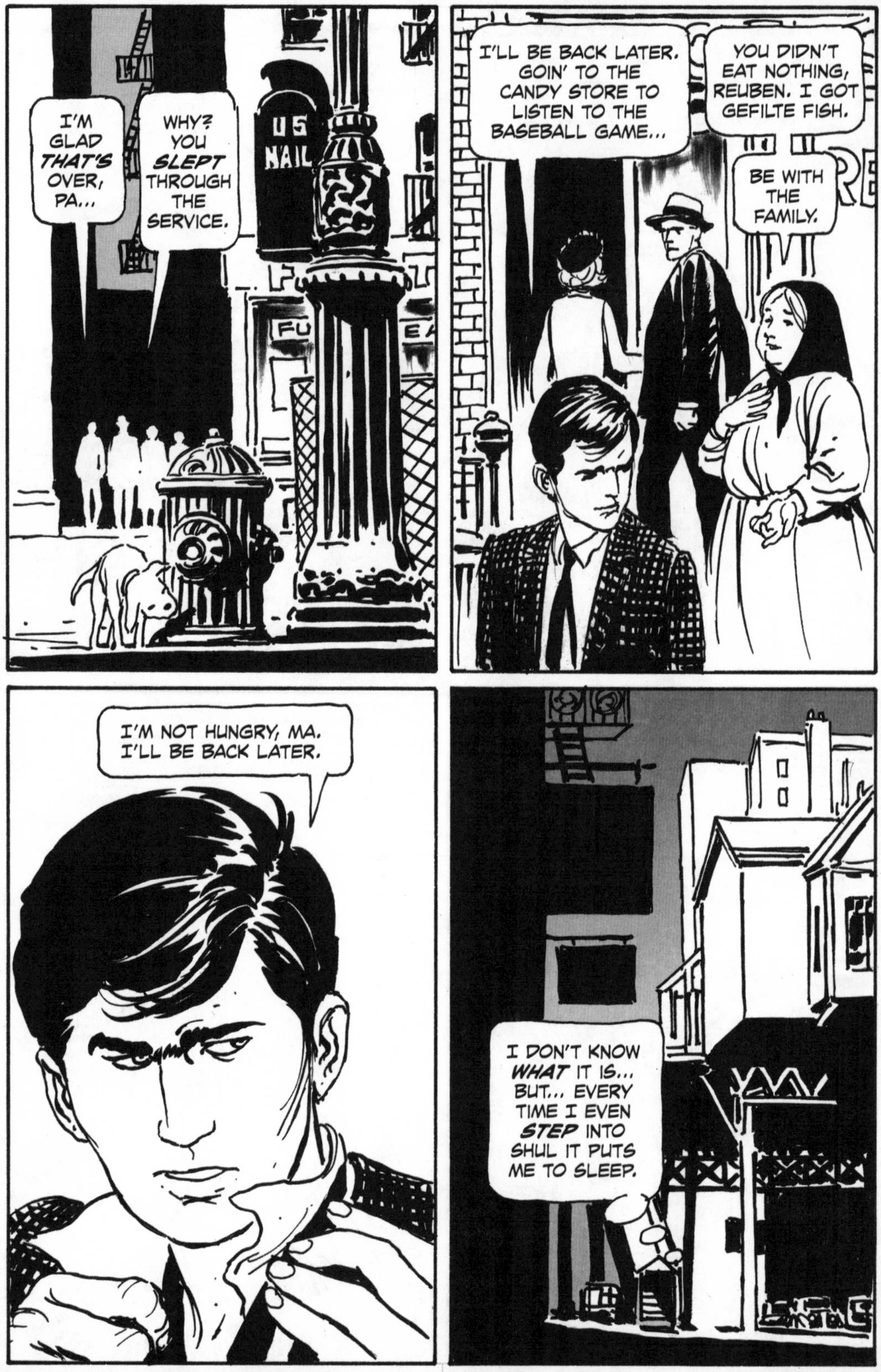
I'M GLAD *THAT'S* OVER, PA...
WHY? YOU *SLEPT* THROUGH THE SERVICE.
US MAIL
I'LL BE BACK LATER. GOIN' TO THE CANDY STORE TO LISTEN TO THE BASEBALL GAME...
YOU DIDN'T EAT NOTHING, REUBEN. I GOT GEFILTE FISH.
BE WITH THE FAMILY.
I'M NOT HUNGRY, MA. I'LL BE BACK LATER.
I DON'T KNOW *WHAT* IT IS... BUT... EVERY TIME I EVEN *STEP* INTO SHUL IT PUTS ME TO SLEEP.

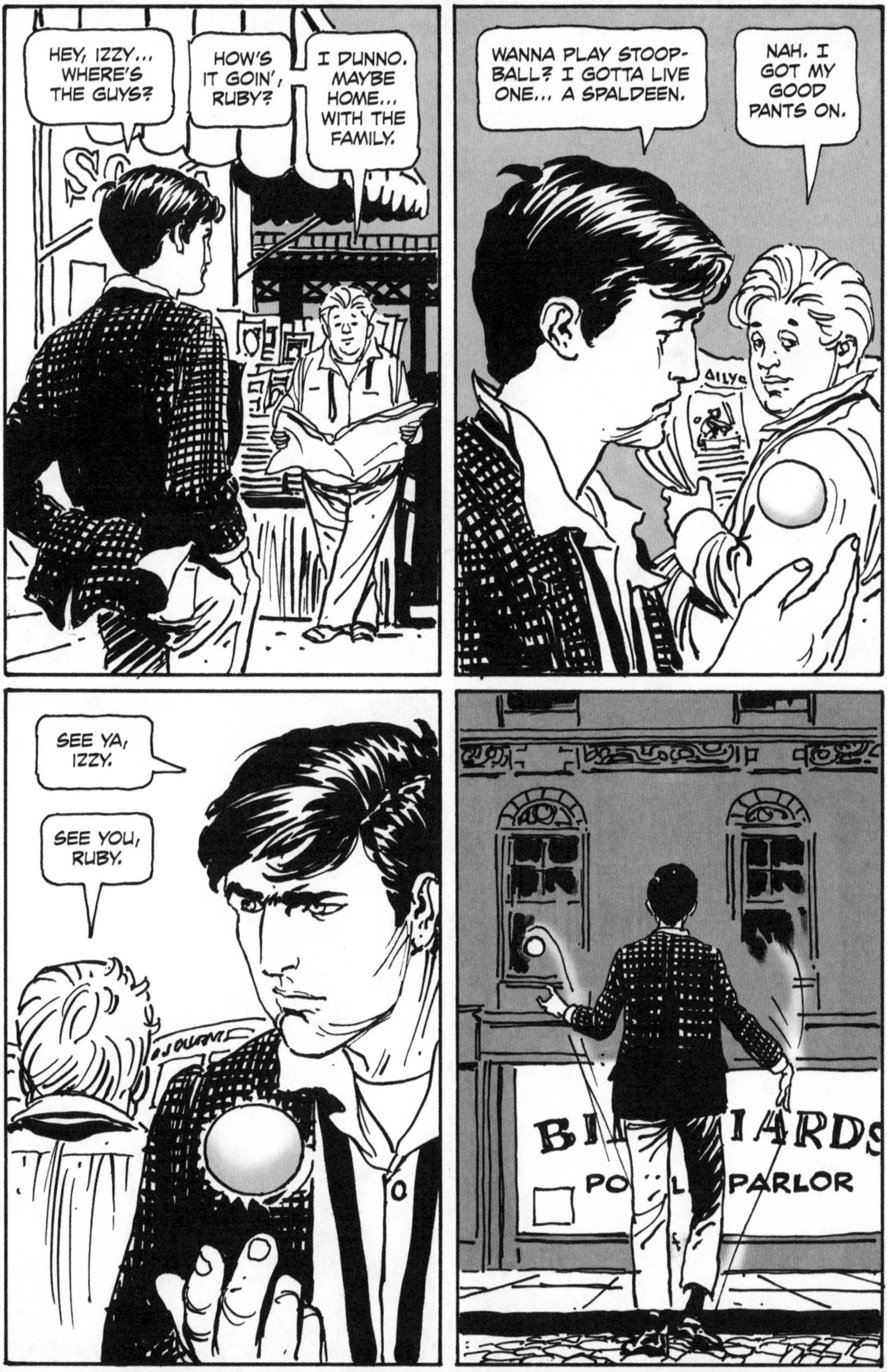
HEY, IZZY... WHERE'S THE GUYS?
HOW'S IT GOIN', RUBY?
I DUNNO. MAYBE HOME... WITH THE FAMILY.
WANNA PLAY STOOP-BALL? I GOTTA LIVE ONE... A SPALDEEN.
NAH. I GOT MY GOOD PANTS ON.
SEE YA, IZZY.
SEE YOU, RUBY.
PARLOR

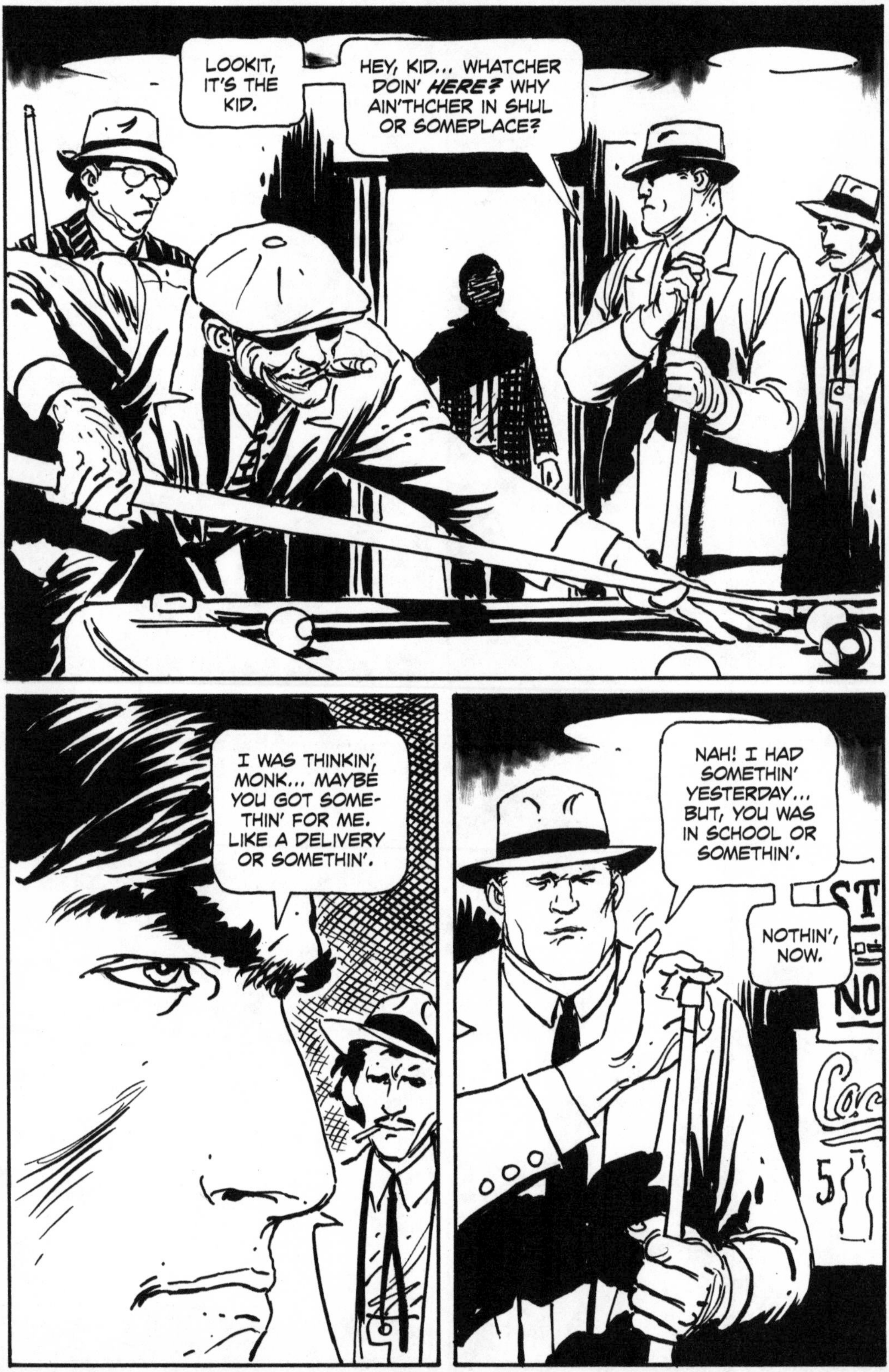
LOOKIT, IT'S THE KID.
HEY, KID... WHATCHER DOIN' *HERE?* WHY AIN'THCHER IN SHUL OR SOMEPLACE?
I WAS THINKIN', MONK... MAYBE YOU GOT SOME-THIN' FOR ME. LIKE A DELIVERY OR SOMETHIN'.
NAH! I HAD SOMETHIN' YESTERDAY... BUT, YOU WAS IN SCHOOL OR SOMETHIN'.
NOTHIN', NOW.

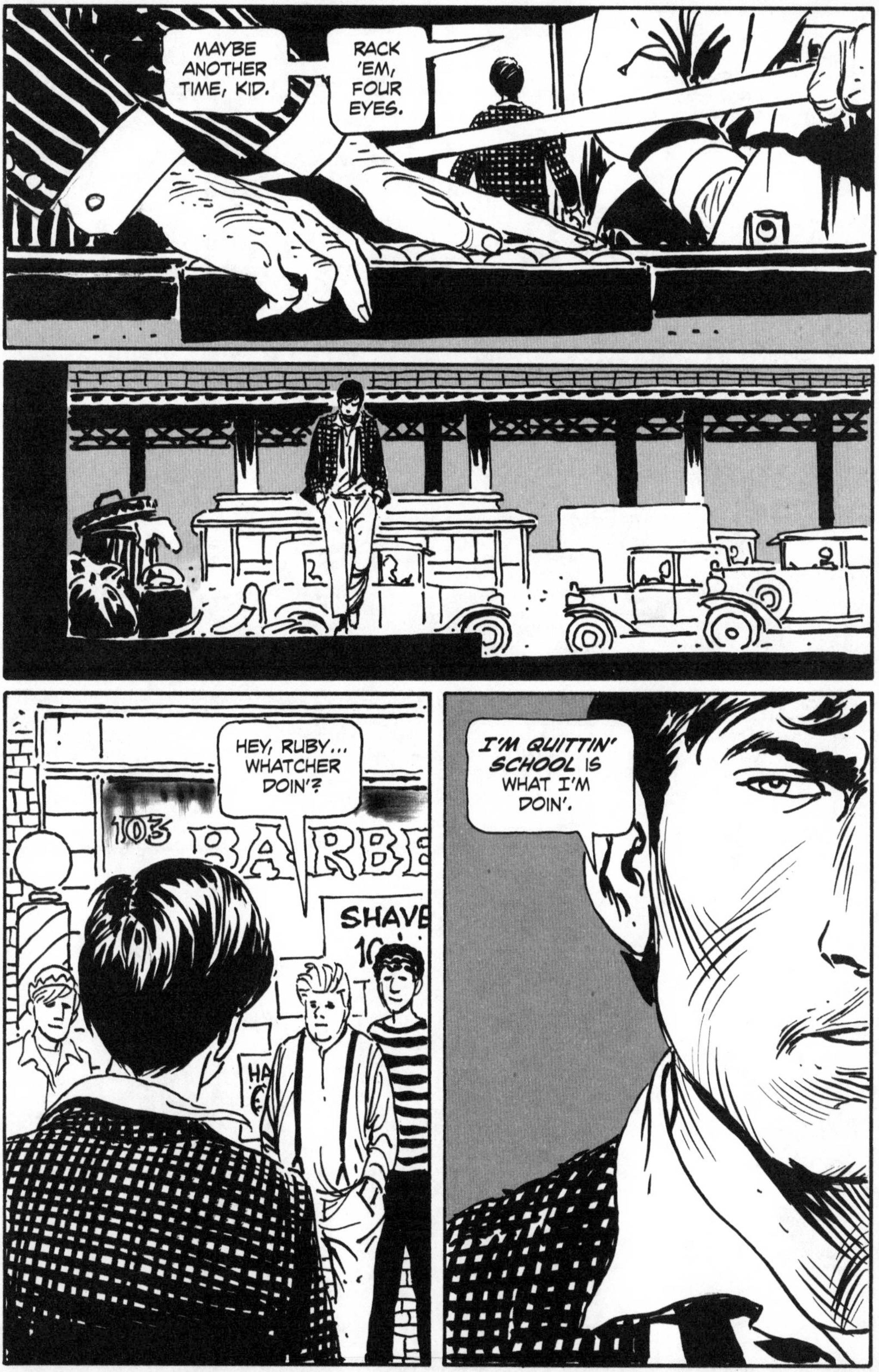
MAYBE ANOTHER TIME, KID.
RACK 'EM, FOUR EYES.
103 BARBE
SHAVE 10
HEY, RUBY... WHATCHER DOIN'?
I'M QUITTIN' SCHOOL IS WHAT I'M DOIN'.

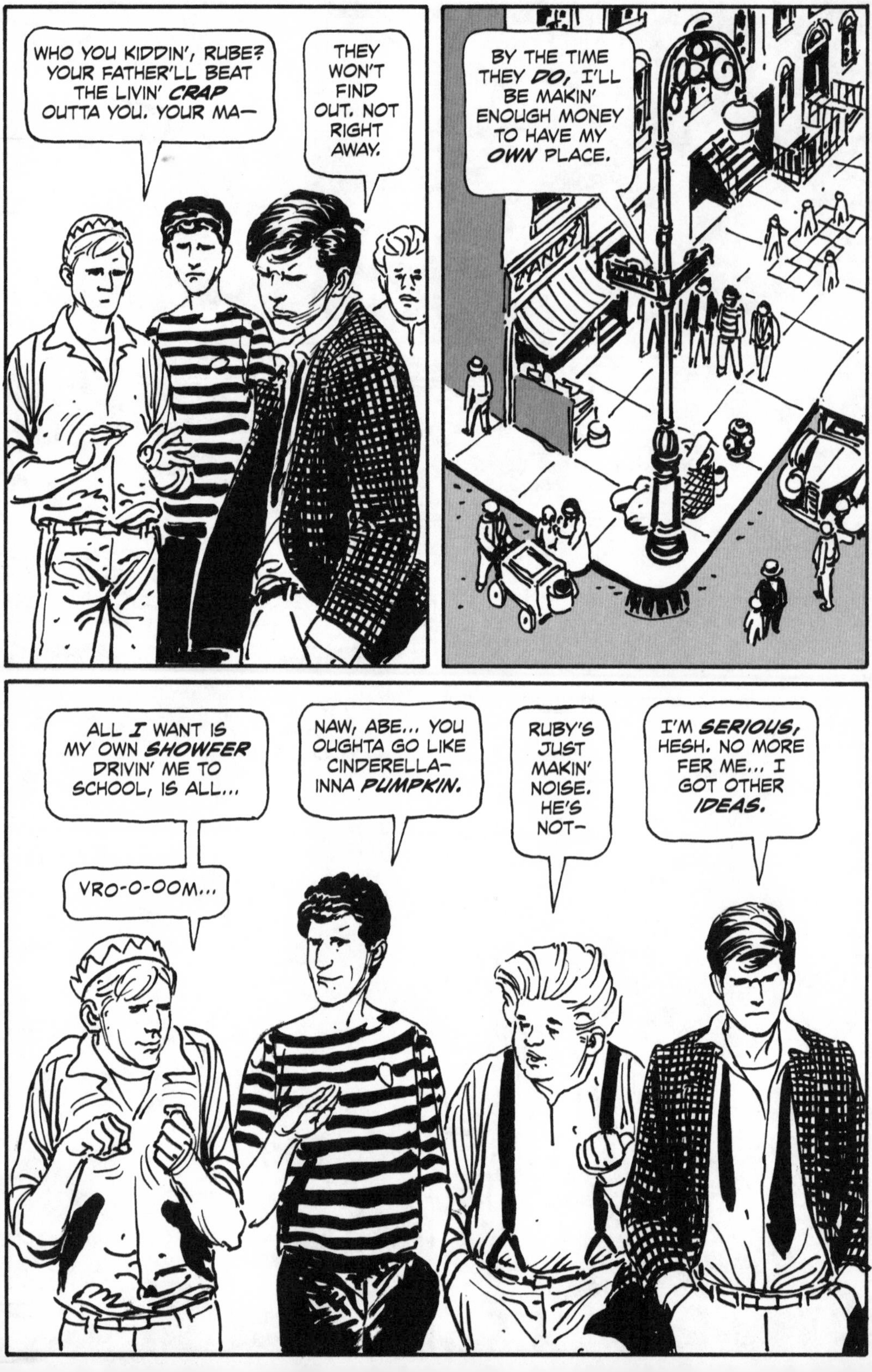
WHO YOU KIDDIN', RUBE? YOUR FATHER'LL BEAT THE LIVIN' CRAP OUTTA YOU. YOUR MA—
THEY WON'T FIND OUT. NOT RIGHT AWAY.
BY THE TIME THEY DO, I'LL BE MAKIN' ENOUGH MONEY TO HAVE MY OWN PLACE.
CANDY
ALL I WANT IS MY OWN SHOWFER DRIVIN' ME TO SCHOOL, IS ALL...
VRO-O-OOM...
NAW, ABE... YOU OUGHTA GO LIKE CINDERELLA-INNA PUMPKIN.
RUBY'S JUST MAKIN' NOISE. HE'S NOT-
I'M SERIOUS, HESH. NO MORE FER ME... I GOT OTHER IDEAS.

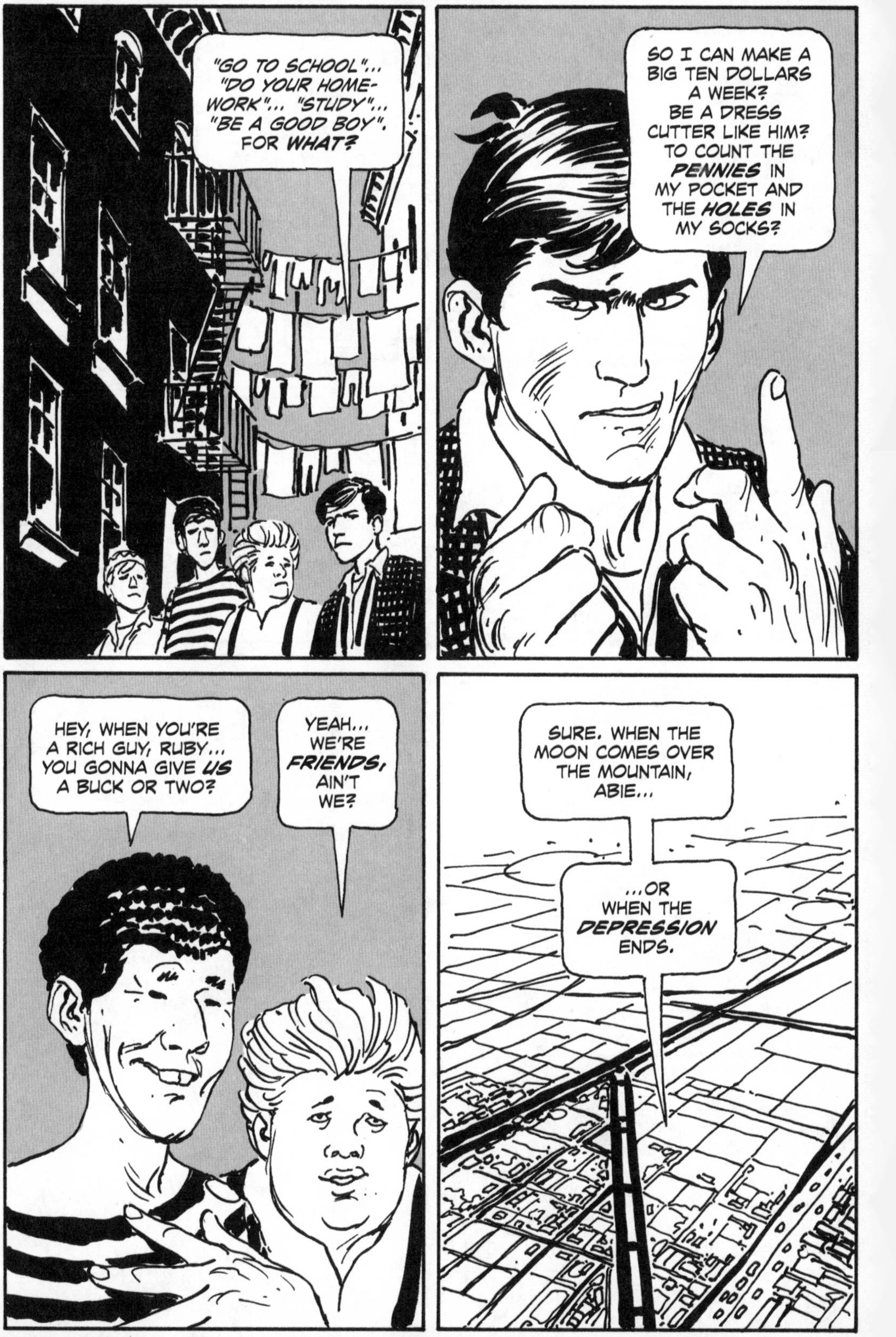
"GO TO SCHOOL"... "DO YOUR HOME-WORK"... "STUDY"... "BE A GOOD BOY". FOR WHAT?
SO I CAN MAKE A BIG TEN DOLLARS A WEEK? BE A DRESS CUTTER LIKE HIM? TO COUNT THE PENNIES IN MY POCKET AND THE HOLES IN MY SOCKS?
HEY, WHEN YOU'RE A RICH GUY, RUBY... YOU GONNA GIVE US A BUCK OR TWO?
YEAH... WE'RE FRIENDS, AIN'T WE?
SURE. WHEN THE MOON COMES OVER THE MOUNTAIN, ABIE...
...OR WHEN THE DEPRESSION ENDS.

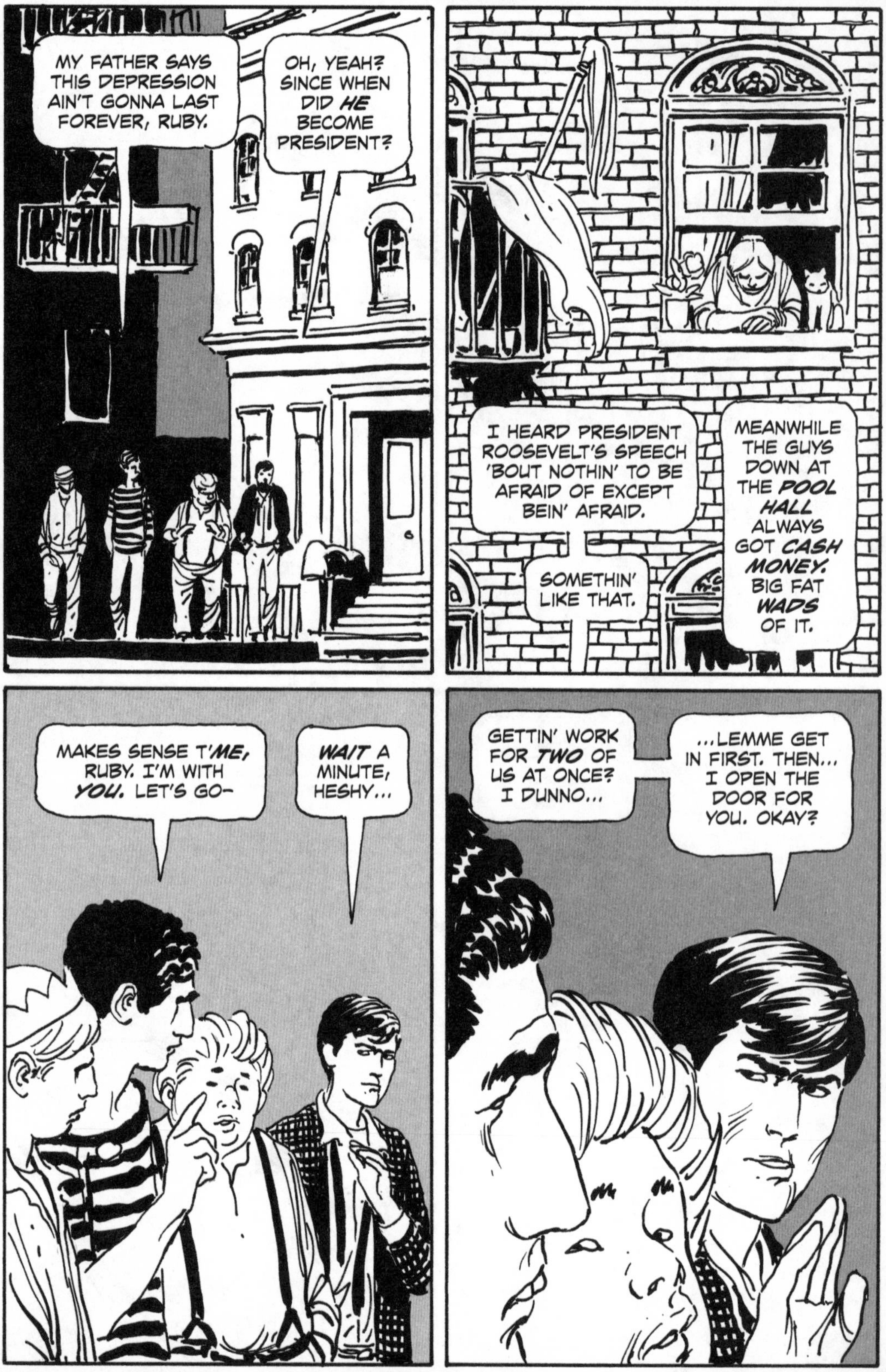
MY FATHER SAYS THIS DEPRESSION AIN'T GONNA LAST FOREVER, RUBY.
OH, YEAH? SINCE WHEN DID HE BECOME PRESIDENT?
I HEARD PRESIDENT ROOSEVELT'S SPEECH 'BOUT NOTHIN' TO BE AFRAID OF EXCEPT BEIN' AFRAID.
SOMETHIN' LIKE THAT.
MEANWHILE THE GUYS DOWN AT THE POOL HALL ALWAYS GOT CASH MONEY. BIG FAT WADS OF IT.
MAKES SENSE T'ME, RUBY. I'M WITH YOU. LET'S GO-
WAIT A MINUTE, HESHY...
GETTIN' WORK FOR TWO OF US AT ONCE? I DUNNO...
...LEMME GET IN FIRST. THEN... I OPEN THE DOOR FOR YOU. OKAY?

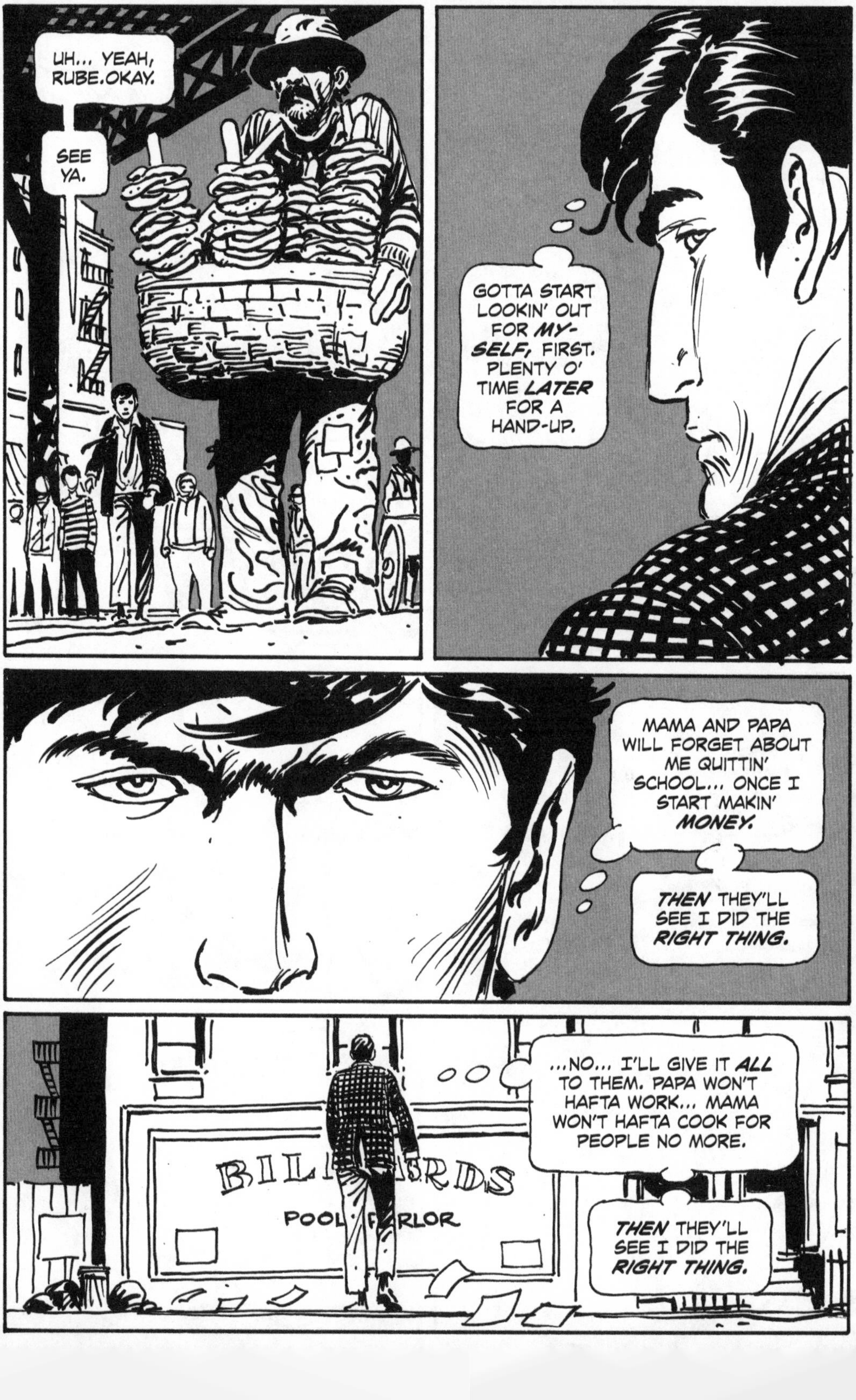
UH... YEAH, RUBE.OKAY.
SEE YA.
GOTTA START LOOKIN' OUT FOR MY-SELF, FIRST. PLENTY O' TIME LATER FOR A HAND-UP.
MAMA AND PAPA WILL FORGET ABOUT ME QUITTIN' SCHOOL... ONCE I START MAKIN' MONEY.
THEN THEY'LL SEE I DID THE RIGHT THING.
...NO... I'LL GIVE IT ALL TO THEM. PAPA WON'T HAFTA WORK... MAMA WON'T HAFTA COOK FOR PEOPLE NO MORE.
THEN THEY'LL SEE I DID THE RIGHT THING.

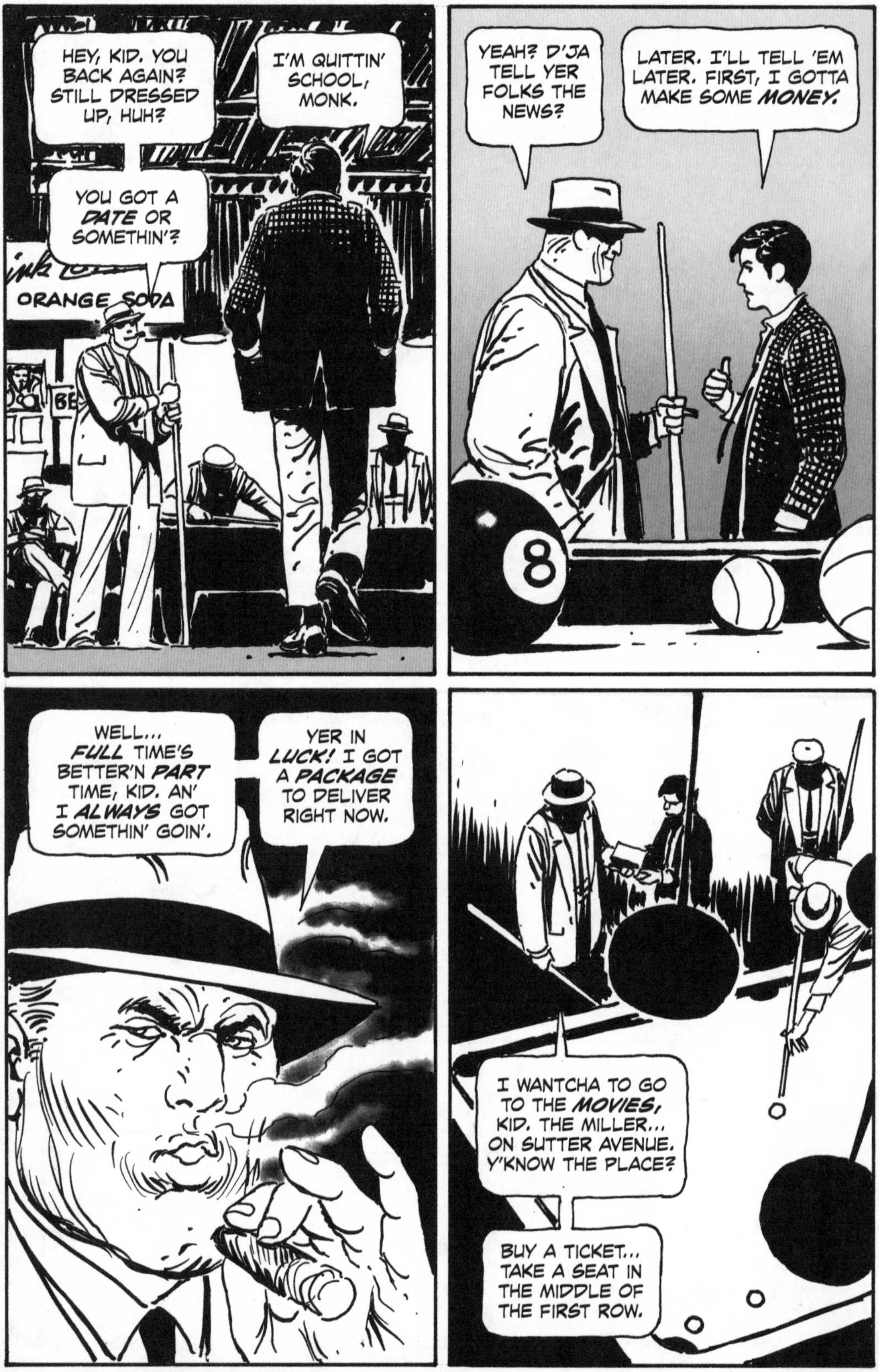
HEY, KID. YOU BACK AGAIN? STILL DRESSED UP, HUH?
I'M QUITTIN' SCHOOL, MONK.
YOU GOT A DATE OR SOMETHIN'?
ORANGE SODA
YEAH? D'JA TELL YER FOLKS THE NEWS?
LATER. I'LL TELL 'EM LATER. FIRST, I GOTTA MAKE SOME MONEY.
WELL... FULL TIME'S BETTER'N PART TIME, KID. AN' I ALWAYS GOT SOMETHIN' GOIN'.
YER IN LUCK! I GOT A PACKAGE TO DELIVER RIGHT NOW.
I WANTCHA TO GO TO THE MOVIES, KID. THE MILLER... ON SUTTER AVENUE. Y'KNOW THE PLACE?
BUY A TICKET... TAKE A SEAT IN THE MIDDLE OF THE FIRST ROW.

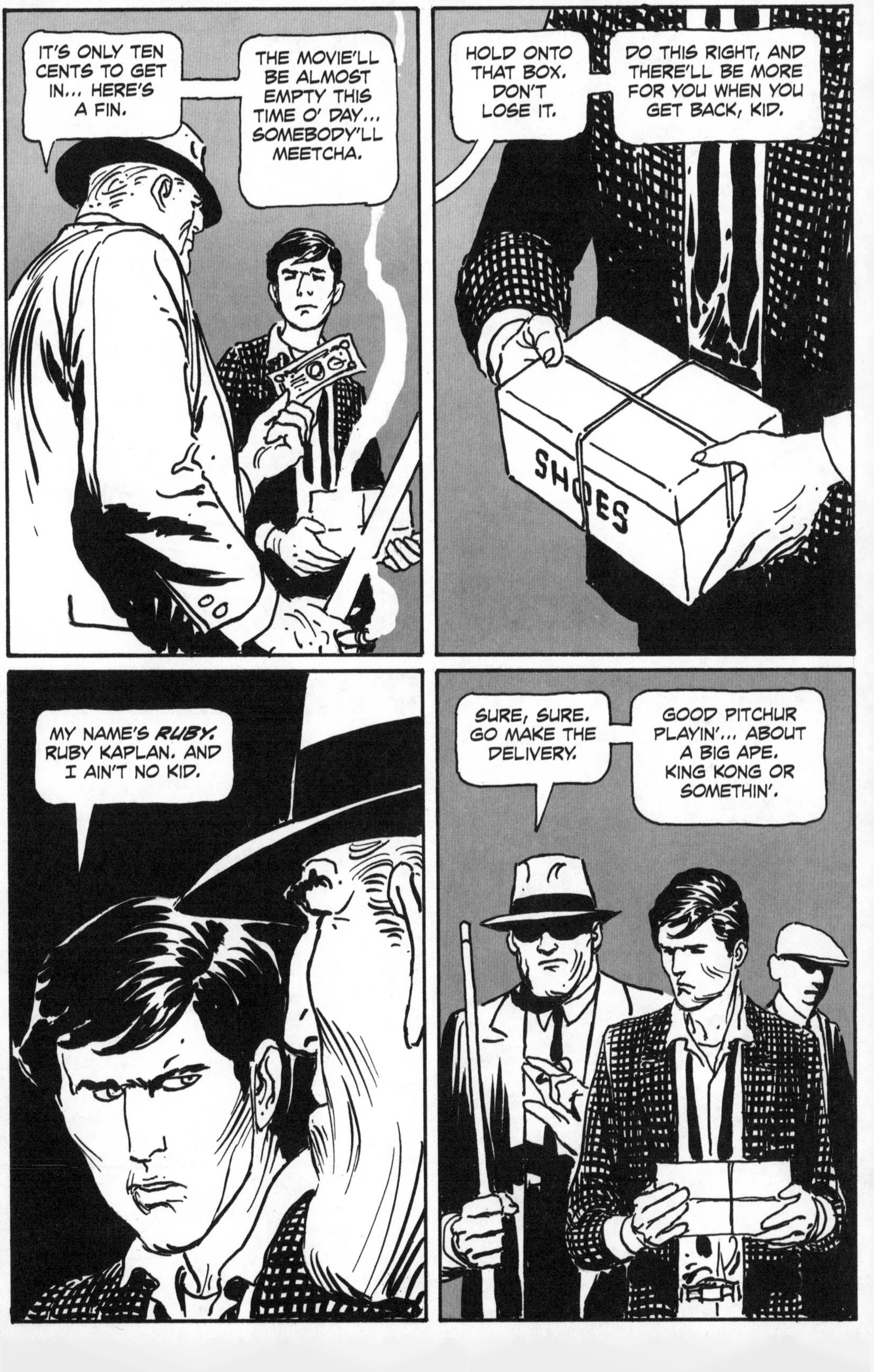
IT'S ONLY TEN CENTS TO GET IN... HERE'S A FIN.
THE MOVIE'LL BE ALMOST EMPTY THIS TIME O' DAY... SOMEBODY'LL MEETCHA.
HOLD ONTO THAT BOX. DON'T LOSE IT.
DO THIS RIGHT, AND THERE'LL BE MORE FOR YOU WHEN YOU GET BACK, KID.
SHOES
MY NAME'S *RUBY.* RUBY KAPLAN. AND I AIN'T NO KID.
SURE, SURE. GO MAKE THE DELIVERY.
GOOD PITCHUR PLAYIN'... ABOUT A BIG APE. KING KONG OR SOMETHIN'.

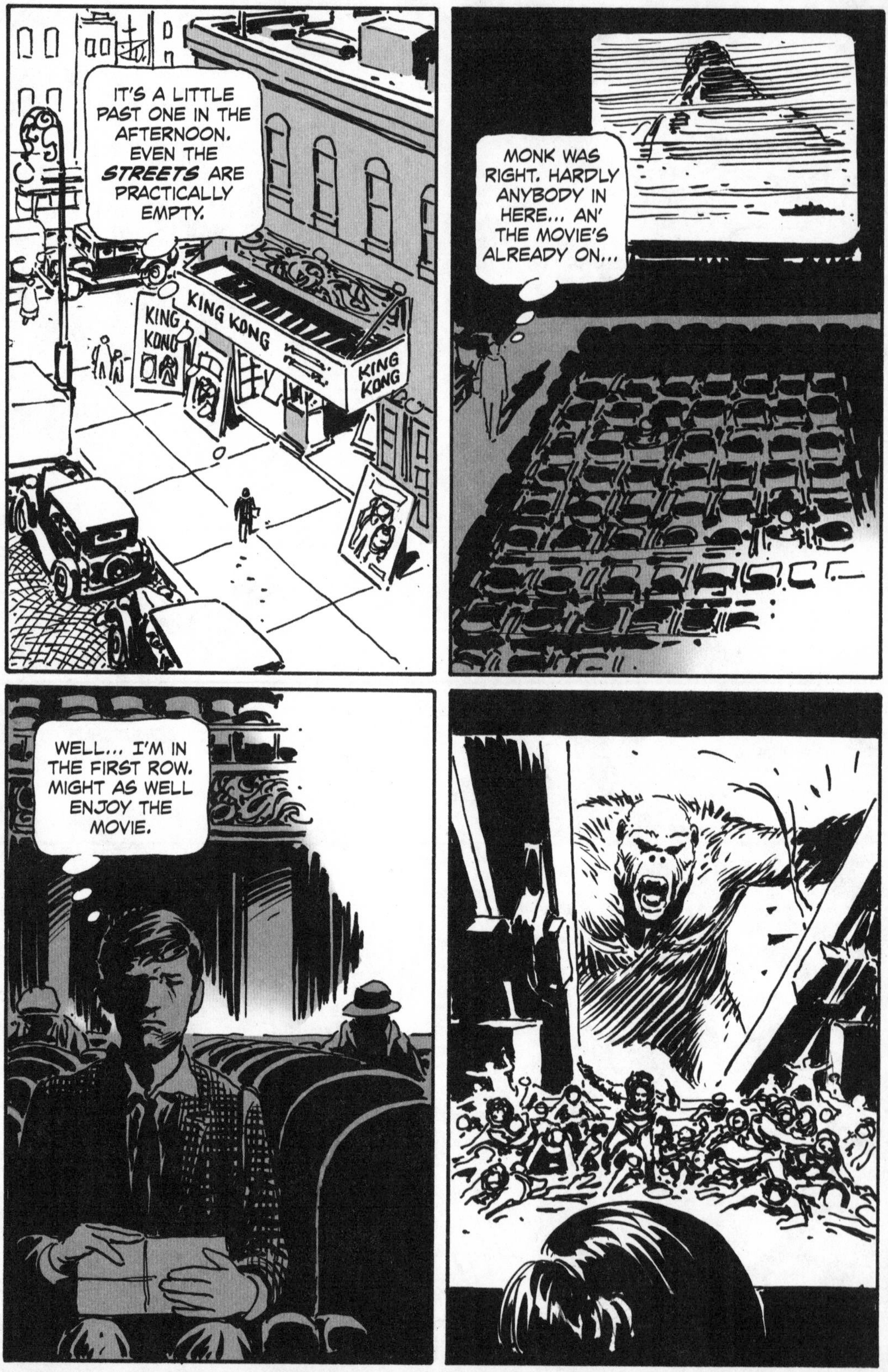
IT'S A LITTLE PAST ONE IN THE AFTERNOON. EVEN THE STREETS ARE PRACTICALLY EMPTY.
KING KONG
KING KONG
KING KONG
KING KONG
MONK WAS RIGHT. HARDLY ANYBODY IN HERE... AN' THE MOVIE'S ALREADY ON...
WELL... I'M IN THE FIRST ROW. MIGHT AS WELL ENJOY THE MOVIE.

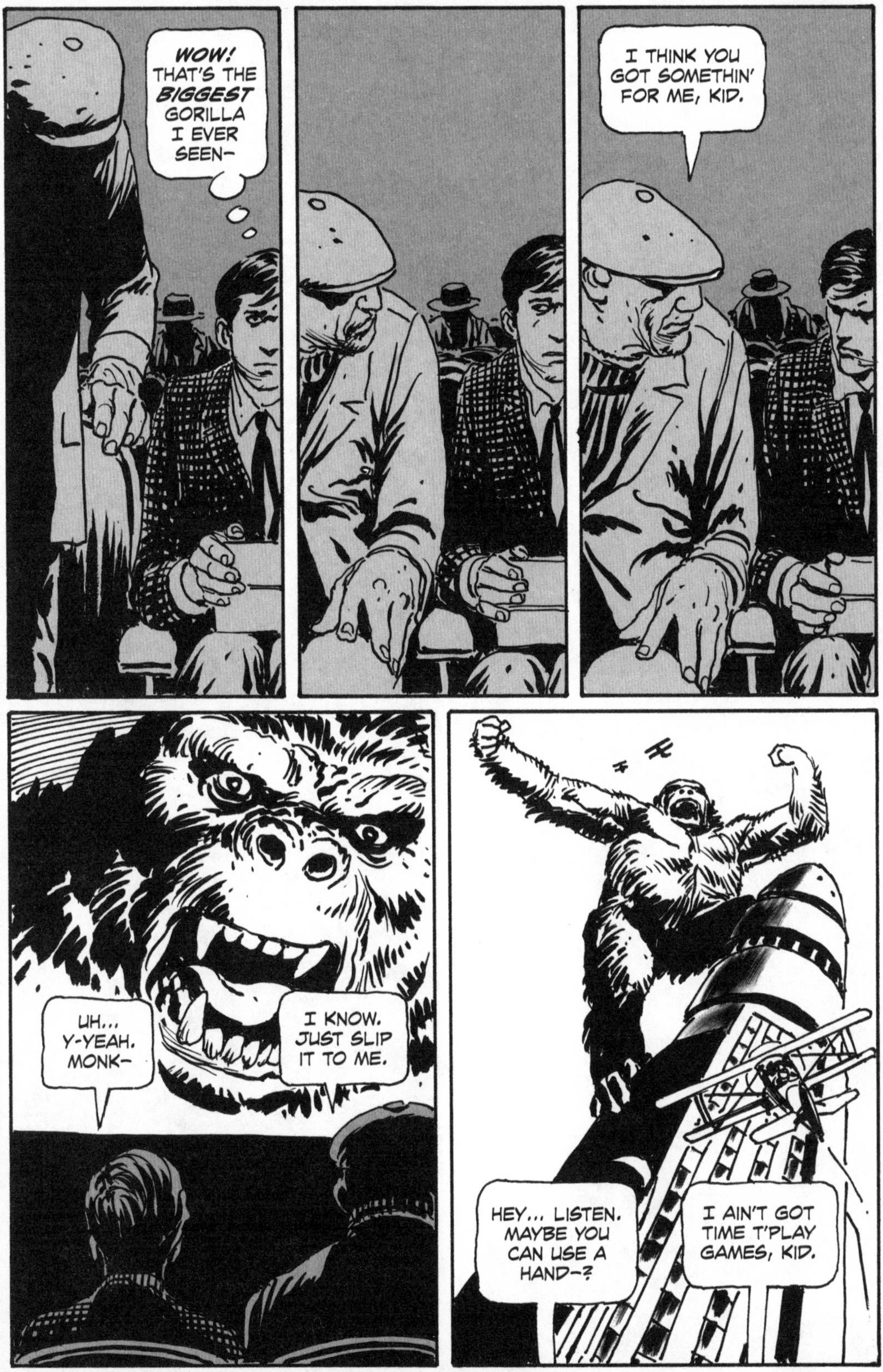
WOW! THAT'S THE BIGGEST GORILLA I EVER SEEN–
I THINK YOU GOT SOMETHIN' FOR ME, KID.
UH... Y-YEAH. MONK–
I KNOW. JUST SLIP IT TO ME.
HEY... LISTEN. MAYBE YOU CAN USE A HAND–?
I AIN'T GOT TIME T'PLAY GAMES, KID.

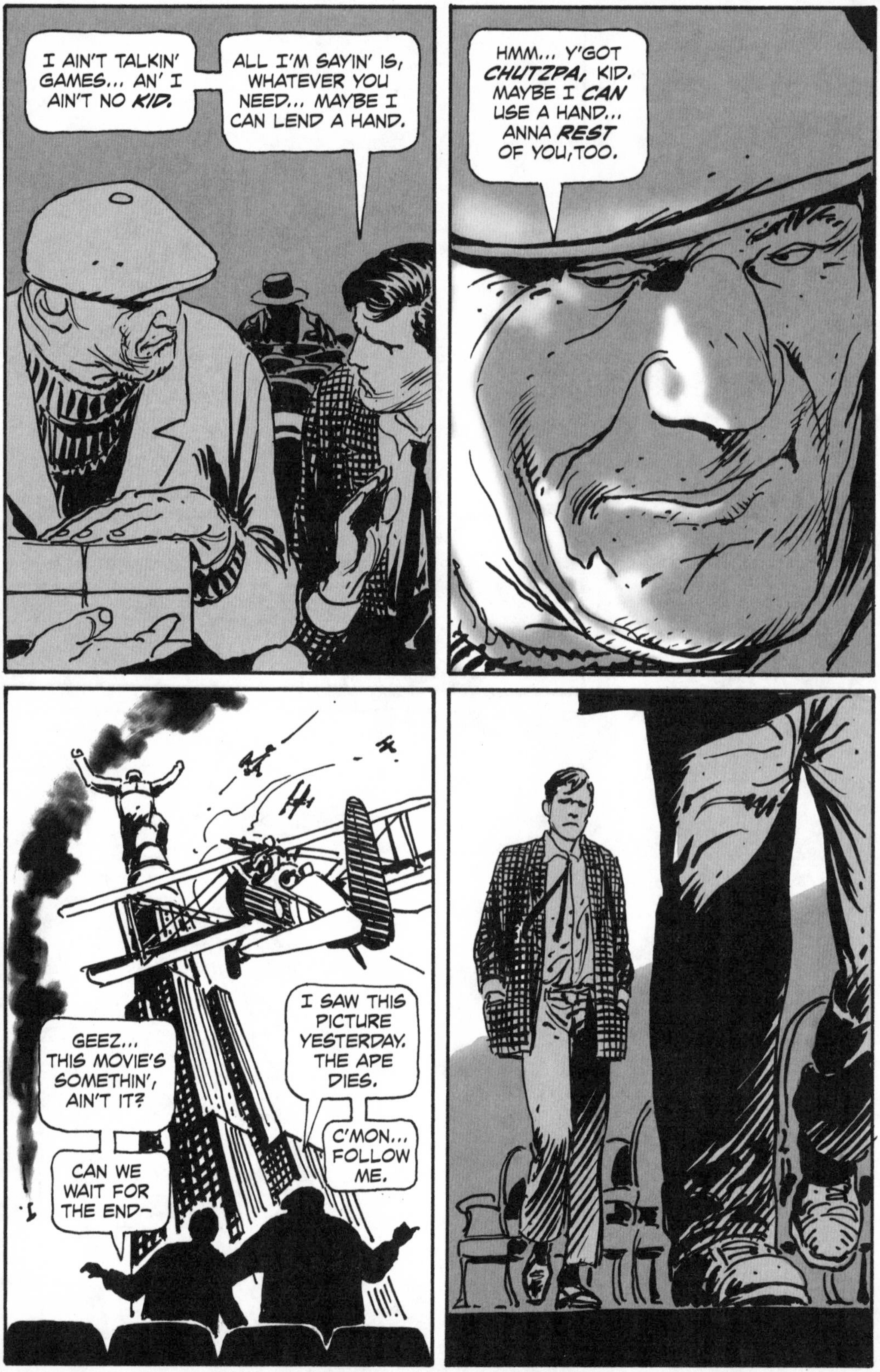

I AIN'T TALKIN' GAMES... AN' I AIN'T NO *KID.*
ALL I'M SAYIN' IS, WHATEVER YOU NEED... MAYBE I CAN LEND A HAND.
HMM... Y'GOT *CHUTZPA,* KID. MAYBE I *CAN* USE A HAND... ANNA *REST* OF YOU,TOO.
GEEZ... THIS MOVIE'S SOMETHIN', AIN'T IT?
CAN WE WAIT FOR THE END–
I SAW THIS PICTURE YESTERDAY. THE APE DIES.
C'MON... FOLLOW ME.

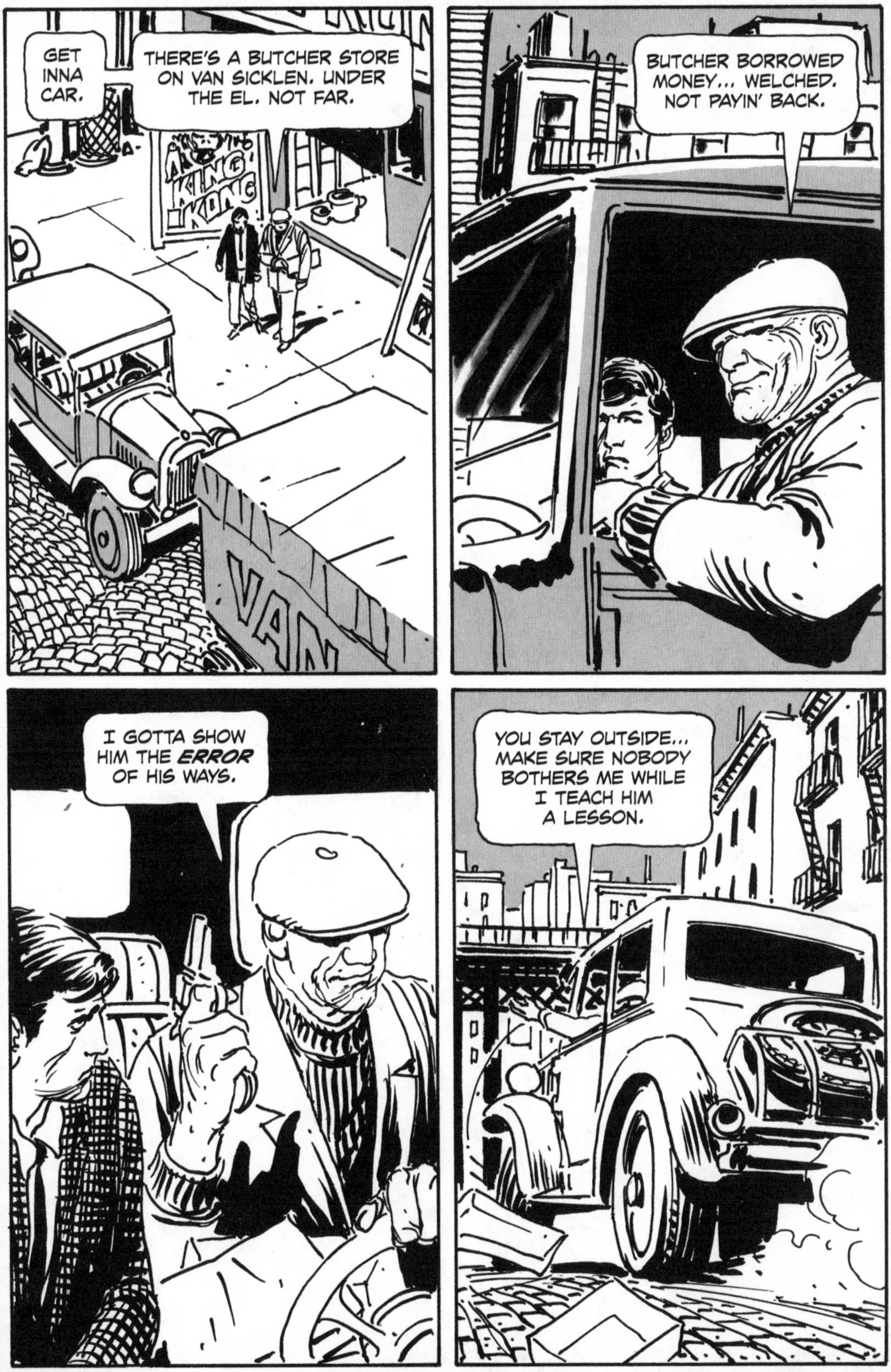
GET INNA CAR.
THERE'S A BUTCHER STORE ON VAN SICKLEN. UNDER THE EL. NOT FAR.
KING KONG
VAN
BUTCHER BORROWED MONEY... WELCHED. NOT PAYIN' BACK.
I GOTTA SHOW HIM THE ERROR OF HIS WAYS.
YOU STAY OUTSIDE... MAKE SURE NOBODY BOTHERS ME WHILE I TEACH HIM A LESSON.

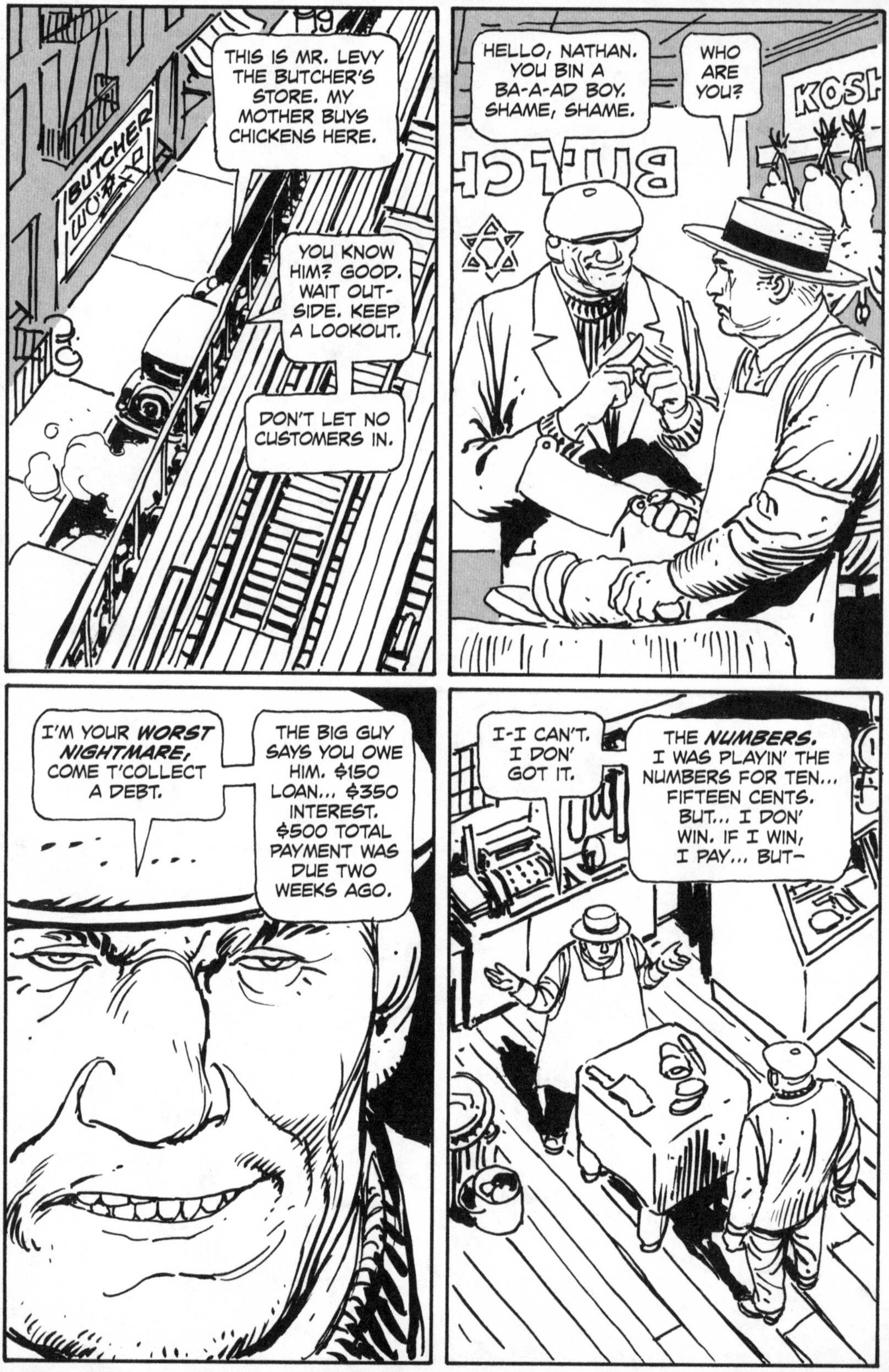

BUTCHER
THIS IS MR. LEVY THE BUTCHER'S STORE. MY MOTHER BUYS CHICKENS HERE.
YOU KNOW HIM? GOOD. WAIT OUTSIDE. KEEP A LOOKOUT.
DON'T LET NO CUSTOMERS IN.
HELLO, NATHAN. YOU BIN A BA-A-AD BOY. SHAME, SHAME.
WHO ARE YOU?
KOSH
I'M YOUR *WORST NIGHTMARE,* COME T'COLLECT A DEBT.
THE BIG GUY SAYS YOU OWE HIM. $150 LOAN... $350 INTEREST. $500 TOTAL PAYMENT WAS DUE TWO WEEKS AGO.
I-I CAN'T. I DON' GOT IT.
THE *NUMBERS.* I WAS PLAYIN' THE NUMBERS FOR TEN... FIFTEEN CENTS. BUT... I DON' WIN. IF I WIN, I PAY... BUT–

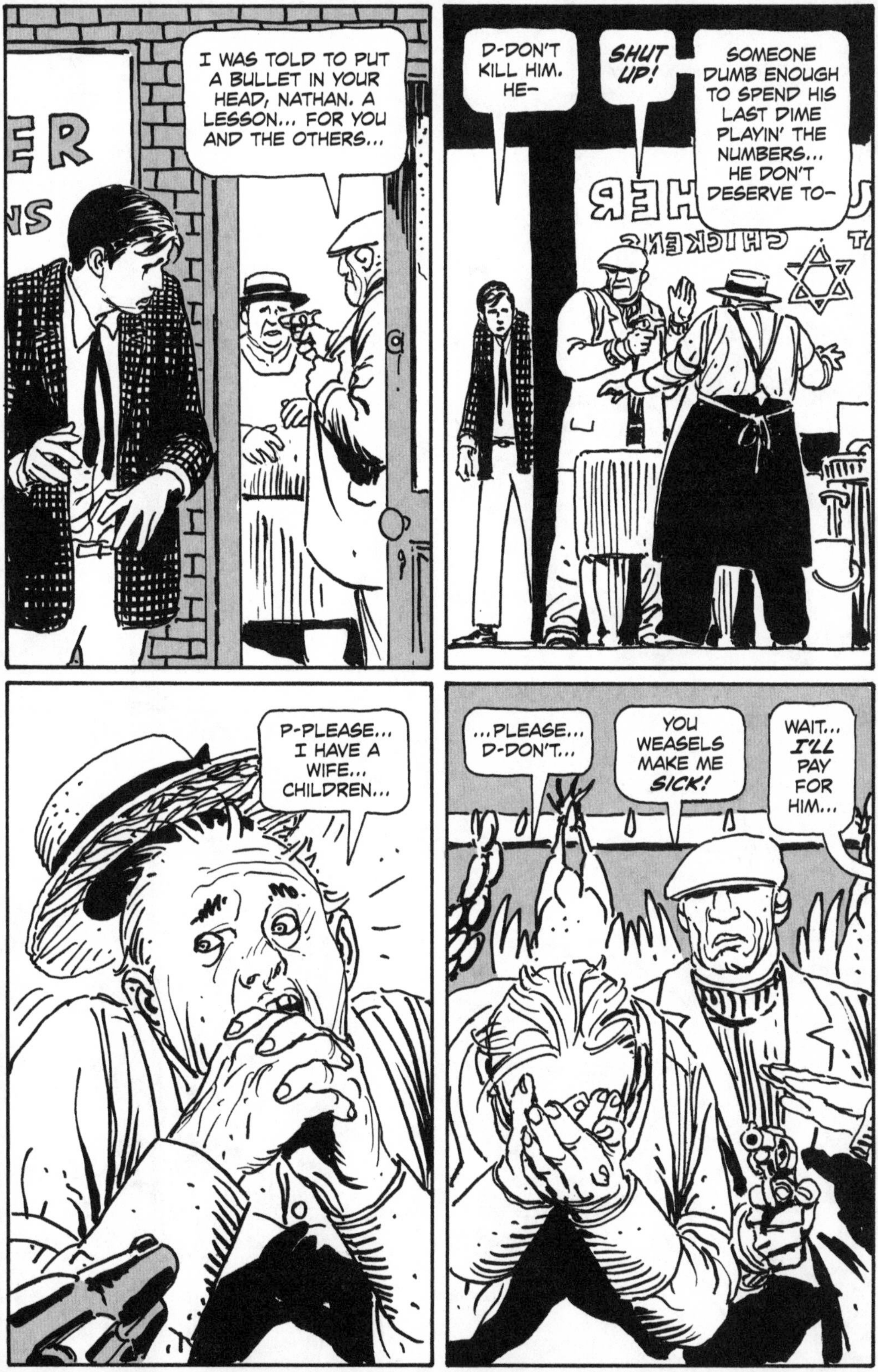
I WAS TOLD TO PUT A BULLET IN YOUR HEAD, NATHAN. A LESSON... FOR YOU AND THE OTHERS...
D-DON'T KILL HIM. HE–
SHUT UP!
SOMEONE DUMB ENOUGH TO SPEND HIS LAST DIME PLAYIN' THE NUMBERS... HE DON'T DESERVE TO–
P-PLEASE... I HAVE A WIFE... CHILDREN...
...PLEASE... D-DON'T...
YOU WEASELS MAKE ME SICK!
WAIT... I'LL PAY FOR HIM...

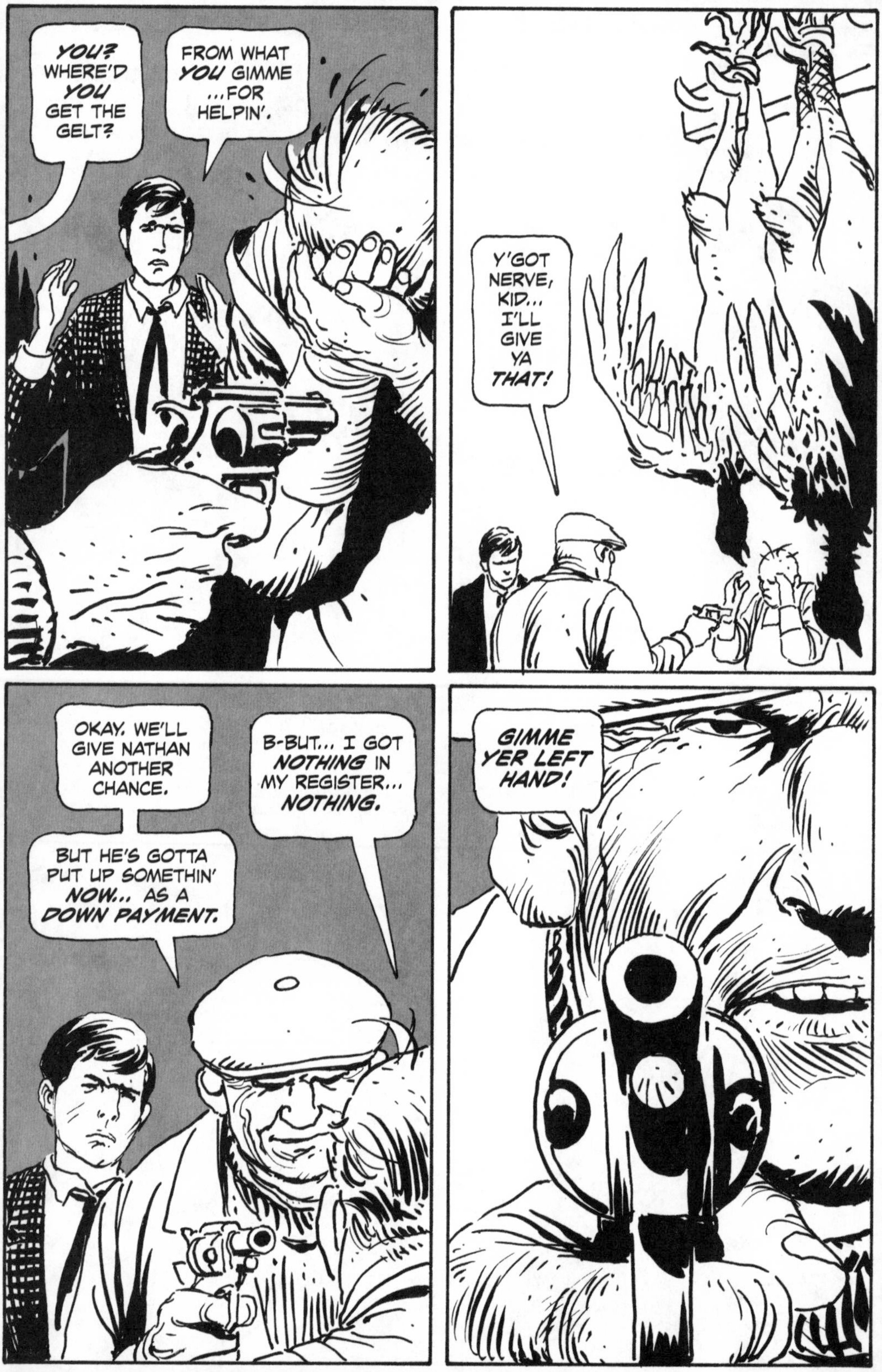
YOU? WHERE'D YOU GET THE GELT?
FROM WHAT YOU GIMME ...FOR HELPIN'.
Y'GOT NERVE, KID... I'LL GIVE YA THAT!
OKAY. WE'LL GIVE NATHAN ANOTHER CHANCE.
BUT HE'S GOTTA PUT UP SOMETHIN' NOW... AS A DOWN PAYMENT.
B-BUT... I GOT NOTHING IN MY REGISTER... NOTHING.
GIMME YER LEFT HAND!

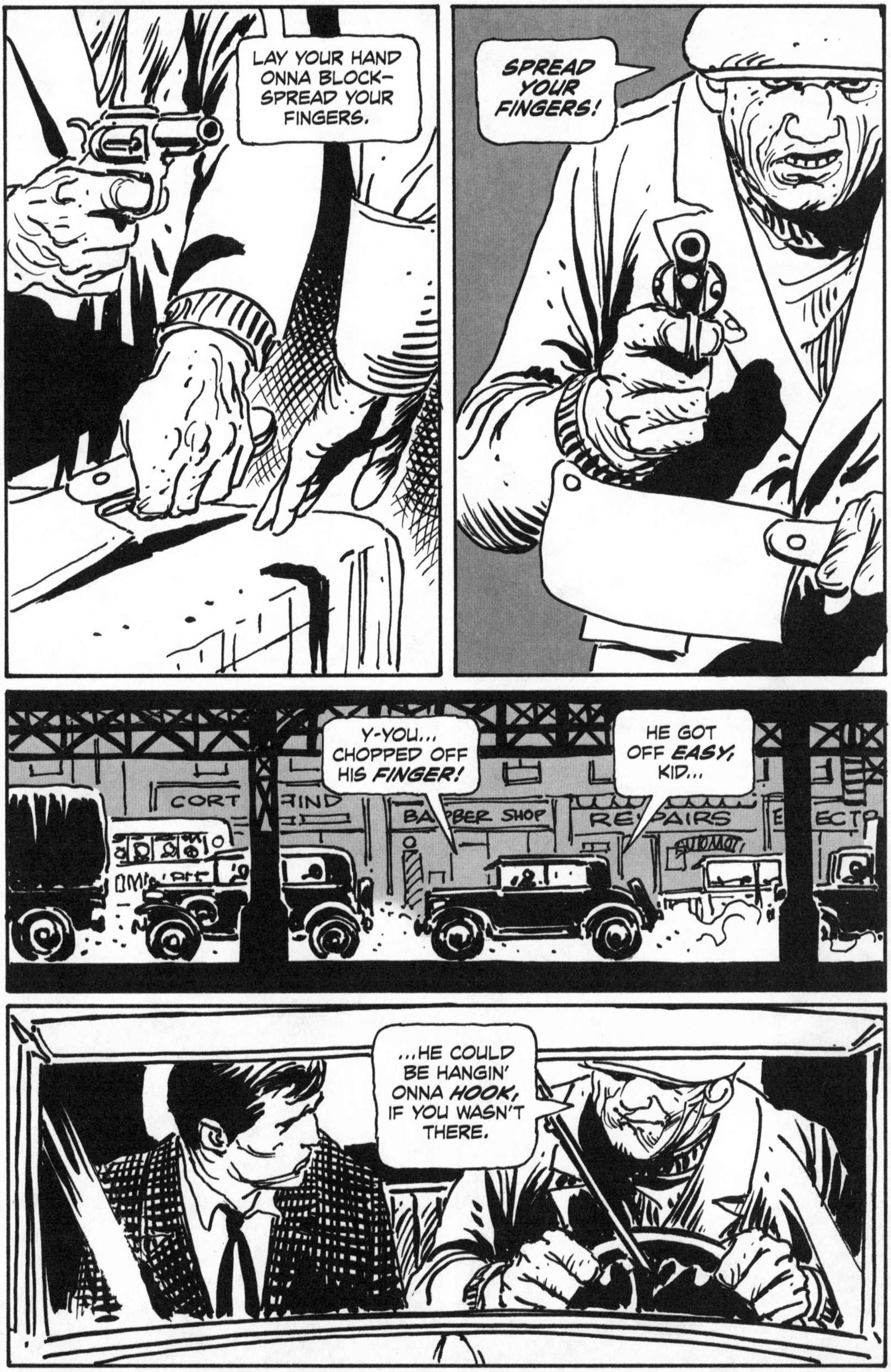
LAY YOUR HAND ONNA BLOCK--SPREAD YOUR FINGERS.
SPREAD YOUR FINGERS!
CORT
BARBER SHOP
REPAIRS
Y-YOU... CHOPPED OFF HIS FINGER!
HE GOT OFF EASY, KID...
...HE COULD BE HANGIN' ONNA HOOK, IF YOU WASN'T THERE.

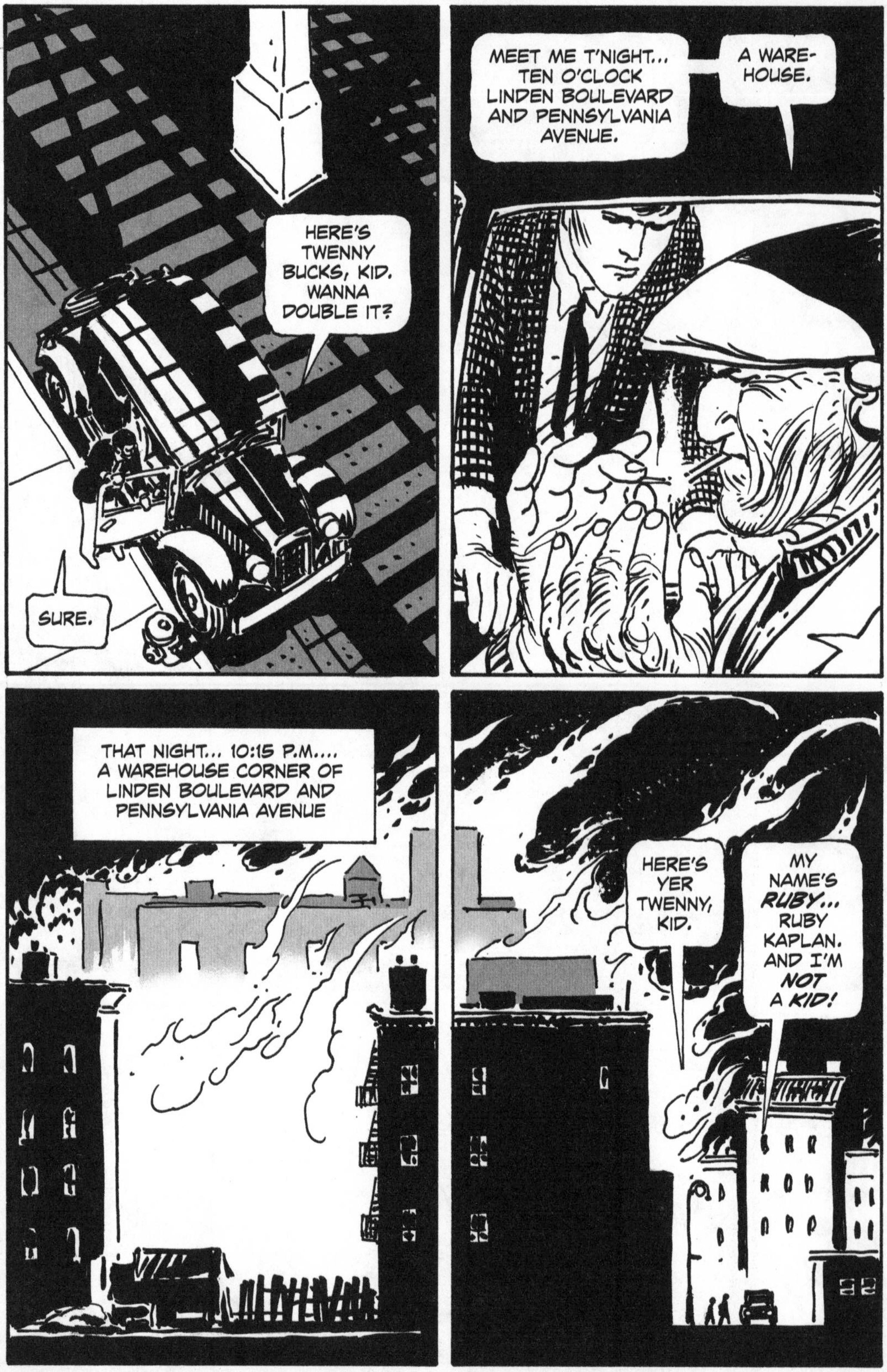
HERE'S TWENNY BUCKS, KID. WANNA DOUBLE IT?
SURE.
MEET ME T'NIGHT... TEN O'CLOCK LINDEN BOULEVARD AND PENNSYLVANIA AVENUE.
A WARE-HOUSE.
THAT NIGHT... 10:15 P.M.... A WAREHOUSE CORNER OF LINDEN BOULEVARD AND PENNSYLVANIA AVENUE
HERE'S YER TWENNY, KID.
MY NAME'S *RUBY*... RUBY KAPLAN. AND I'M *NOT* A *KID!*

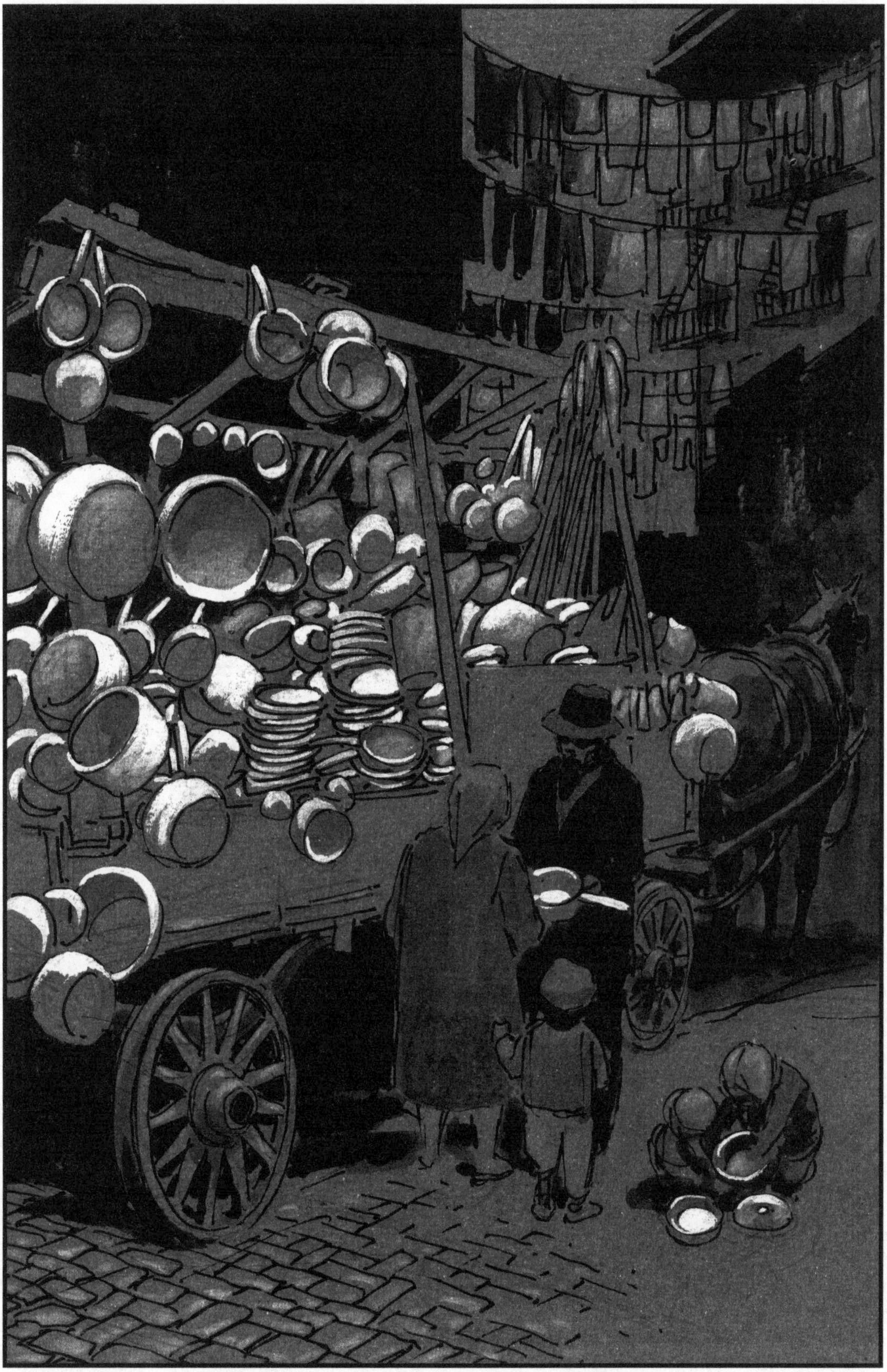

Tinware on the Hoof — Brooklyn

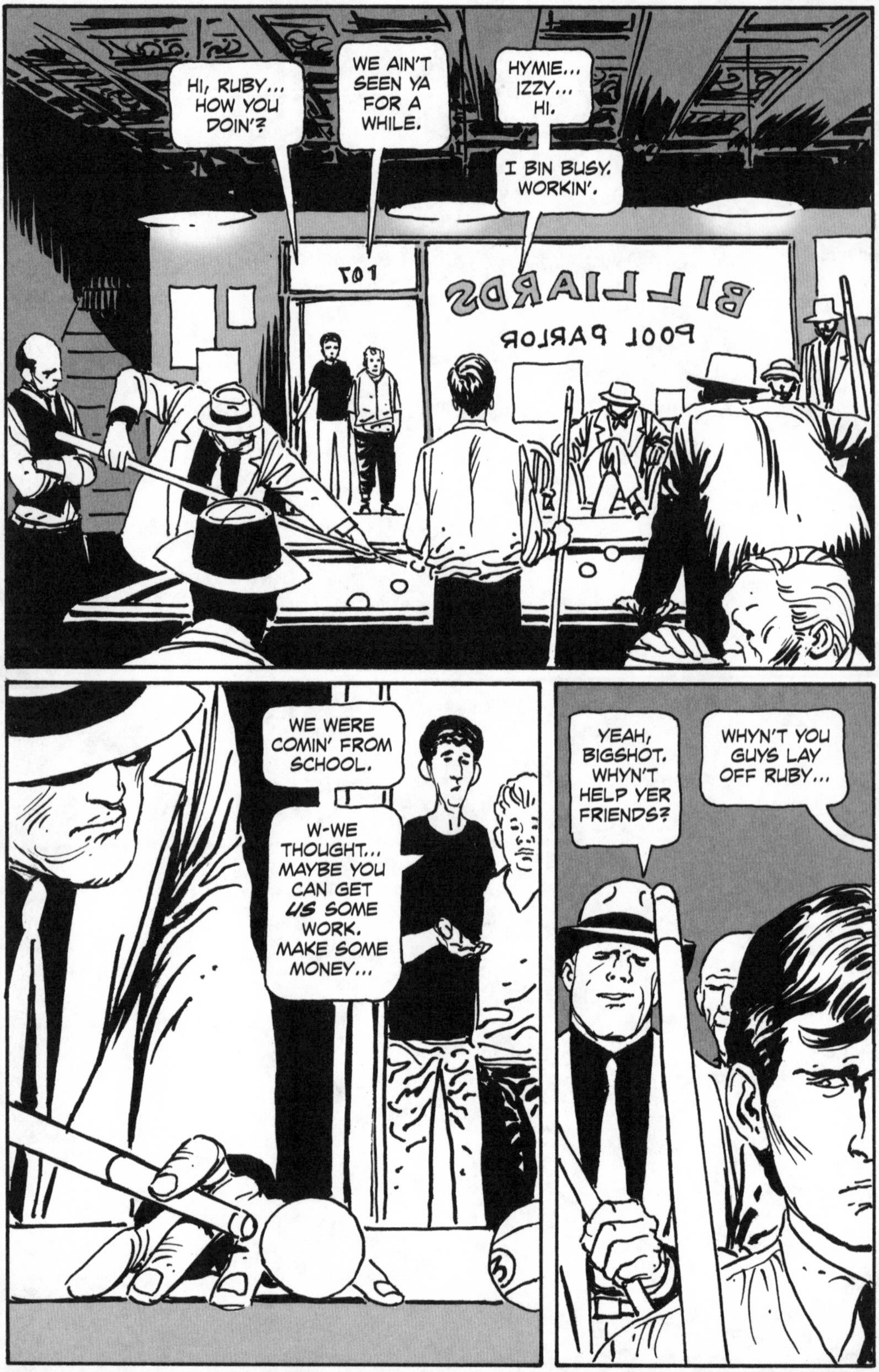
HI, RUBY... HOW YOU DOIN'?
WE AIN'T SEEN YA FOR A WHILE.
HYMIE... IZZY... HI.
I BIN BUSY. WORKIN'.
101
BILLIARDS
POOL PARLOR
WE WERE COMIN' FROM SCHOOL.
W-WE THOUGHT... MAYBE YOU CAN GET US SOME WORK. MAKE SOME MONEY...
YEAH, BIGSHOT. WHYN'T HELP YER FRIENDS?
WHYN'T YOU GUYS LAY OFF RUBY...

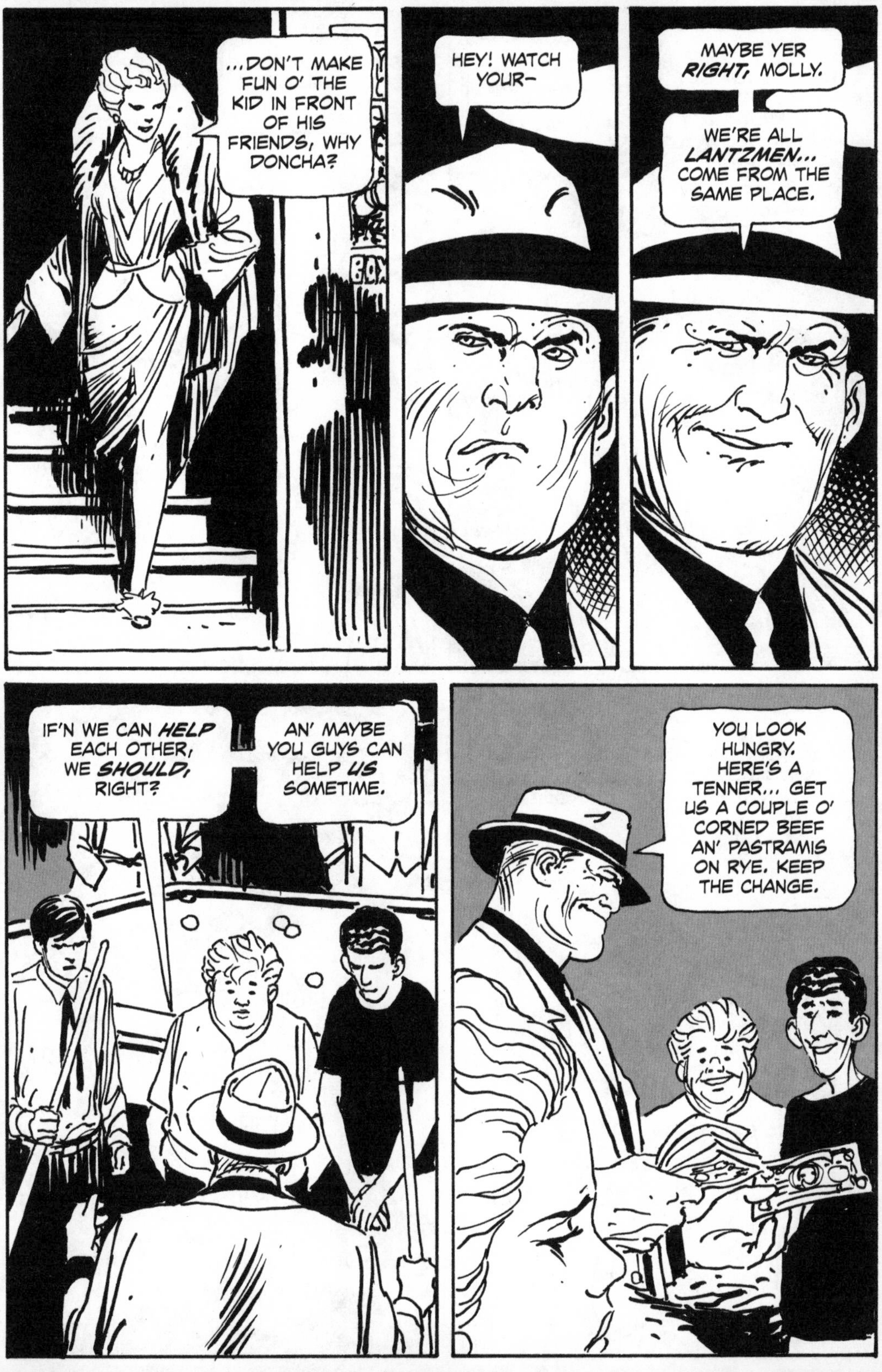
...DON'T MAKE FUN O' THE KID IN FRONT OF HIS FRIENDS, WHY DONCHA?
HEY! WATCH YOUR—
MAYBE YER RIGHT, MOLLY.
WE'RE ALL LANTZMEN... COME FROM THE SAME PLACE.
IF'N WE CAN HELP EACH OTHER, WE SHOULD, RIGHT?
AN' MAYBE YOU GUYS CAN HELP US SOMETIME.
YOU LOOK HUNGRY. HERE'S A TENNER... GET US A COUPLE O' CORNED BEEF AN' PASTRAMIS ON RYE. KEEP THE CHANGE.

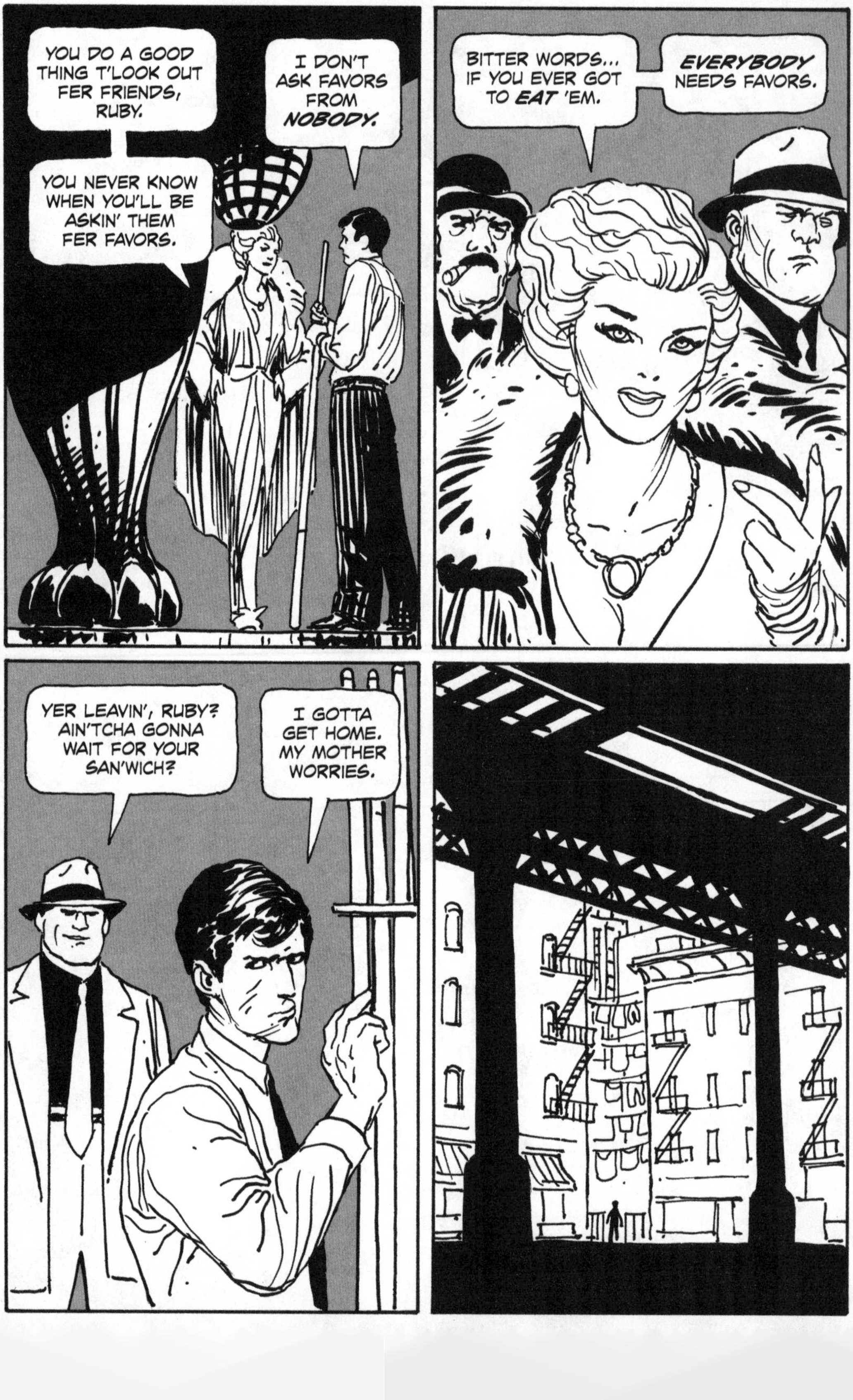
YOU DO A GOOD THING T'LOOK OUT FER FRIENDS, RUBY.
YOU NEVER KNOW WHEN YOU'LL BE ASKIN' THEM FER FAVORS.
I DON'T ASK FAVORS FROM NOBODY.
BITTER WORDS... IF YOU EVER GOT TO EAT 'EM.
EVERYBODY NEEDS FAVORS.
YER LEAVIN', RUBY? AIN'TCHA GONNA WAIT FOR YOUR SAN'WICH?
I GOTTA GET HOME. MY MOTHER WORRIES.

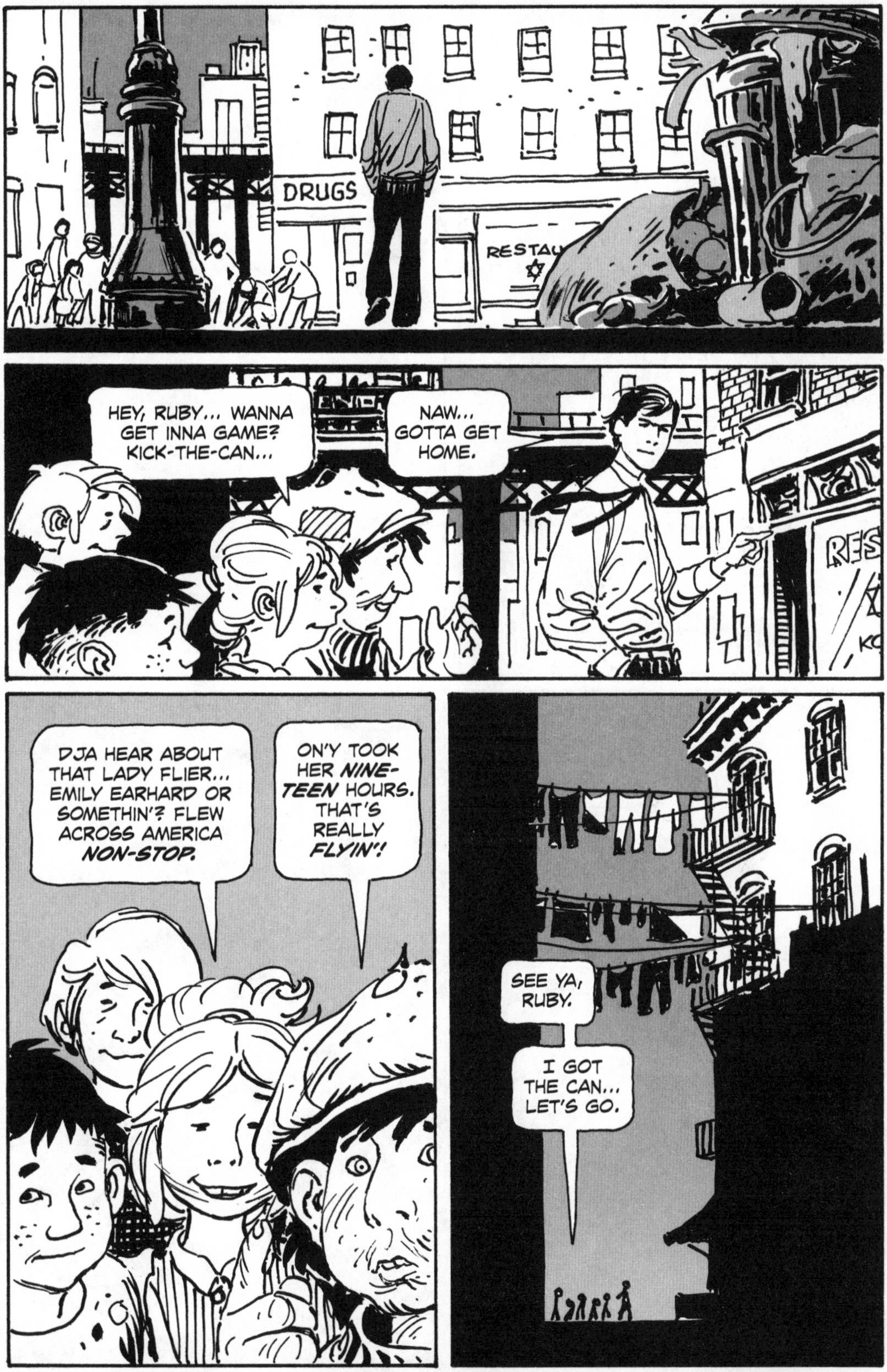
DRUGS
RESTAU
HEY, RUBY... WANNA GET INNA GAME? KICK-THE-CAN...
NAW... GOTTA GET HOME.
DJA HEAR ABOUT THAT LADY FLIER... EMILY EARHARD OR SOMETHIN'? FLEW ACROSS AMERICA *NON-STOP.*
ON'Y TOOK HER *NINE-TEEN* HOURS. THAT'S REALLY *FLYIN'!*
SEE YA, RUBY.
I GOT THE CAN... LET'S GO.

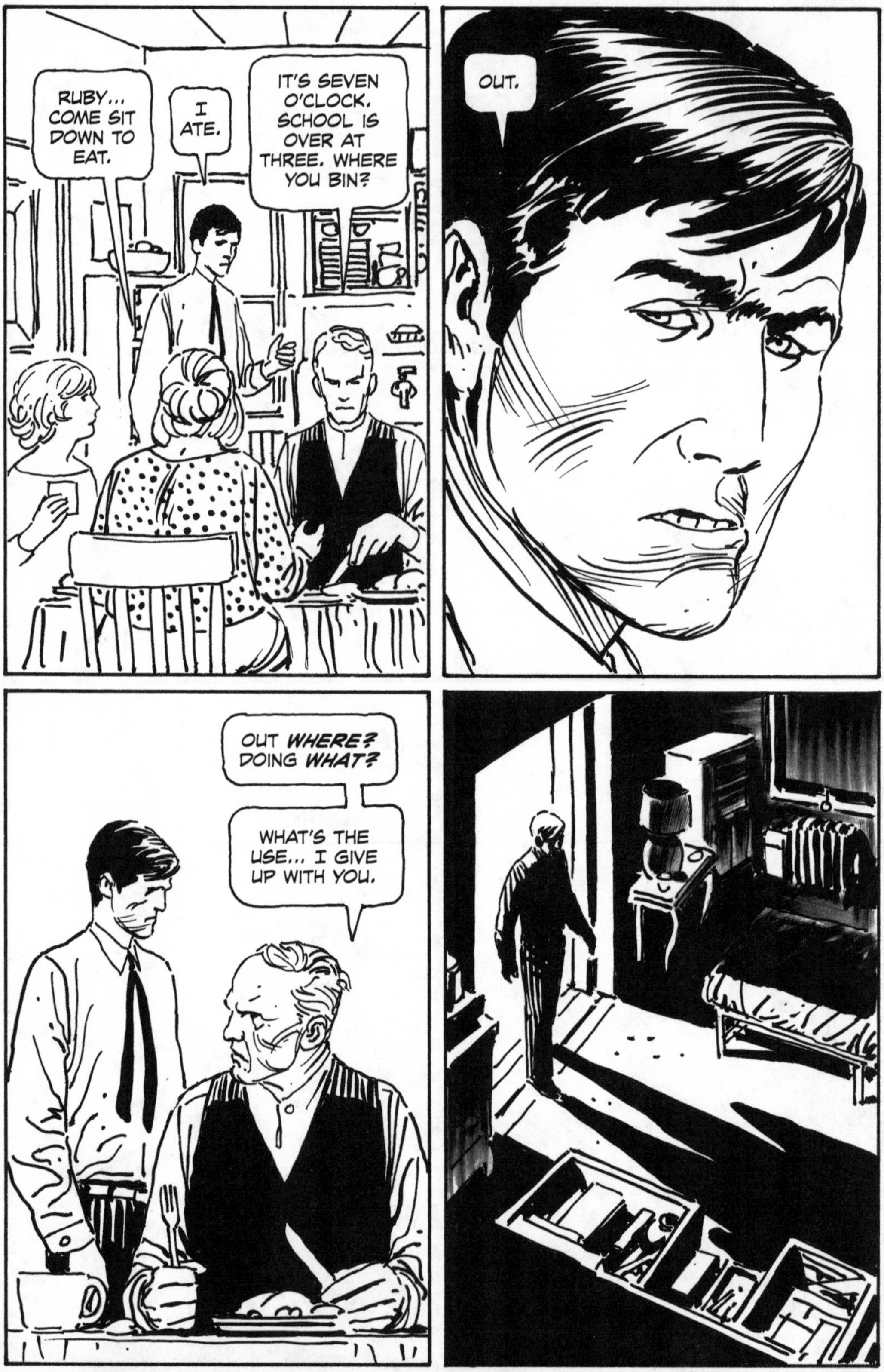
RUBY... COME SIT DOWN TO EAT.
I ATE.
IT'S SEVEN O'CLOCK. SCHOOL IS OVER AT THREE. WHERE YOU BIN?
OUT.
OUT *WHERE?* DOING *WHAT?*
WHAT'S THE USE... I GIVE UP WITH YOU.

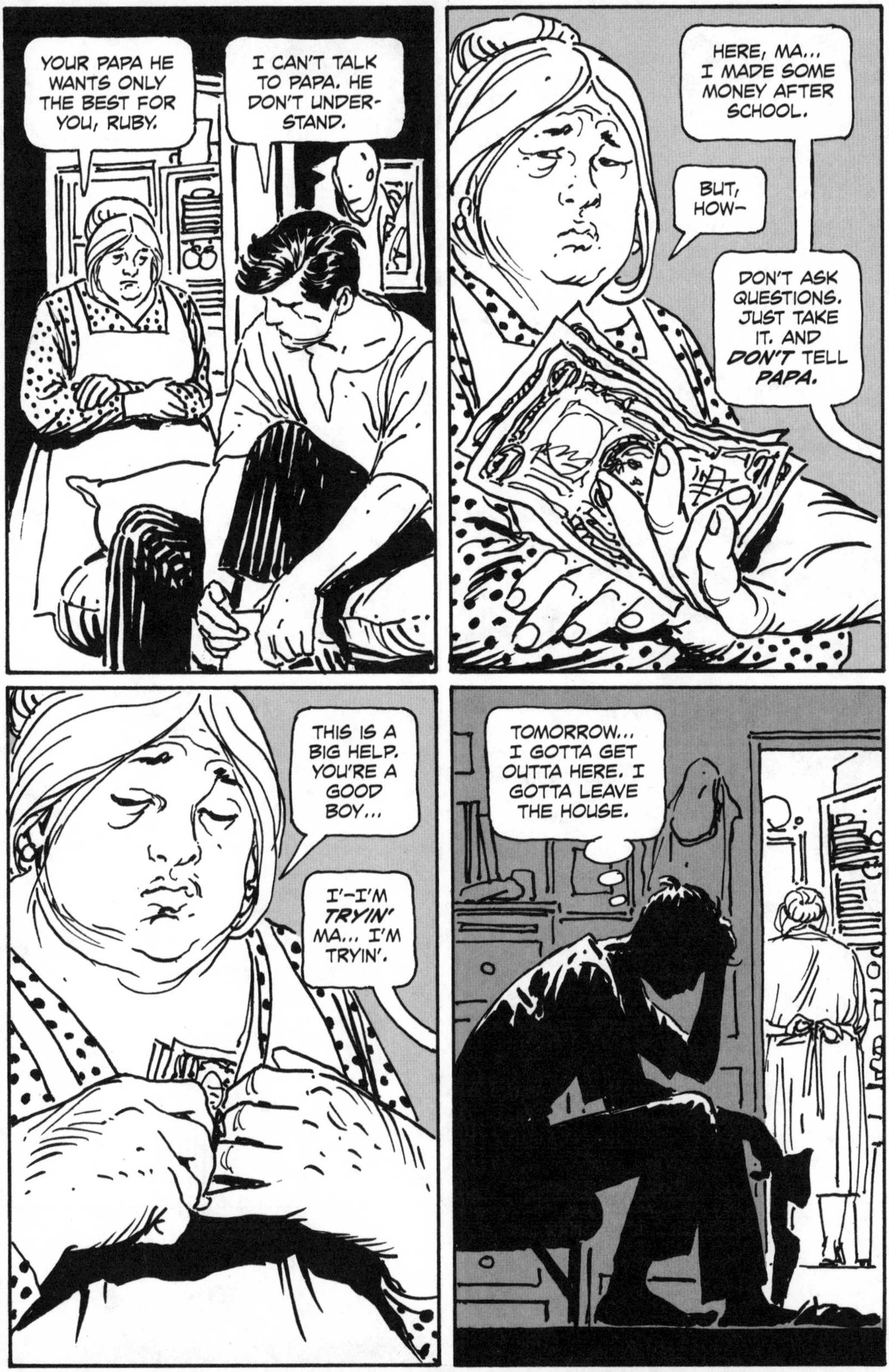
YOUR PAPA HE WANTS ONLY THE BEST FOR YOU, RUBY.
I CAN'T TALK TO PAPA. HE DON'T UNDER-STAND.
HERE, MA... I MADE SOME MONEY AFTER SCHOOL.
BUT, HOW-
DON'T ASK QUESTIONS. JUST TAKE IT. AND DON'T TELL PAPA.
THIS IS A BIG HELP. YOU'RE A GOOD BOY...
I'-I'M TRYIN' MA... I'M TRYIN'.
TOMORROW... I GOTTA GET OUTTA HERE. I GOTTA LEAVE THE HOUSE.

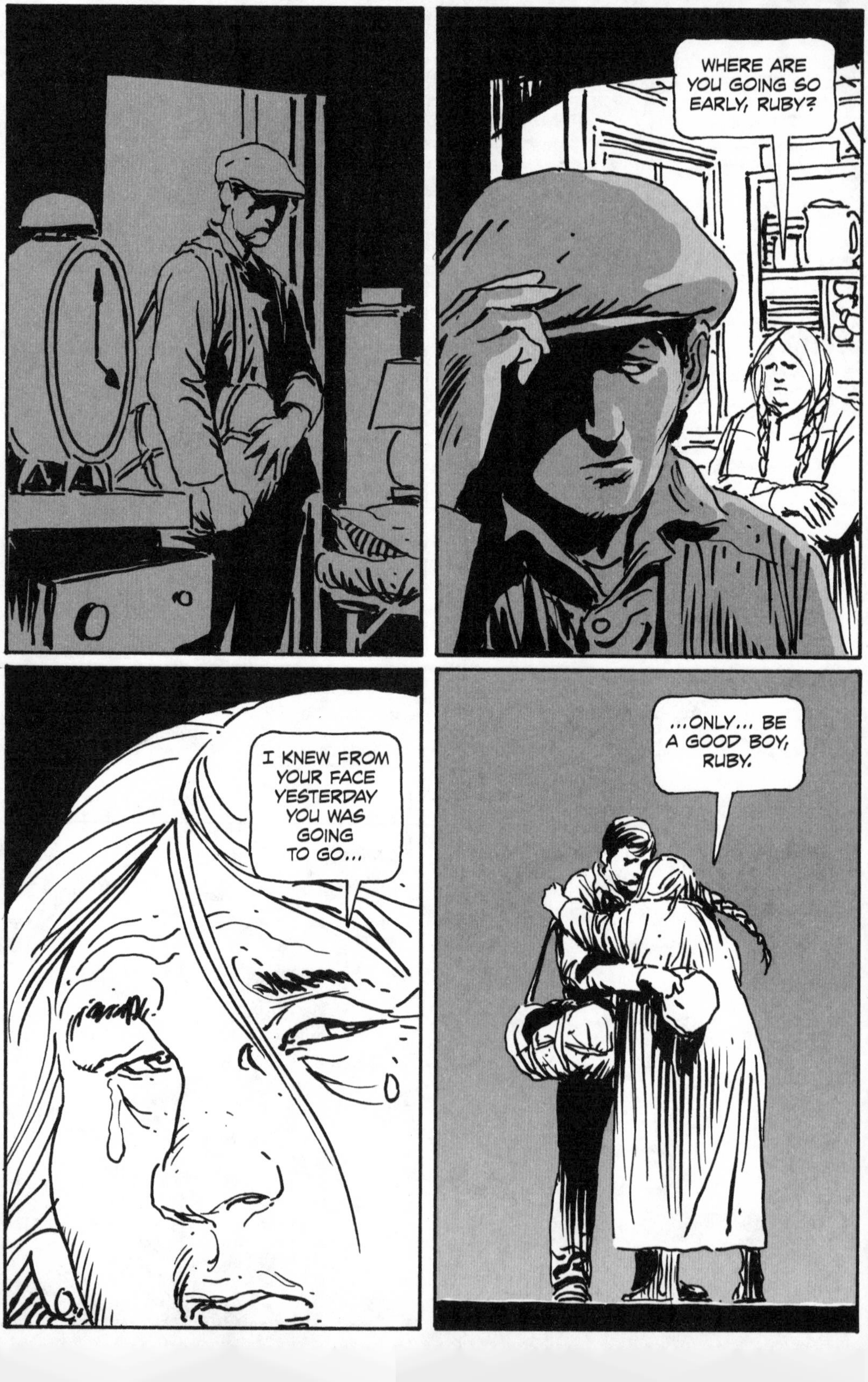
WHERE ARE YOU GOING SO EARLY, RUBY?
I KNEW FROM YOUR FACE YESTERDAY YOU WAS GOING TO GO...
...ONLY... BE A GOOD BOY, RUBY.

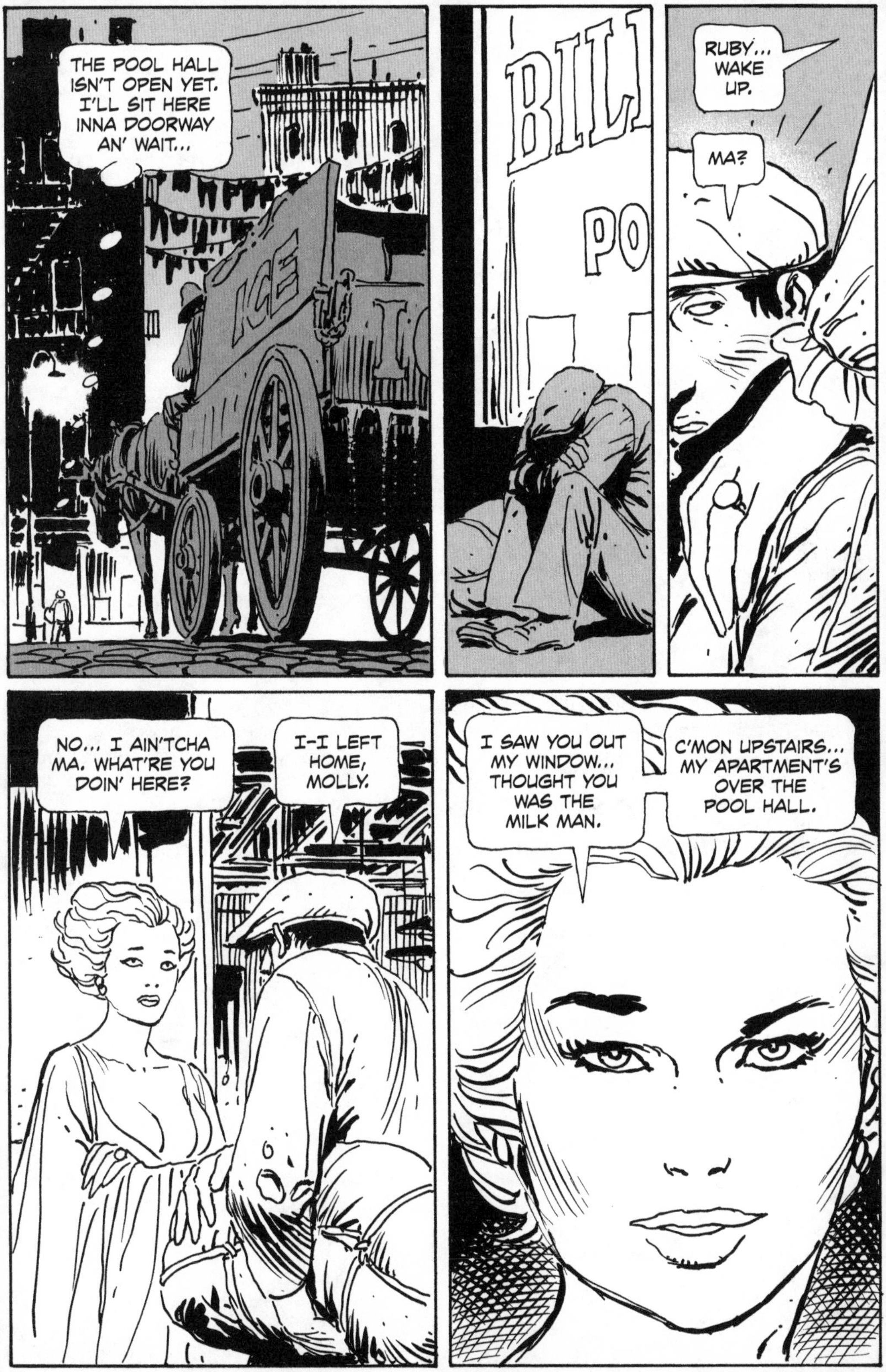
THE POOL HALL ISN'T OPEN YET. I'LL SIT HERE INNA DOORWAY AN' WAIT...
ICE
BILL
PO
RUBY... WAKE UP.
MA?
NO... I AIN'TCHA MA. WHAT'RE YOU DOIN' HERE?
I-I LEFT HOME, MOLLY.
I SAW YOU OUT MY WINDOW... THOUGHT YOU WAS THE MILK MAN.
C'MON UPSTAIRS... MY APARTMENT'S OVER THE POOL HALL.

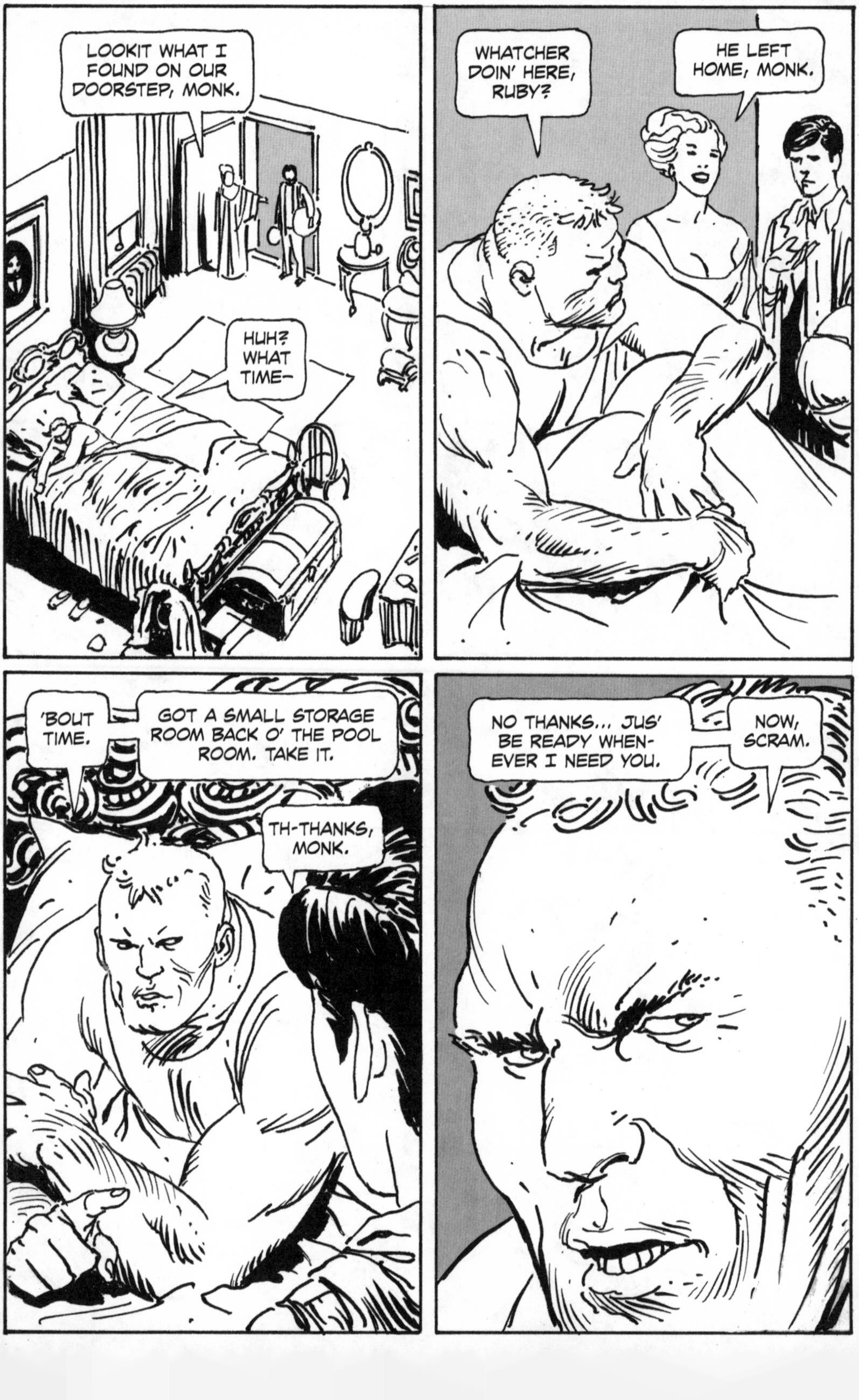
LOOKIT WHAT I FOUND ON OUR DOORSTEP, MONK.
HUH? WHAT TIME–
WHATCHER DOIN' HERE, RUBY?
HE LEFT HOME, MONK.
'BOUT TIME.
GOT A SMALL STORAGE ROOM BACK O' THE POOL ROOM. TAKE IT.
TH-THANKS, MONK.
NO THANKS... JUS' BE READY WHEN-EVER I NEED YOU.
NOW, SCRAM.

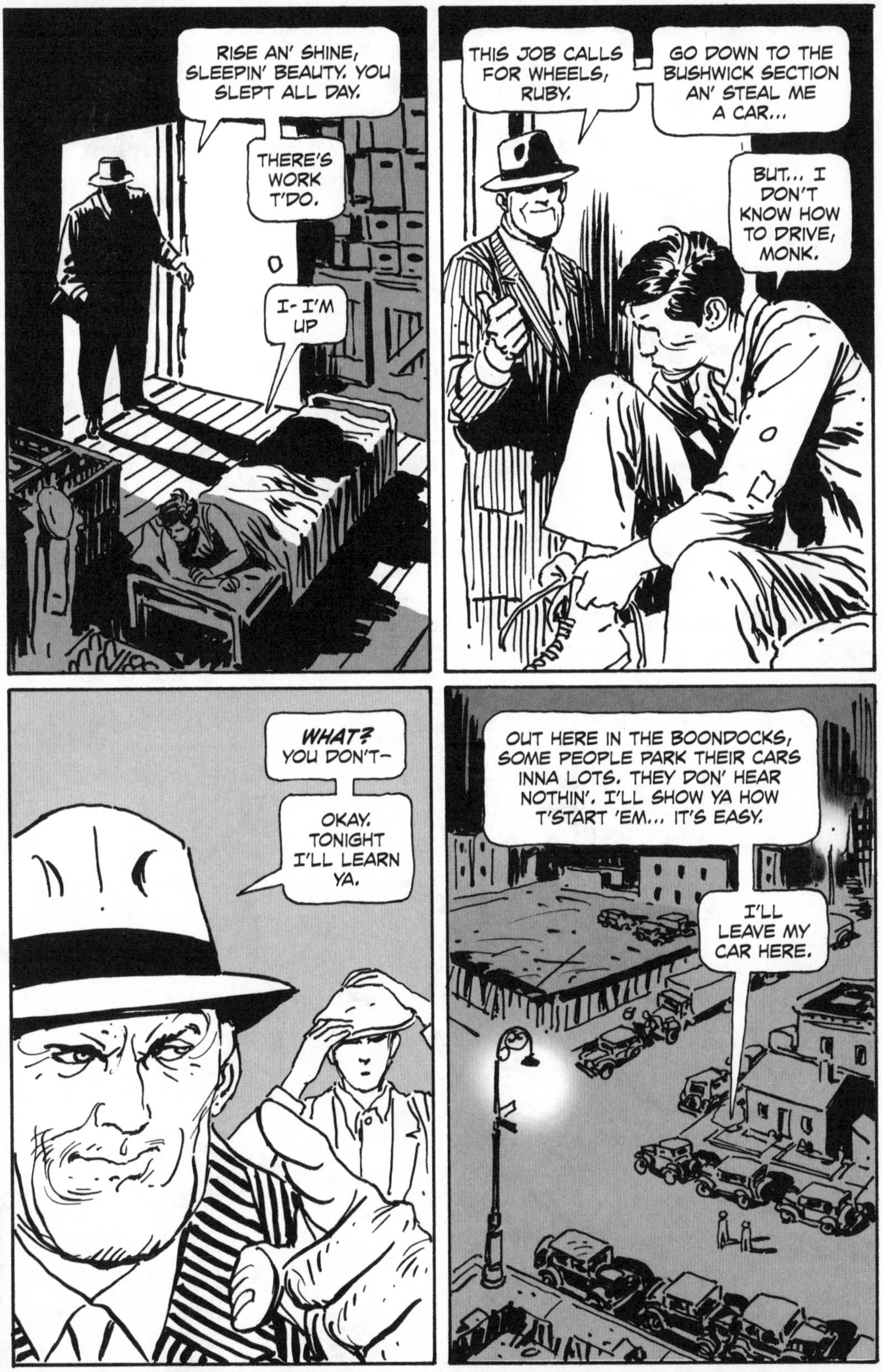
RISE AN' SHINE, SLEEPIN' BEAUTY. YOU SLEPT ALL DAY.
THERE'S WORK T'DO.
I- I'M UP
THIS JOB CALLS FOR WHEELS, RUBY.
GO DOWN TO THE BUSHWICK SECTION AN' STEAL ME A CAR...
BUT... I DON'T KNOW HOW TO DRIVE, MONK.
WHAT? YOU DON'T-
OKAY. TONIGHT I'LL LEARN YA.
OUT HERE IN THE BOONDOCKS, SOME PEOPLE PARK THEIR CARS INNA LOTS. THEY DON' HEAR NOTHIN'. I'LL SHOW YA HOW T'START 'EM... IT'S EASY.
I'LL LEAVE MY CAR HERE.

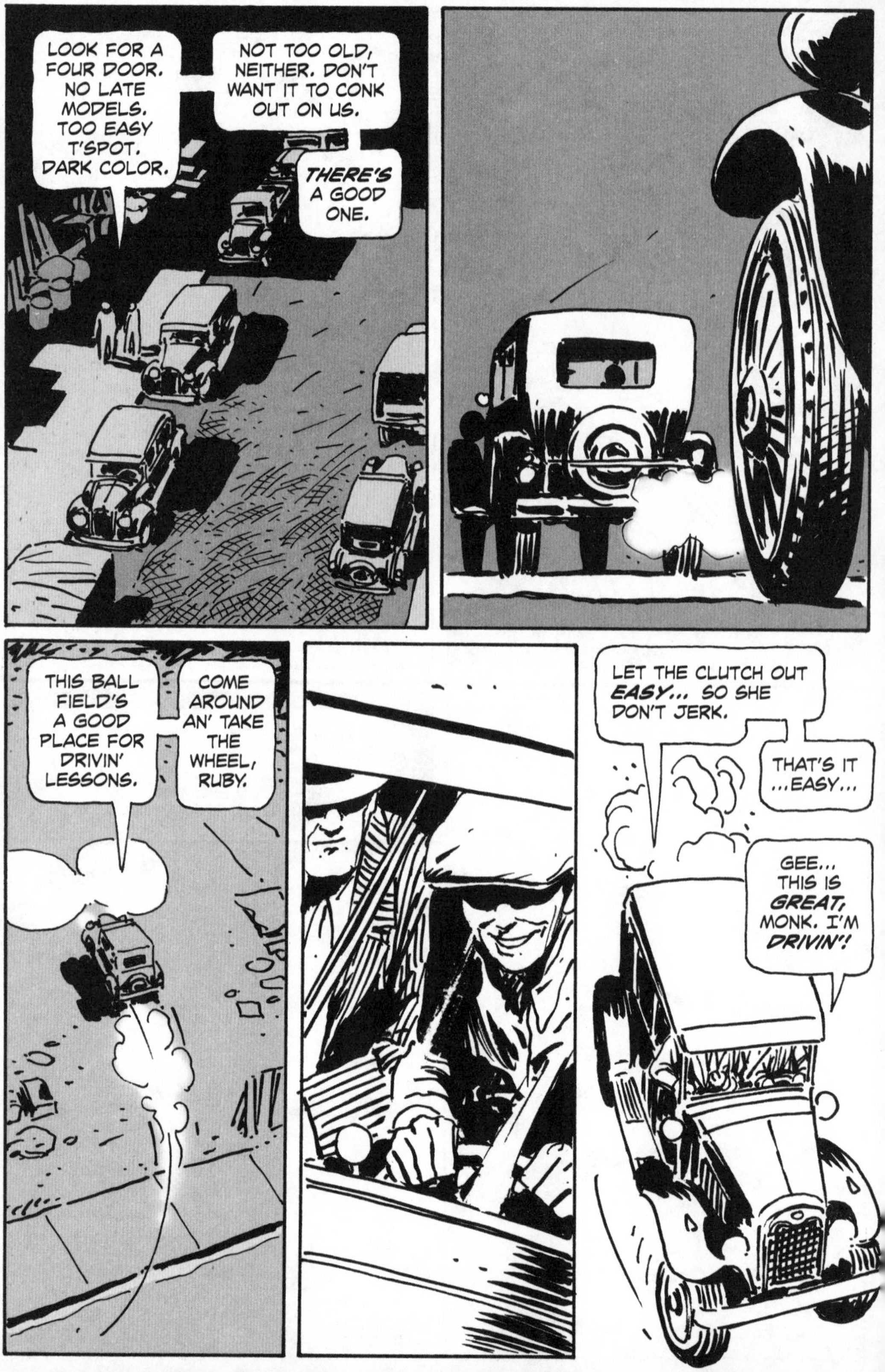
LOOK FOR A FOUR DOOR. NO LATE MODELS. TOO EASY T'SPOT. DARK COLOR.
NOT TOO OLD, NEITHER. DON'T WANT IT TO CONK OUT ON US.
THERE'S A GOOD ONE.
THIS BALL FIELD'S A GOOD PLACE FOR DRIVIN' LESSONS.
COME AROUND AN' TAKE THE WHEEL, RUBY.
LET THE CLUTCH OUT EASY... SO SHE DON'T JERK.
THAT'S IT ...EASY...
GEE... THIS IS GREAT, MONK. I'M DRIVIN'!

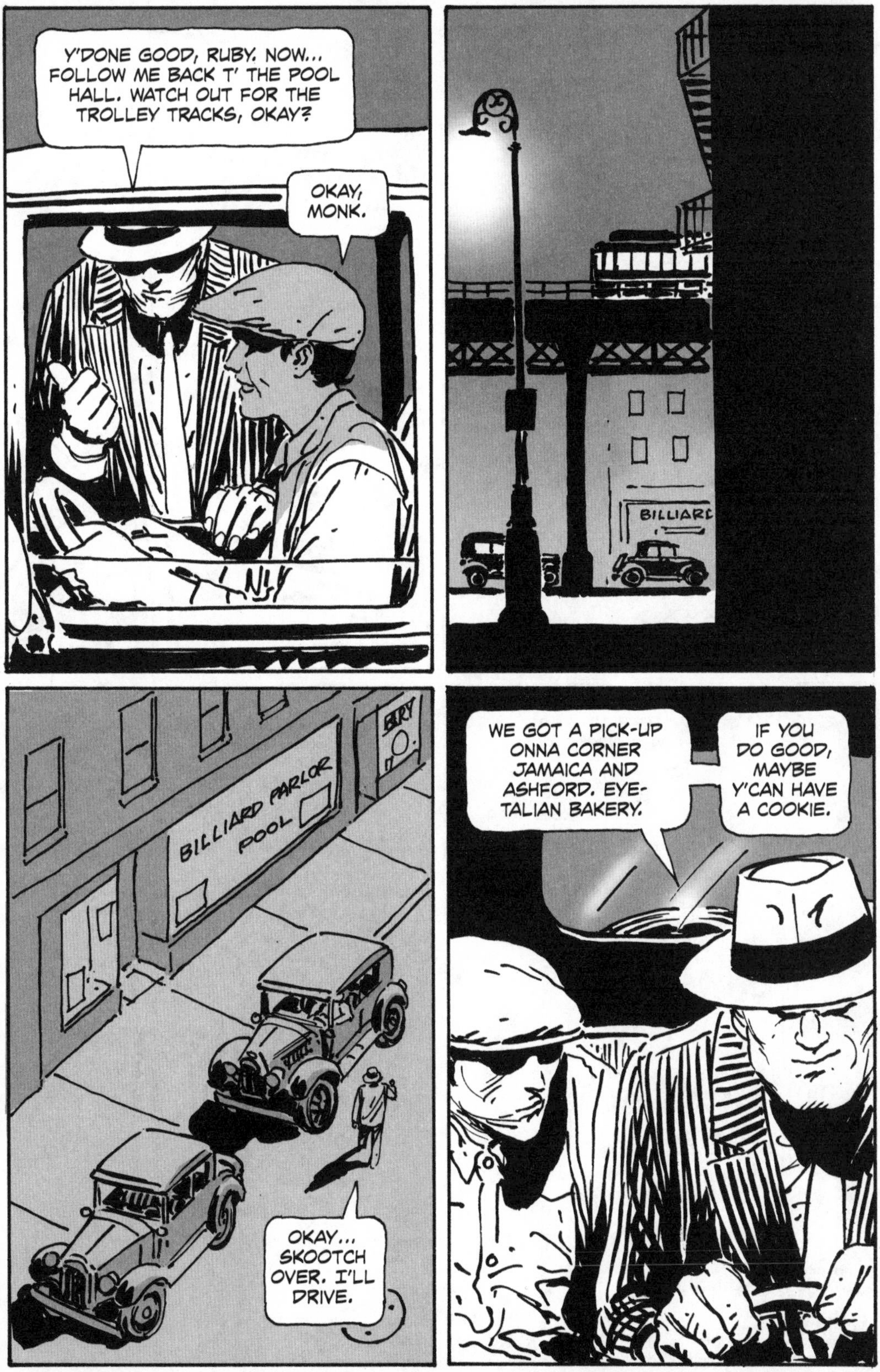
Y'DONE GOOD, RUBY. NOW... FOLLOW ME BACK T' THE POOL HALL. WATCH OUT FOR THE TROLLEY TRACKS, OKAY?
OKAY, MONK.
BILLIARD
BILLIARD PARLOR
POOL
OKAY... SKOOTCH OVER. I'LL DRIVE.
WE GOT A PICK-UP ONNA CORNER JAMAICA AND ASHFORD. EYE-TALIAN BAKERY.
IF YOU DO GOOD, MAYBE Y'CAN HAVE A COOKIE.

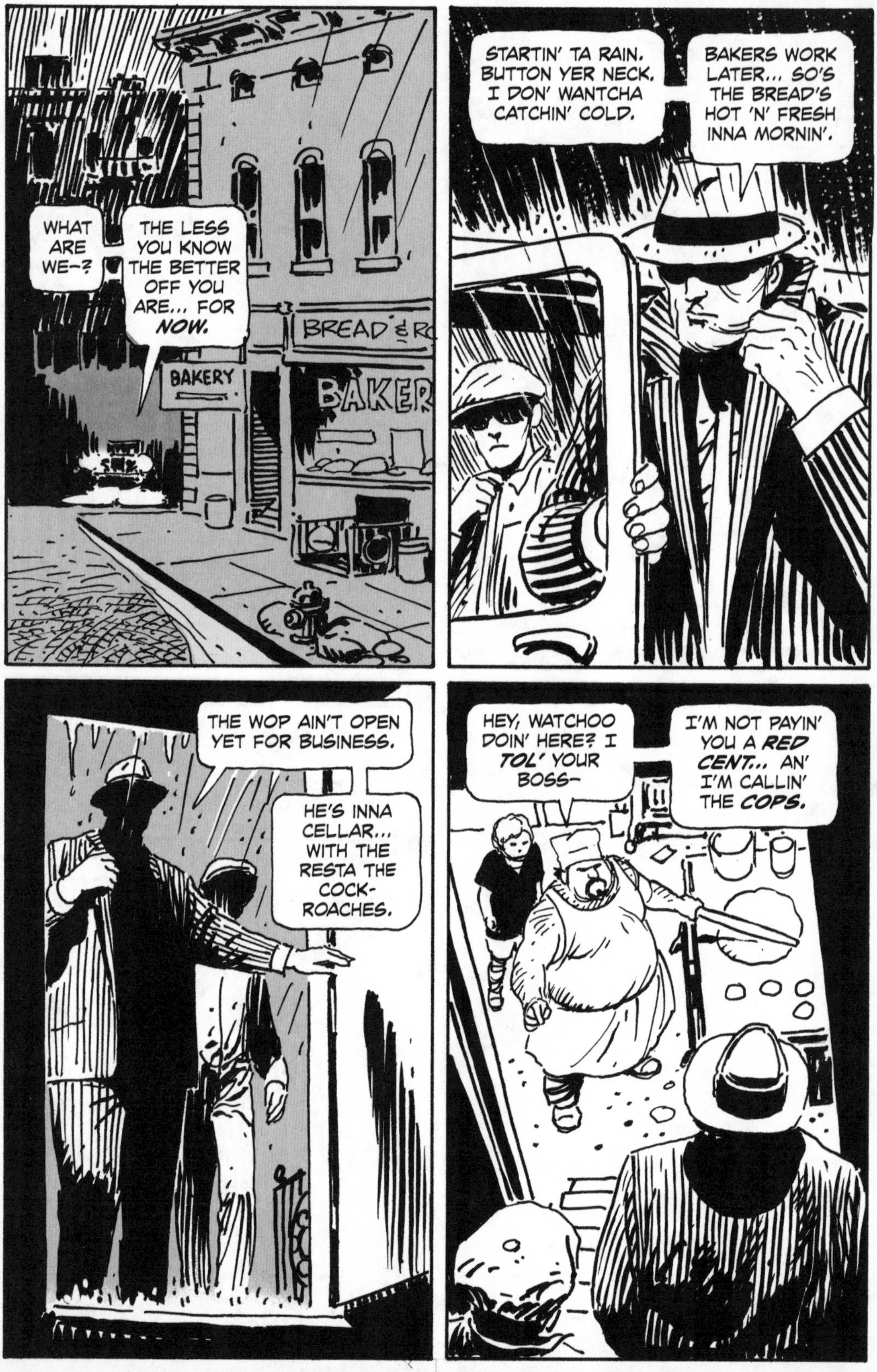
WHAT ARE WE-?
THE LESS YOU KNOW THE BETTER OFF YOU ARE... FOR NOW.
BREAD & RO
BAKERY
BAKER
STARTIN' TA RAIN. BUTTON YER NECK. I DON' WANTCHA CATCHIN' COLD.
BAKERS WORK LATER... SO'S THE BREAD'S HOT 'N' FRESH INNA MORNIN'.
THE WOP AIN'T OPEN YET FOR BUSINESS.
HE'S INNA CELLAR... WITH THE RESTA THE COCK-ROACHES.
HEY, WATCHOO DOIN' HERE? I TOL' YOUR BOSS-
I'M NOT PAYIN' YOU A RED CENT... AN' I'M CALLIN' THE COPS.

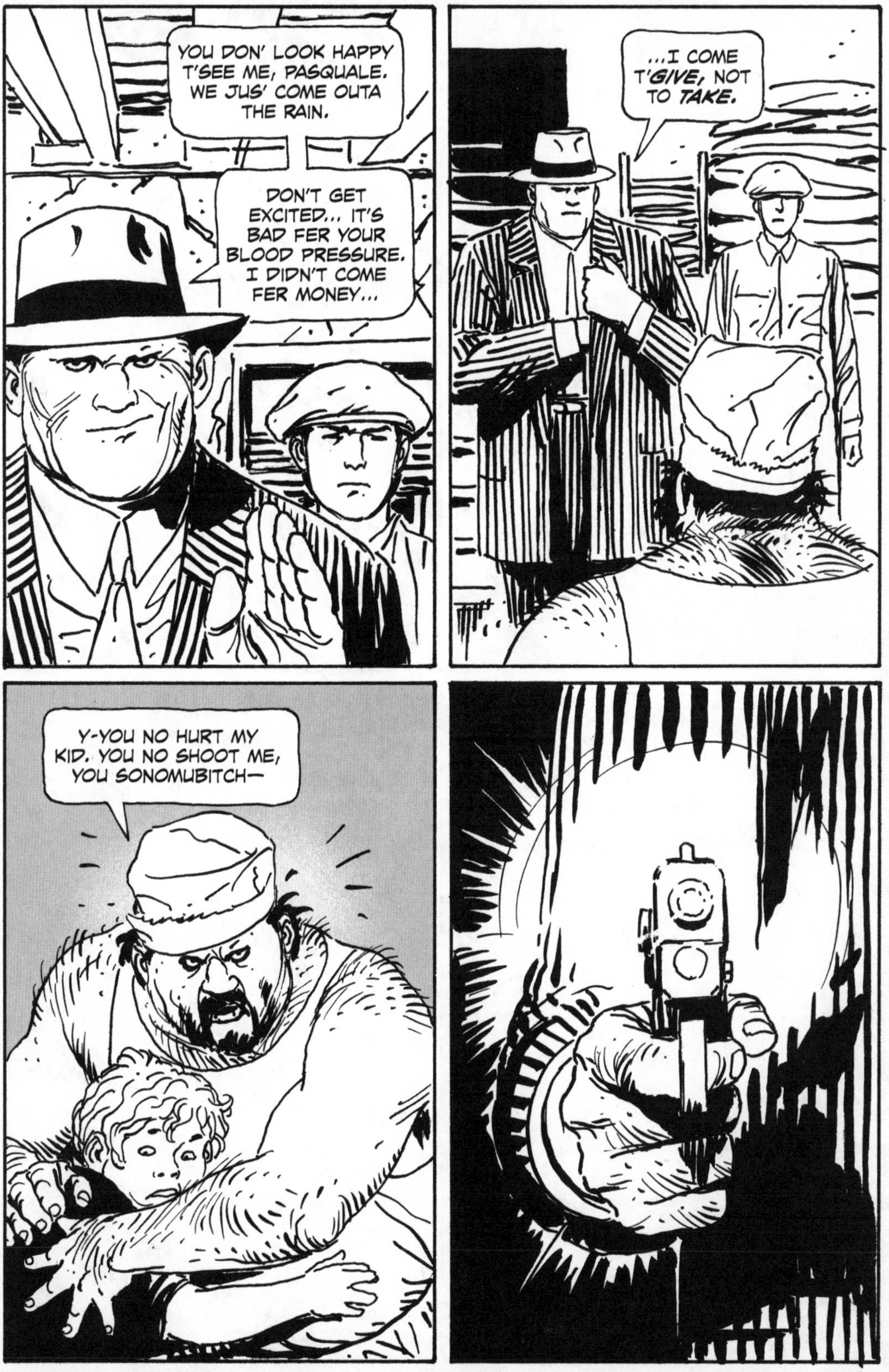
YOU DON' LOOK HAPPY T'SEE ME, PASQUALE. WE JUS' COME OUTA THE RAIN.
DON'T GET EXCITED... IT'S BAD FER YOUR BLOOD PRESSURE. I DIDN'T COME FER MONEY...
...I COME T'GIVE, NOT TO TAKE.
Y-YOU NO HURT MY KID. YOU NO SHOOT ME, YOU SONOMUBITCH—

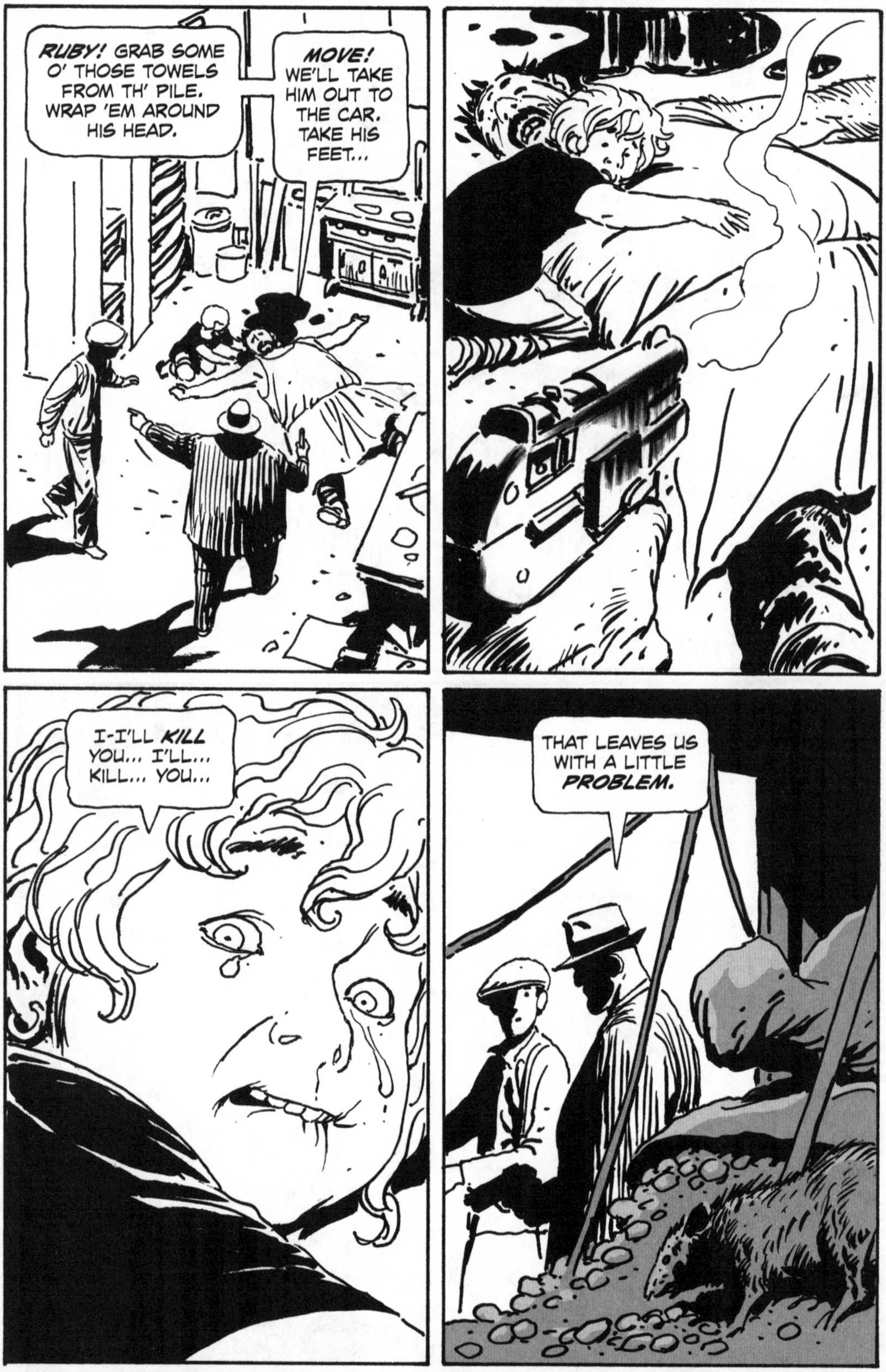
RUBY! GRAB SOME O' THOSE TOWELS FROM TH' PILE. WRAP 'EM AROUND HIS HEAD.
MOVE! WE'LL TAKE HIM OUT TO THE CAR. TAKE HIS FEET...
I-I'LL KILL YOU... I'LL... KILL... YOU...
THAT LEAVES US WITH A LITTLE PROBLEM.

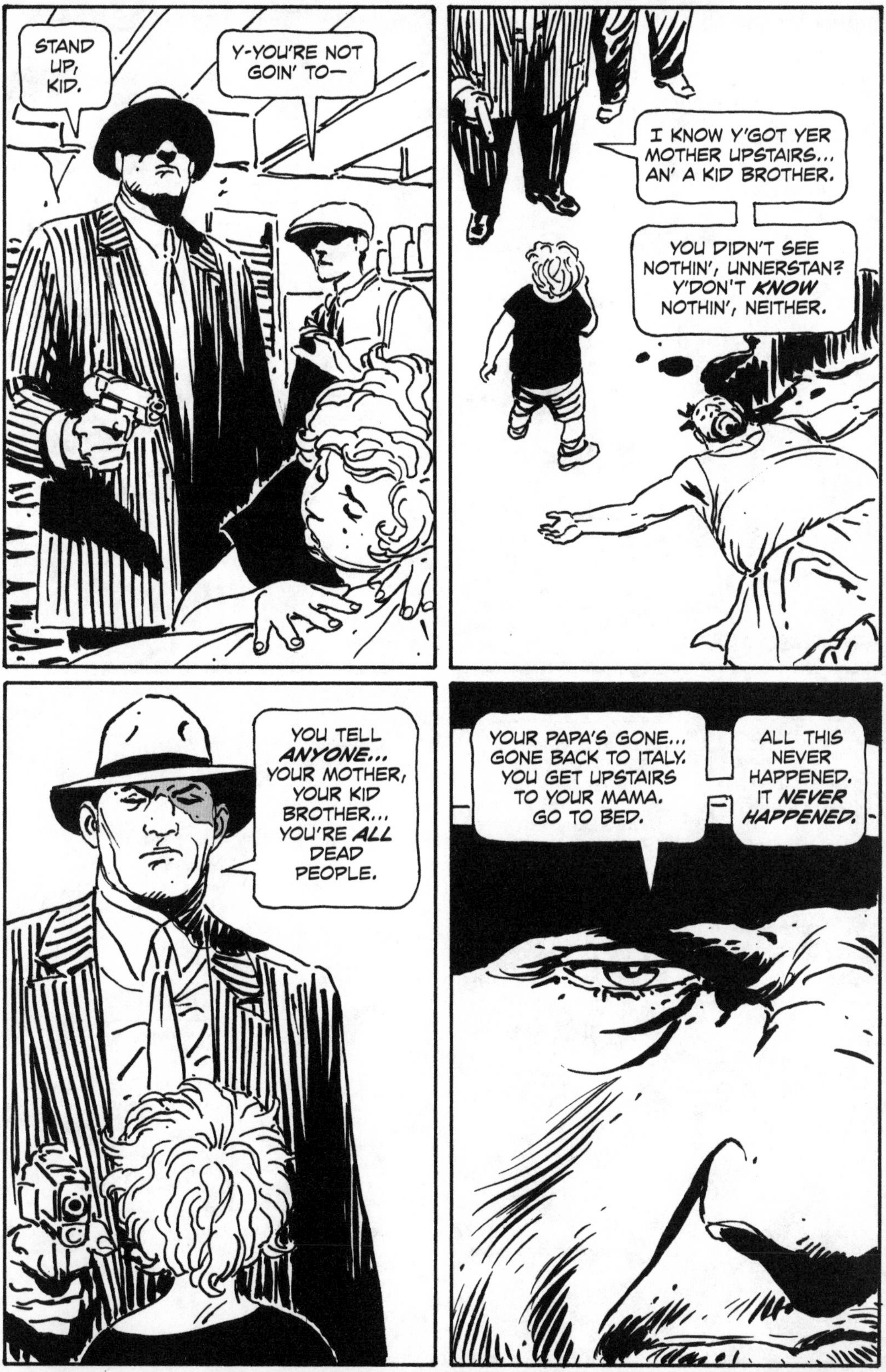
STAND UP, KID.
Y-YOU'RE NOT GOIN' TO—
I KNOW Y'GOT YER MOTHER UPSTAIRS... AN' A KID BROTHER.
YOU DIDN'T SEE NOTHIN', UNNERSTAN? Y'DON'T KNOW NOTHIN', NEITHER.
YOU TELL ANYONE... YOUR MOTHER, YOUR KID BROTHER... YOU'RE ALL DEAD PEOPLE.
YOUR PAPA'S GONE... GONE BACK TO ITALY. YOU GET UPSTAIRS TO YOUR MAMA. GO TO BED.
ALL THIS NEVER HAPPENED. IT NEVER HAPPENED.

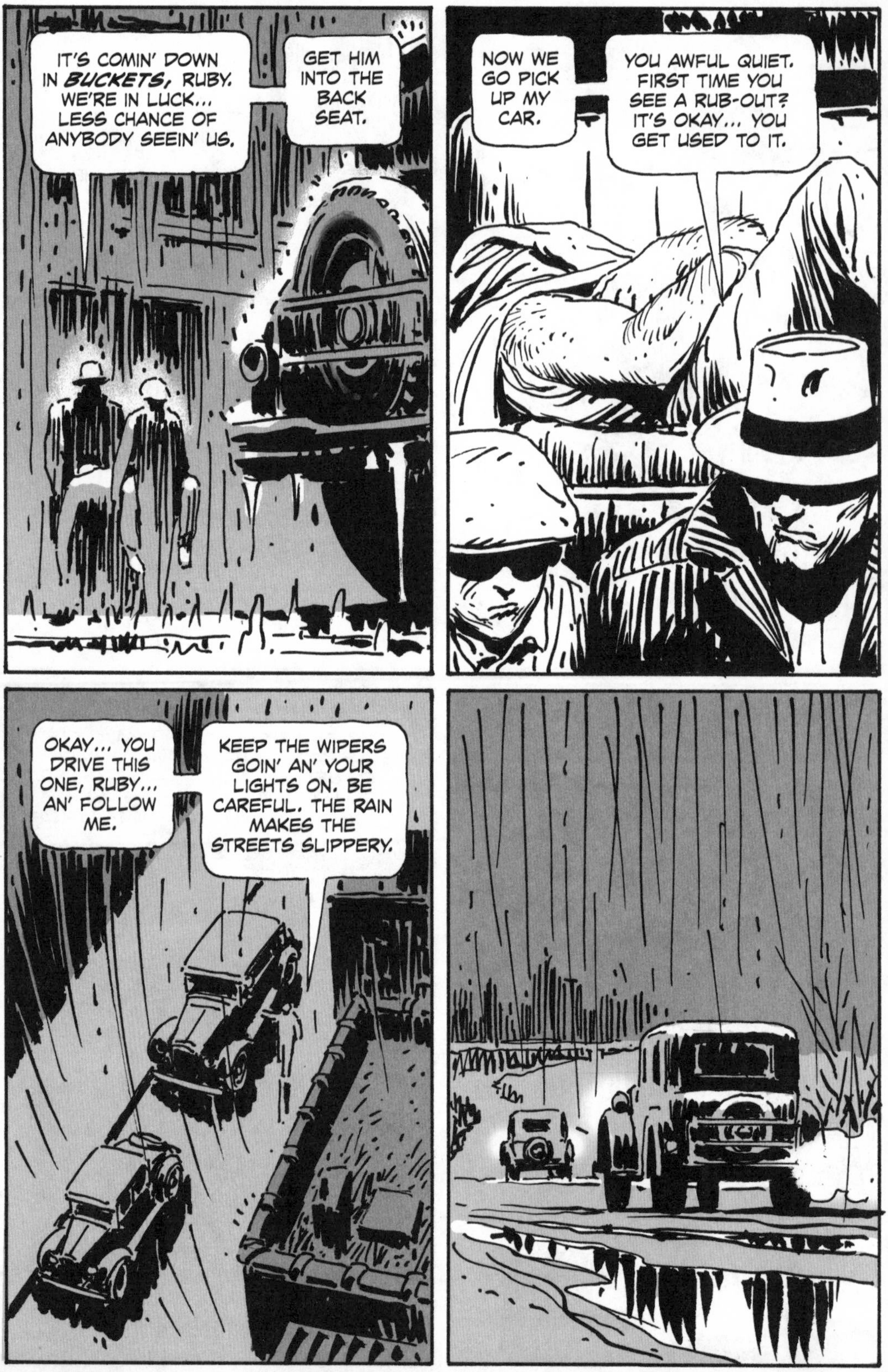

IT'S COMIN' DOWN IN BUCKETS, RUBY. WE'RE IN LUCK... LESS CHANCE OF ANYBODY SEEIN' US.
GET HIM INTO THE BACK SEAT.
NOW WE GO PICK UP MY CAR.
YOU AWFUL QUIET. FIRST TIME YOU SEE A RUB-OUT? IT'S OKAY... YOU GET USED TO IT.
OKAY... YOU DRIVE THIS ONE, RUBY... AN' FOLLOW ME.
KEEP THE WIPERS GOIN' AN' YOUR LIGHTS ON. BE CAREFUL. THE RAIN MAKES THE STREETS SLIPPERY.

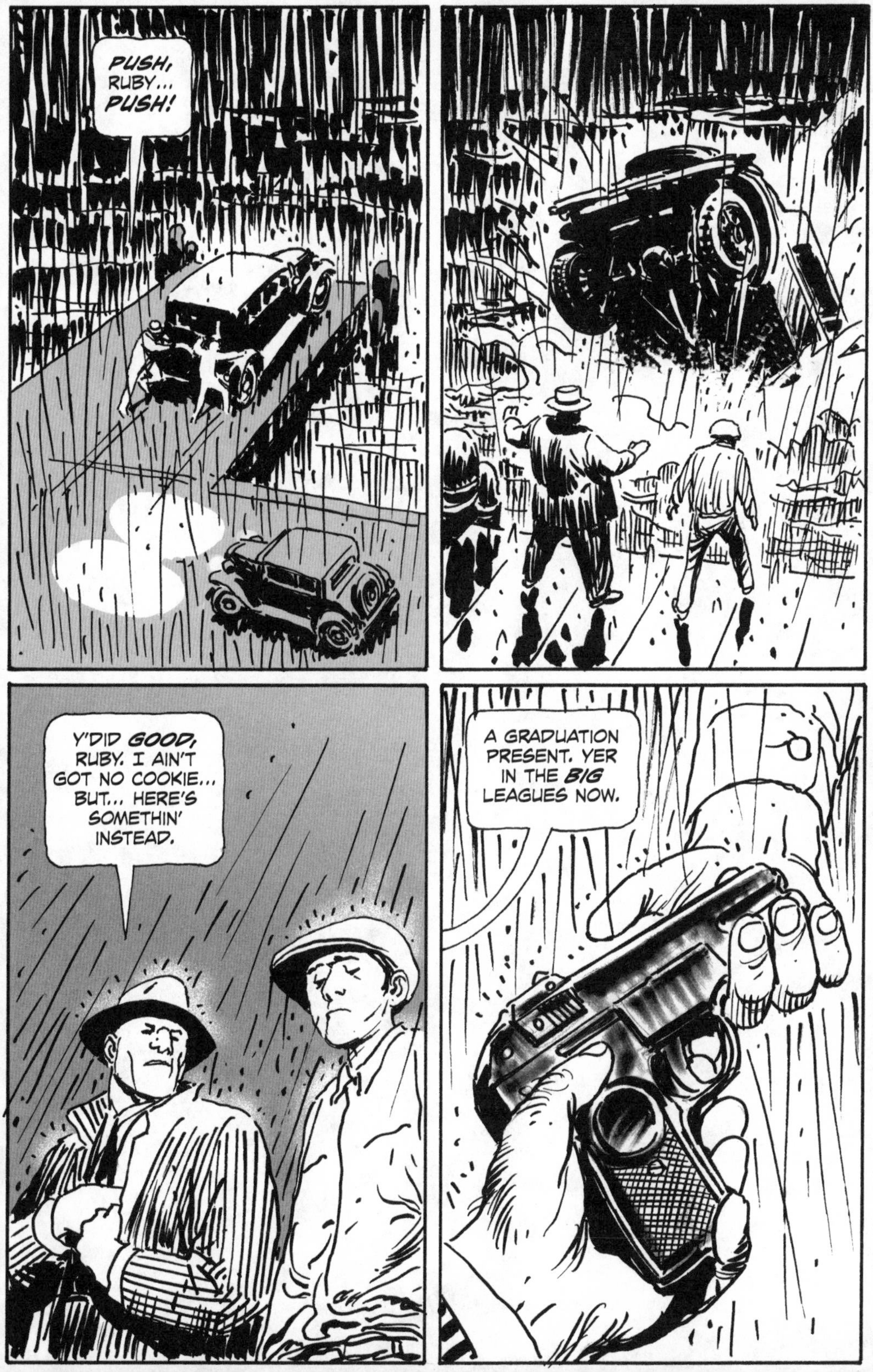
PUSH, RUBY... PUSH!
Y'DID GOOD, RUBY. I AIN'T GOT NO COOKIE... BUT... HERE'S SOMETHIN' INSTEAD.
A GRADUATION PRESENT. YER IN THE BIG LEAGUES NOW.

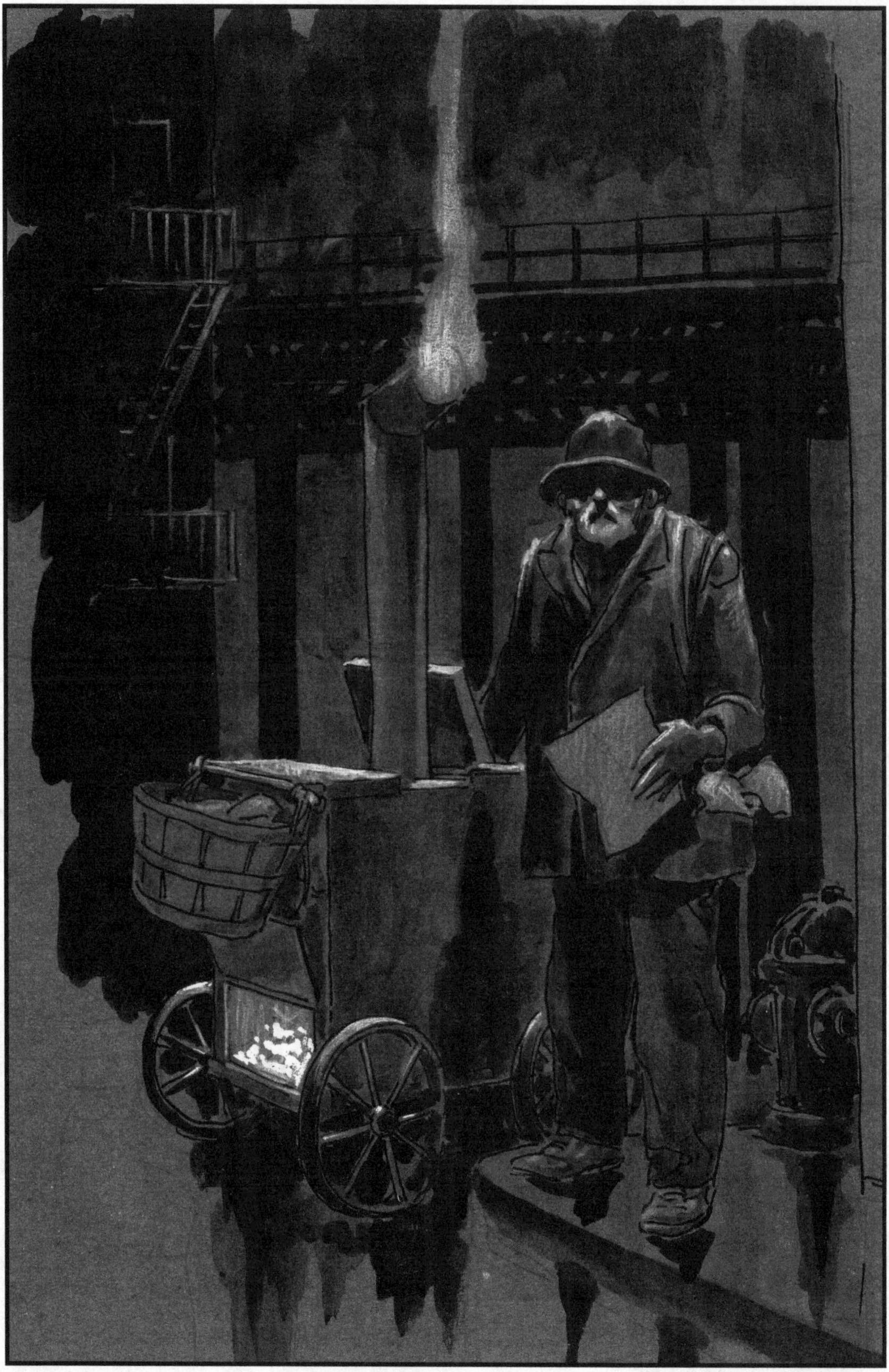

A Change of Seasons

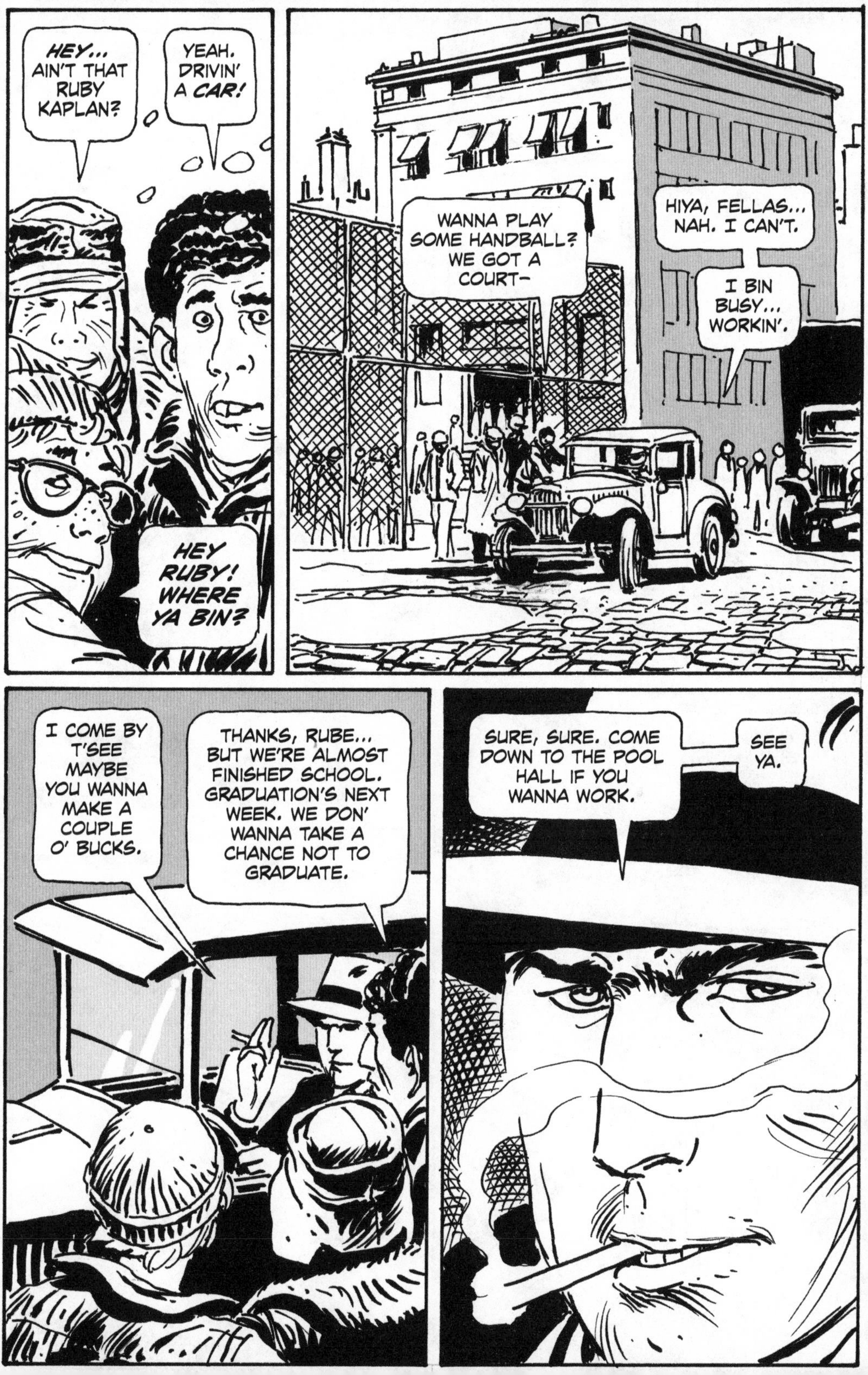
HEY... AIN'T THAT RUBY KAPLAN?
YEAH. DRIVIN' A CAR!
HEY RUBY! WHERE YA BIN?
WANNA PLAY SOME HANDBALL? WE GOT A COURT-
HIYA, FELLAS... NAH. I CAN'T.
I BIN BUSY... WORKIN'.
I COME BY T'SEE MAYBE YOU WANNA MAKE A COUPLE O' BUCKS.
THANKS, RUBE... BUT WE'RE ALMOST FINISHED SCHOOL. GRADUATION'S NEXT WEEK. WE DON' WANNA TAKE A CHANCE NOT TO GRADUATE.
SURE, SURE. COME DOWN TO THE POOL HALL IF YOU WANNA WORK.
SEE YA.

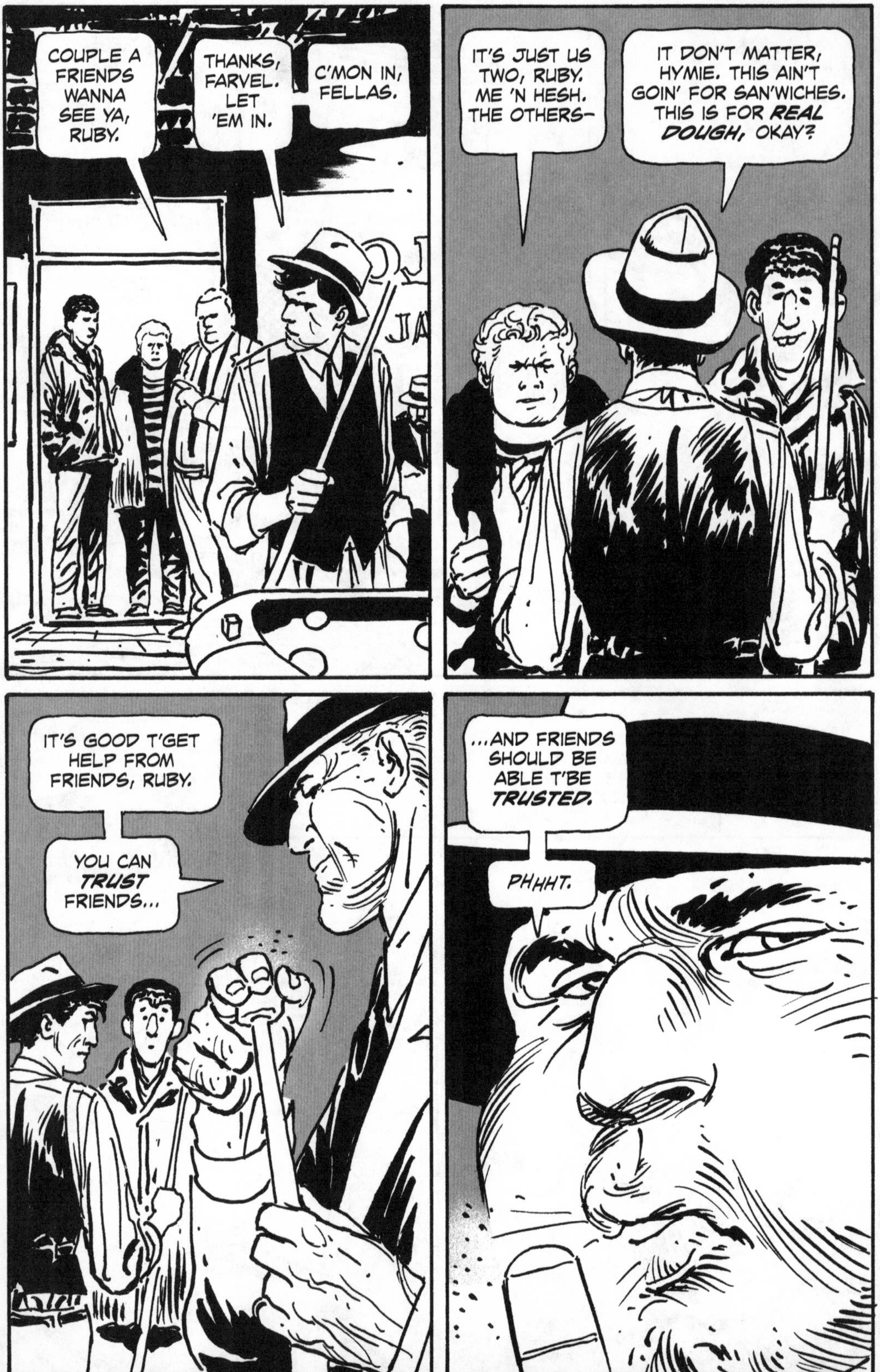
COUPLE A FRIENDS WANNA SEE YA, RUBY.
THANKS, FARVEL. LET 'EM IN.
C'MON IN, FELLAS.
IT'S JUST US TWO, RUBY. ME 'N HESH. THE OTHERS–
IT DON'T MATTER, HYMIE. THIS AIN'T GOIN' FOR SAN'WICHES. THIS IS FOR REAL DOUGH, OKAY?
IT'S GOOD T'GET HELP FROM FRIENDS, RUBY.
YOU CAN TRUST FRIENDS...
...AND FRIENDS SHOULD BE ABLE T'BE TRUSTED.
PHHHT.

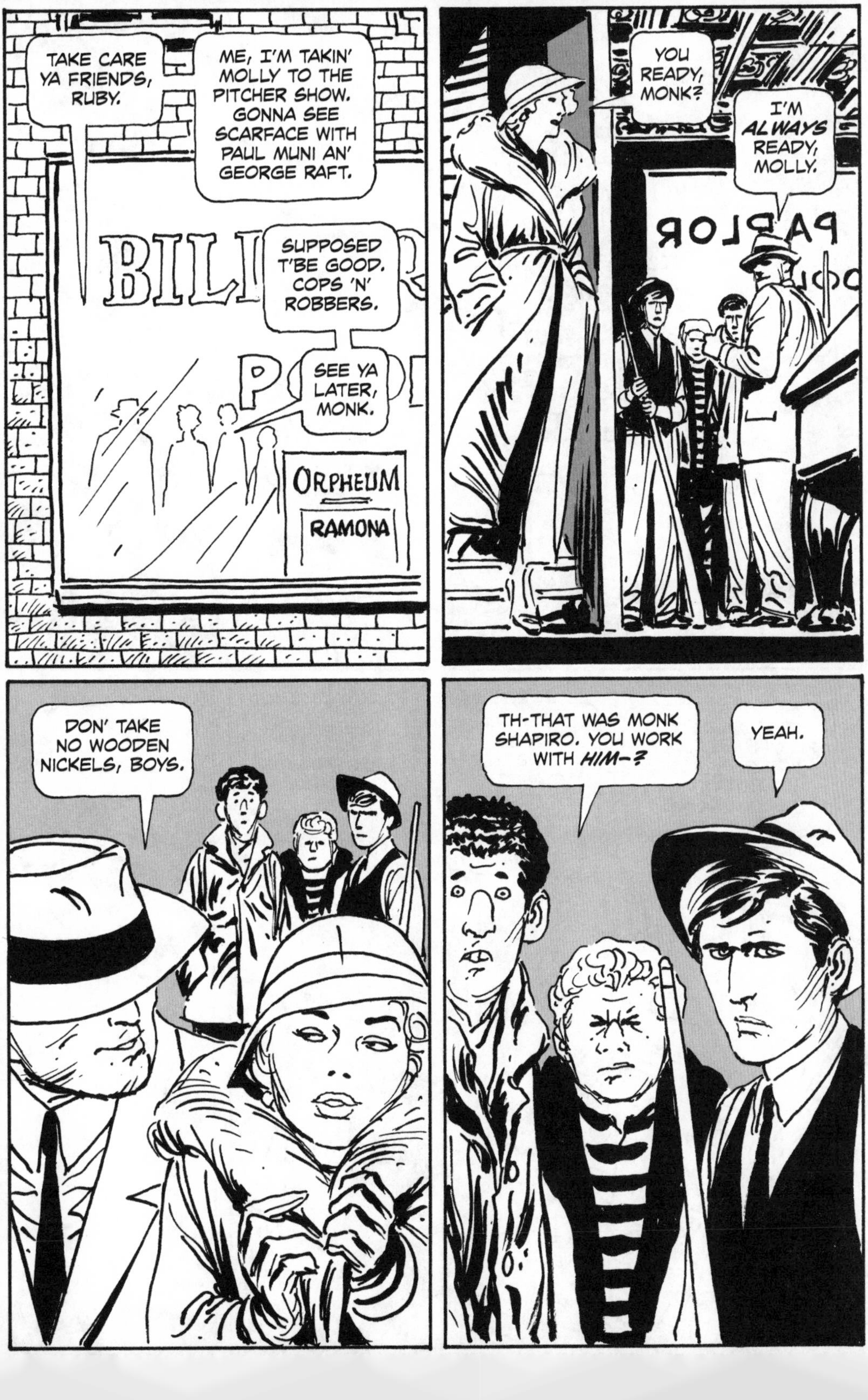
TAKE CARE YA FRIENDS, RUBY.
ME, I'M TAKIN' MOLLY TO THE PITCHER SHOW. GONNA SEE SCARFACE WITH PAUL MUNI AN' GEORGE RAFT.
BILL
SUPPOSED T'BE GOOD. COPS 'N' ROBBERS.
SEE YA LATER, MONK.
ORPHEUM
RAMONA
YOU READY, MONK?
I'M ALWAYS READY, MOLLY.
PARLOR
DON' TAKE NO WOODEN NICKELS, BOYS.
TH-THAT WAS MONK SHAPIRO. YOU WORK WITH HIM-?
YEAH.

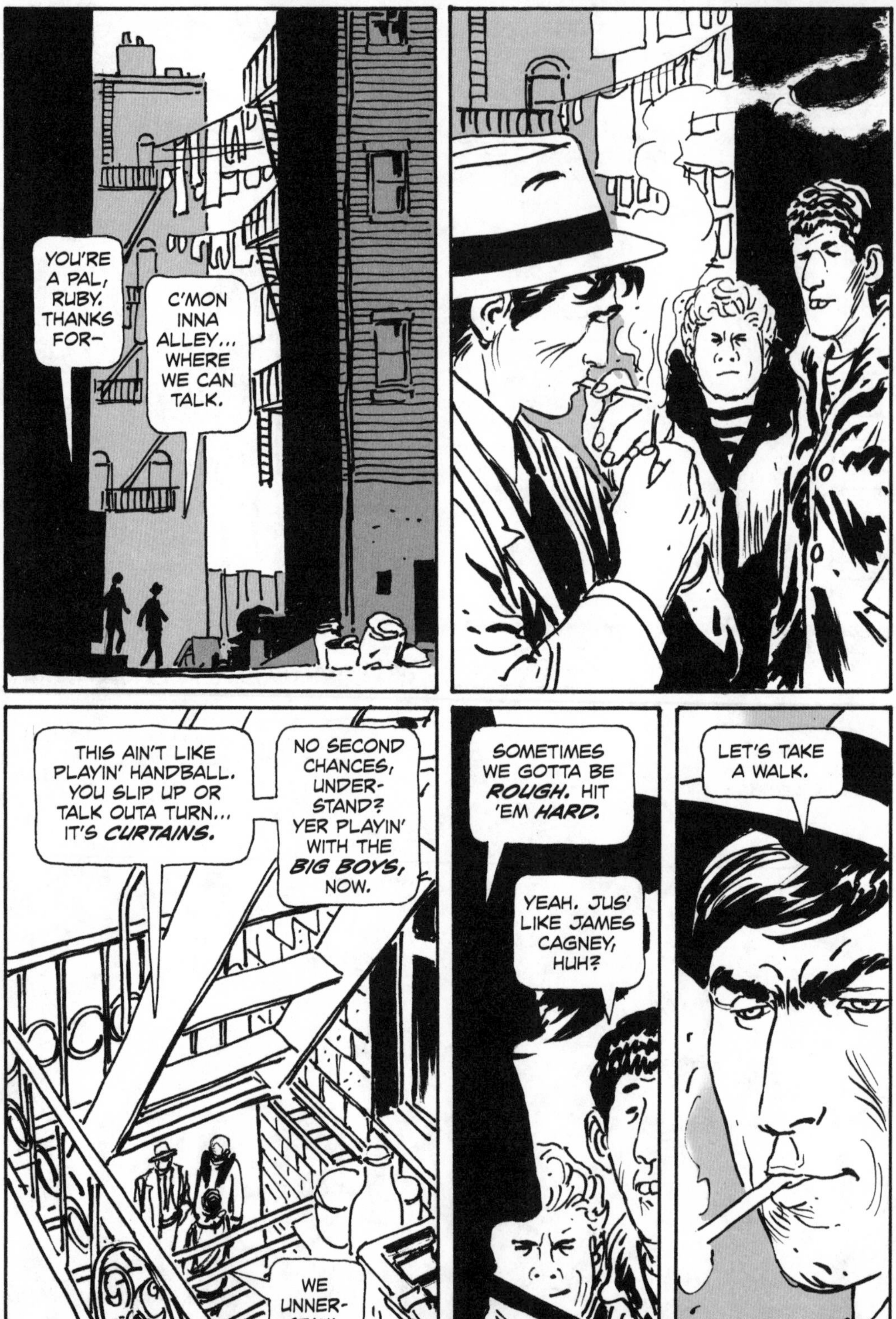
YOU'RE A PAL, RUBY. THANKS FOR–
C'MON INNA ALLEY... WHERE WE CAN TALK.
THIS AIN'T LIKE PLAYIN' HANDBALL. YOU SLIP UP OR TALK OUTA TURN... IT'S CURTAINS.
NO SECOND CHANCES, UNDER-STAND? YER PLAYIN' WITH THE BIG BOYS, NOW.
WE UNNER-STAN', RUBY.
SOMETIMES WE GOTTA BE ROUGH. HIT 'EM HARD.
YEAH. JUS' LIKE JAMES CAGNEY, HUH?
LET'S TAKE A WALK.

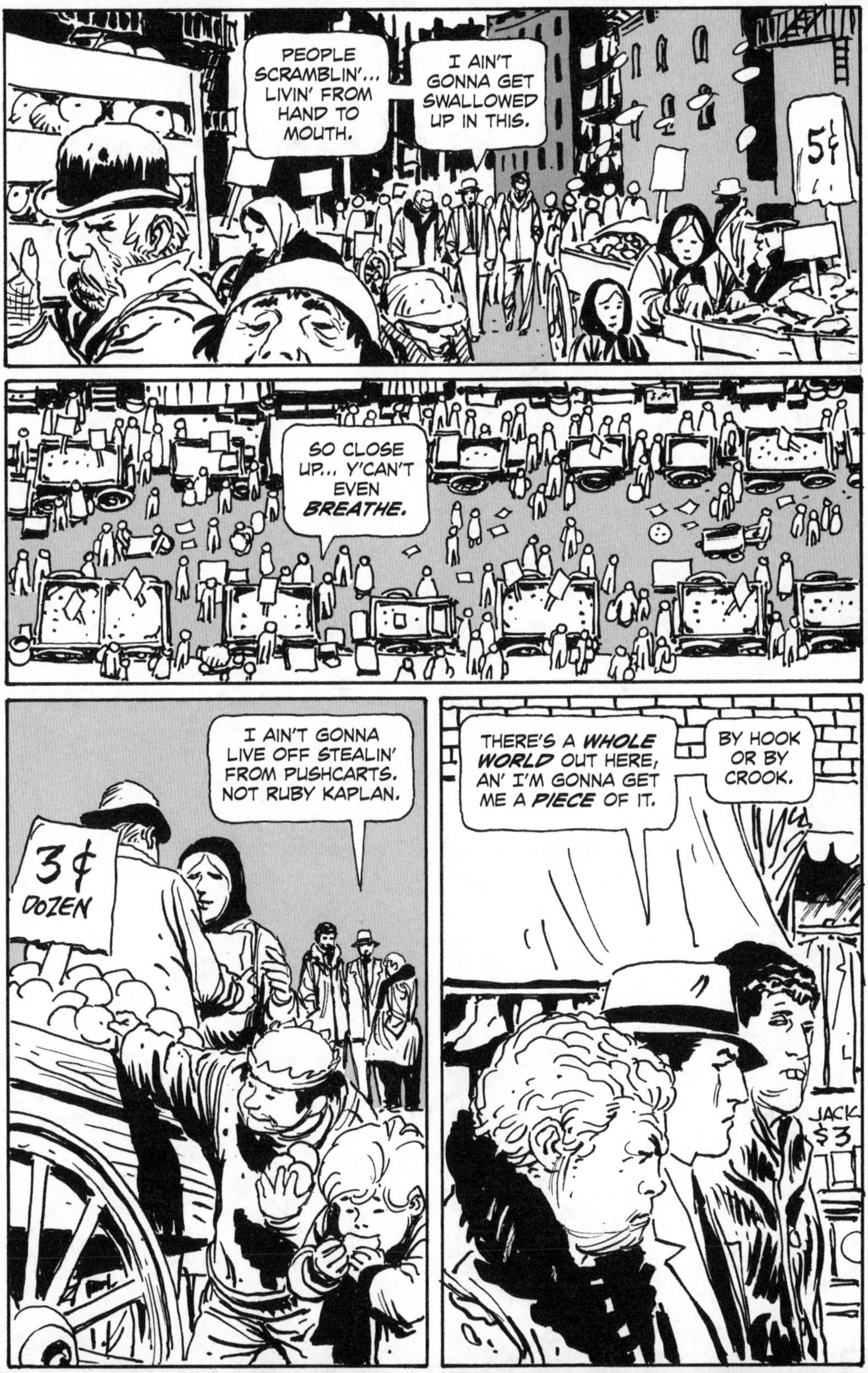
PEOPLE SCRAMBLIN'... LIVIN' FROM HAND TO MOUTH.
I AIN'T GONNA GET SWALLOWED UP IN THIS.
5¢
SO CLOSE UP... Y'CAN'T EVEN BREATHE.
I AIN'T GONNA LIVE OFF STEALIN' FROM PUSHCARTS. NOT RUBY KAPLAN.
3¢ DOZEN
THERE'S A WHOLE WORLD OUT HERE, AN' I'M GONNA GET ME A PIECE OF IT.
BY HOOK OR BY CROOK.
JACK $3

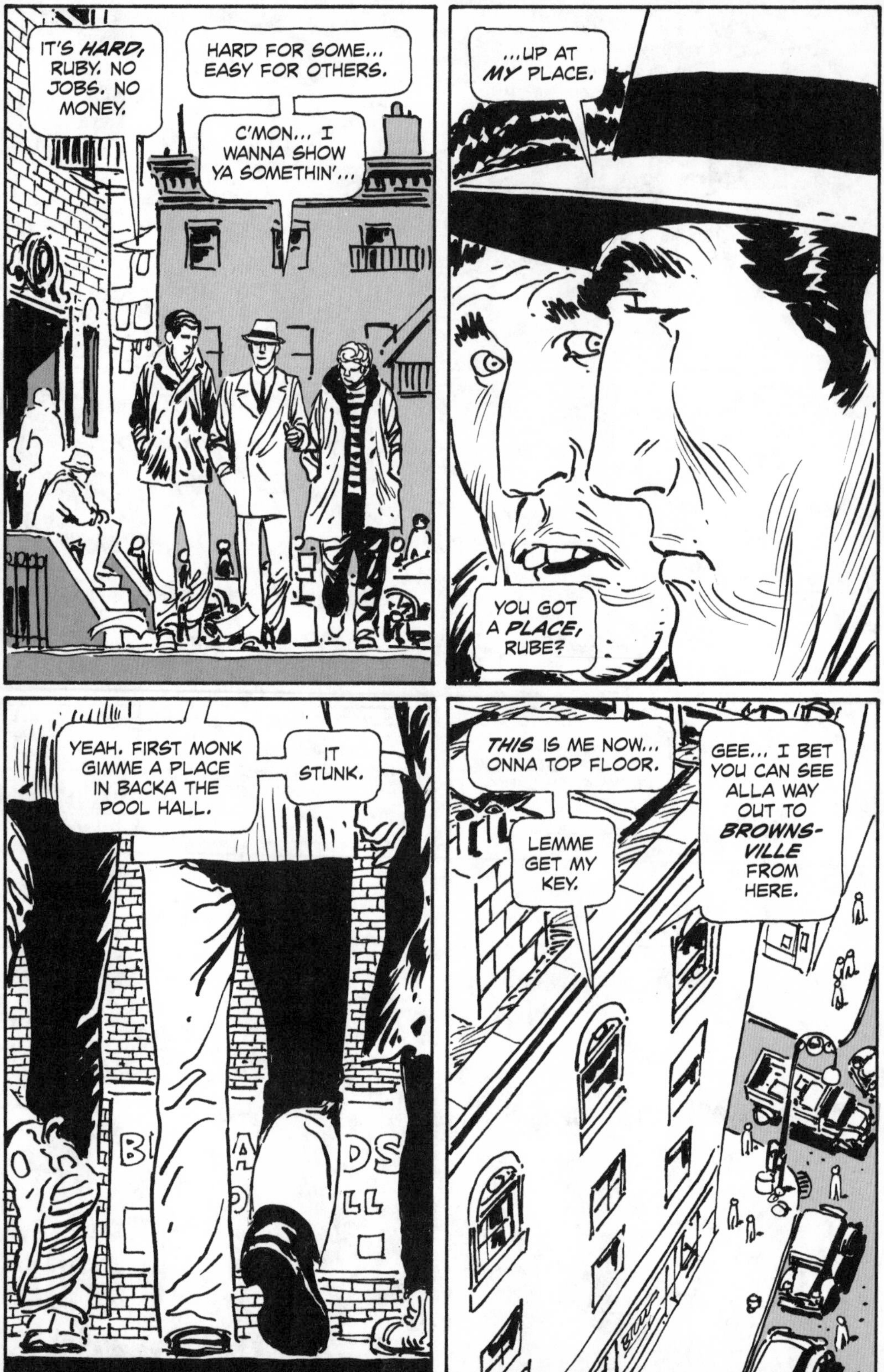
IT'S HARD, RUBY. NO JOBS. NO MONEY.
HARD FOR SOME... EASY FOR OTHERS.
C'MON... I WANNA SHOW YA SOMETHIN'...
...UP AT MY PLACE.
YOU GOT A PLACE, RUBE?
YEAH. FIRST MONK GIMME A PLACE IN BACKA THE POOL HALL.
IT STUNK.
THIS IS ME NOW... ONNA TOP FLOOR.
LEMME GET MY KEY.
GEE... I BET YOU CAN SEE ALLA WAY OUT TO BROWNSVILLE FROM HERE.

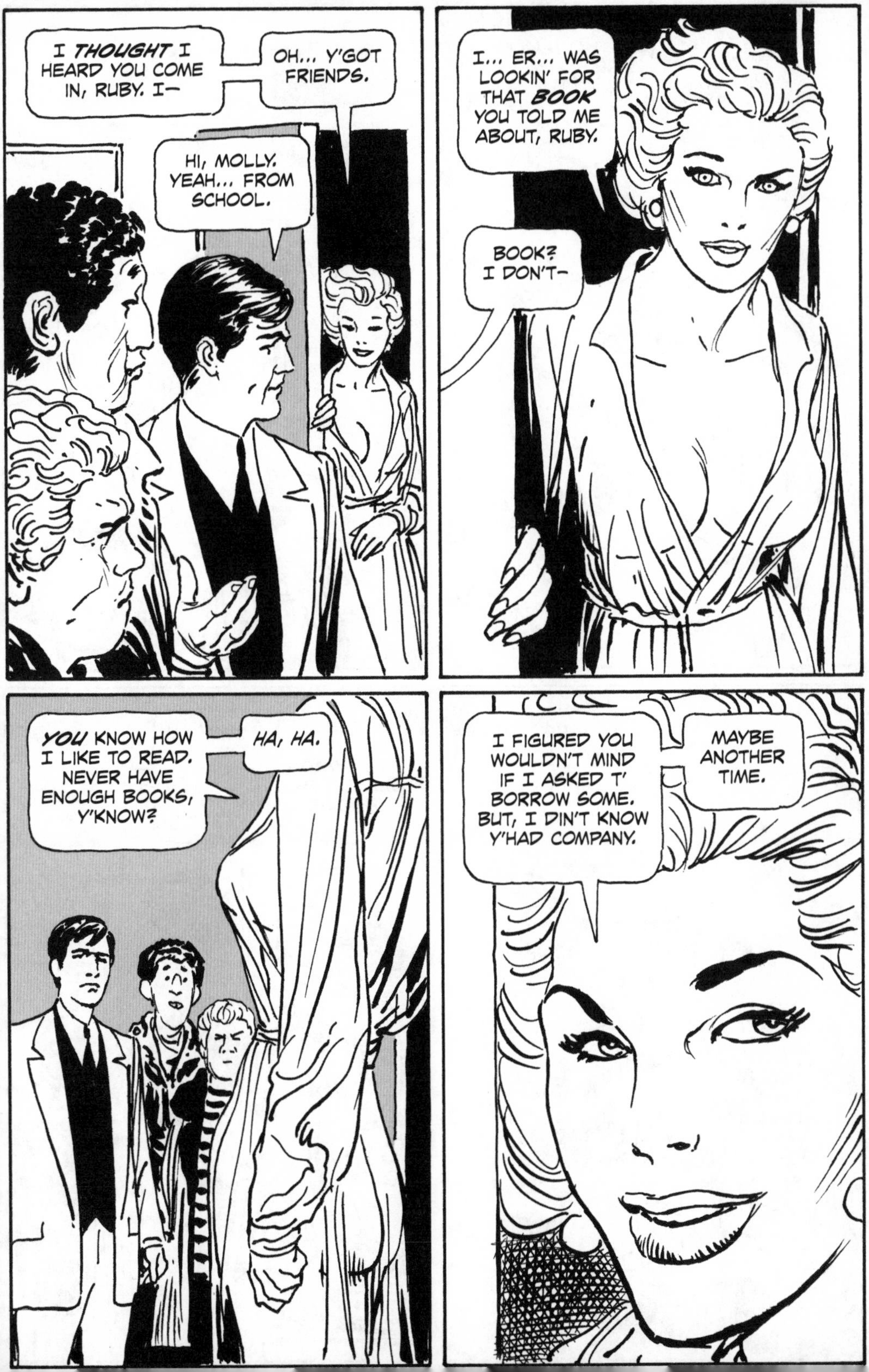
I *THOUGHT* I HEARD YOU COME IN, RUBY. I—
OH... Y'GOT FRIENDS.
HI, MOLLY. YEAH... FROM SCHOOL.
I... ER... WAS LOOKIN' FOR THAT *BOOK* YOU TOLD ME ABOUT, RUBY.
BOOK? I DON'T—
YOU KNOW HOW I LIKE TO READ. NEVER HAVE ENOUGH BOOKS, Y'KNOW?
HA, HA.
I FIGURED YOU WOULDN'T MIND IF I ASKED T' BORROW SOME. BUT, I DIN'T KNOW Y'HAD COMPANY.
MAYBE ANOTHER TIME.

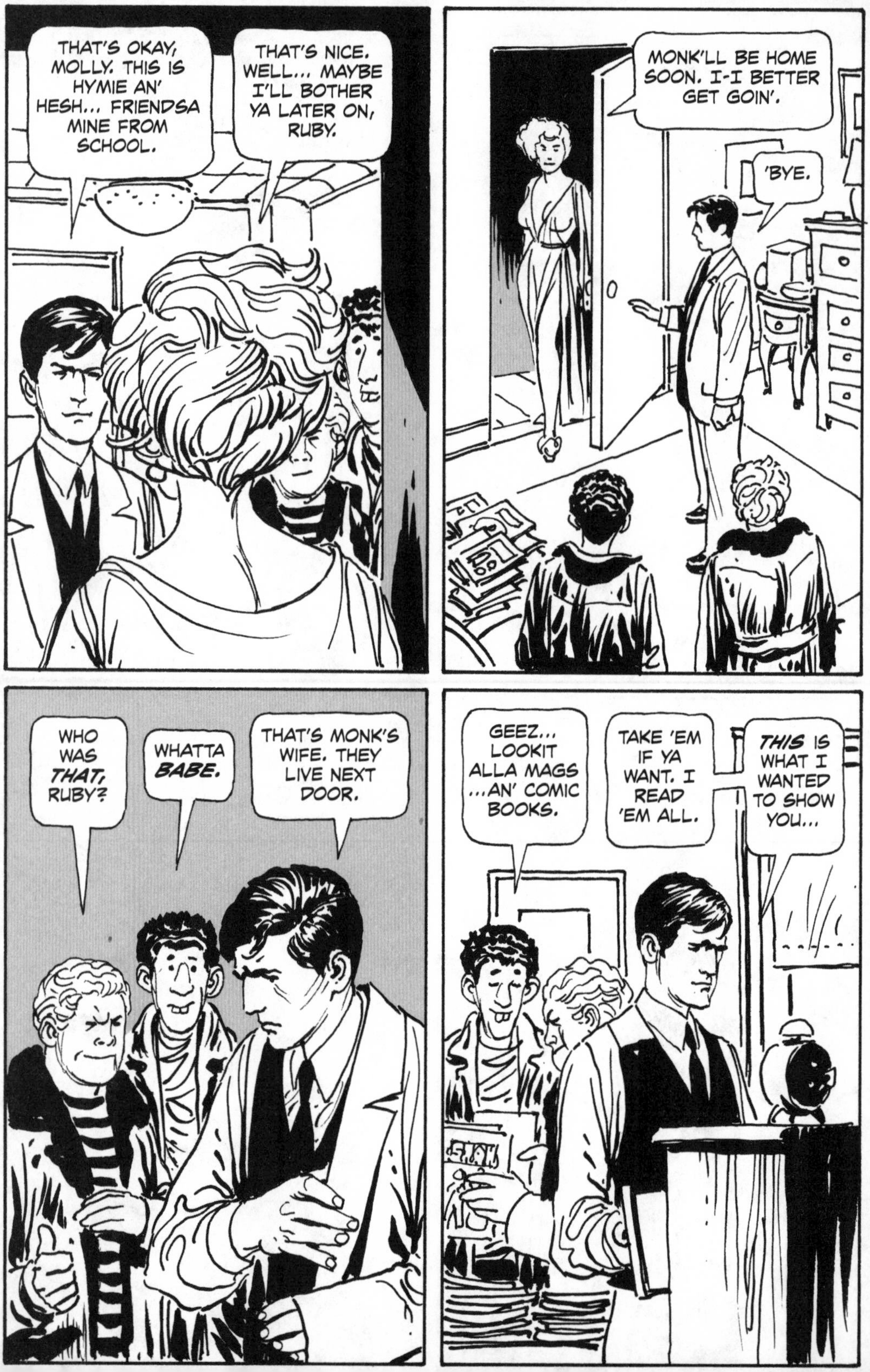
THAT'S OKAY, MOLLY. THIS IS HYMIE AN' HESH... FRIENDSA MINE FROM SCHOOL.
THAT'S NICE. WELL... MAYBE I'LL BOTHER YA LATER ON, RUBY.
MONK'LL BE HOME SOON. I-I BETTER GET GOIN'.
'BYE.
WHO WAS *THAT,* RUBY?
WHATTA *BABE.*
THAT'S MONK'S WIFE. THEY LIVE NEXT DOOR.
GEEZ... LOOKIT ALLA MAGS ...AN' COMIC BOOKS.
TAKE 'EM IF YA WANT. I READ 'EM ALL.
THIS IS WHAT I WANTED TO SHOW YOU...

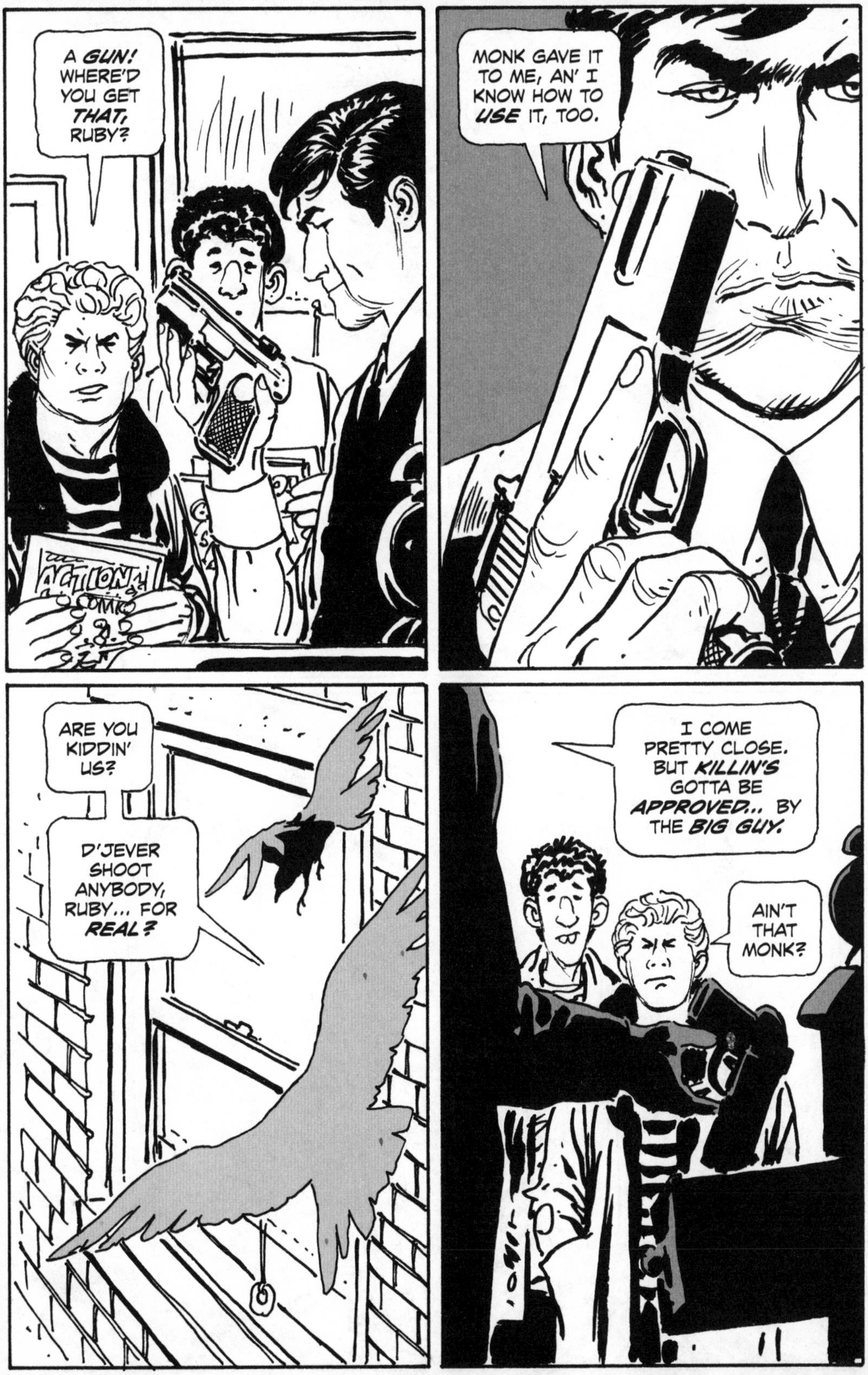
A GUN! WHERE'D YOU GET THAT, RUBY?
MONK GAVE IT TO ME, AN' I KNOW HOW TO USE IT, TOO.
ARE YOU KIDDIN' US?
D'JEVER SHOOT ANYBODY, RUBY... FOR REAL?
I COME PRETTY CLOSE. BUT KILLIN'S GOTTA BE APPROVED... BY THE BIG GUY.
AIN'T THAT MONK?

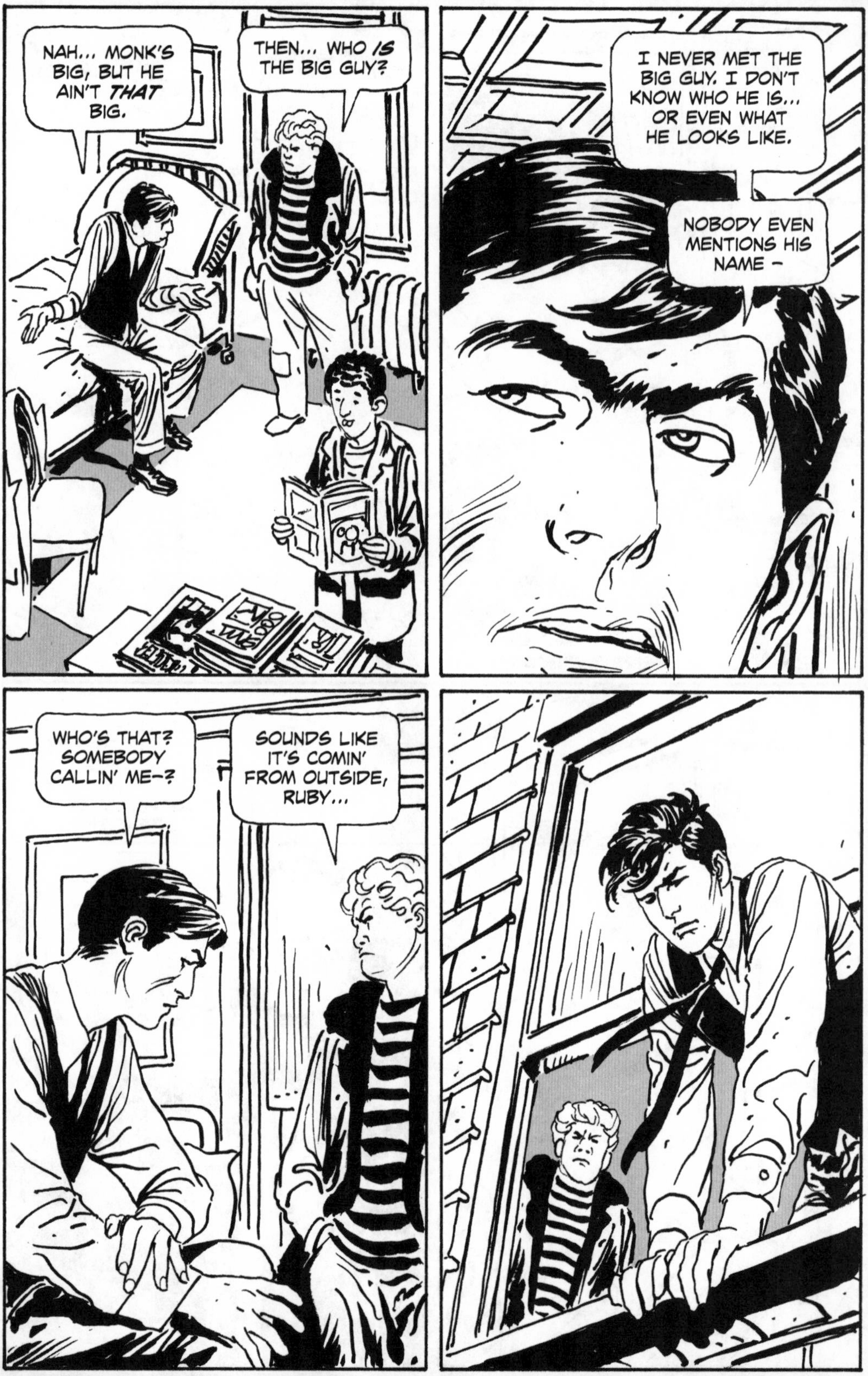
NAH... MONK'S BIG, BUT HE AIN'T *THAT* BIG.
THEN... WHO *IS* THE BIG GUY?
I NEVER MET THE BIG GUY. I DON'T KNOW WHO HE IS... OR EVEN WHAT HE LOOKS LIKE.
NOBODY EVEN MENTIONS HIS NAME –
WHO'S THAT? SOMEBODY CALLIN' ME–?
SOUNDS LIKE IT'S COMIN' FROM OUTSIDE, RUBY...

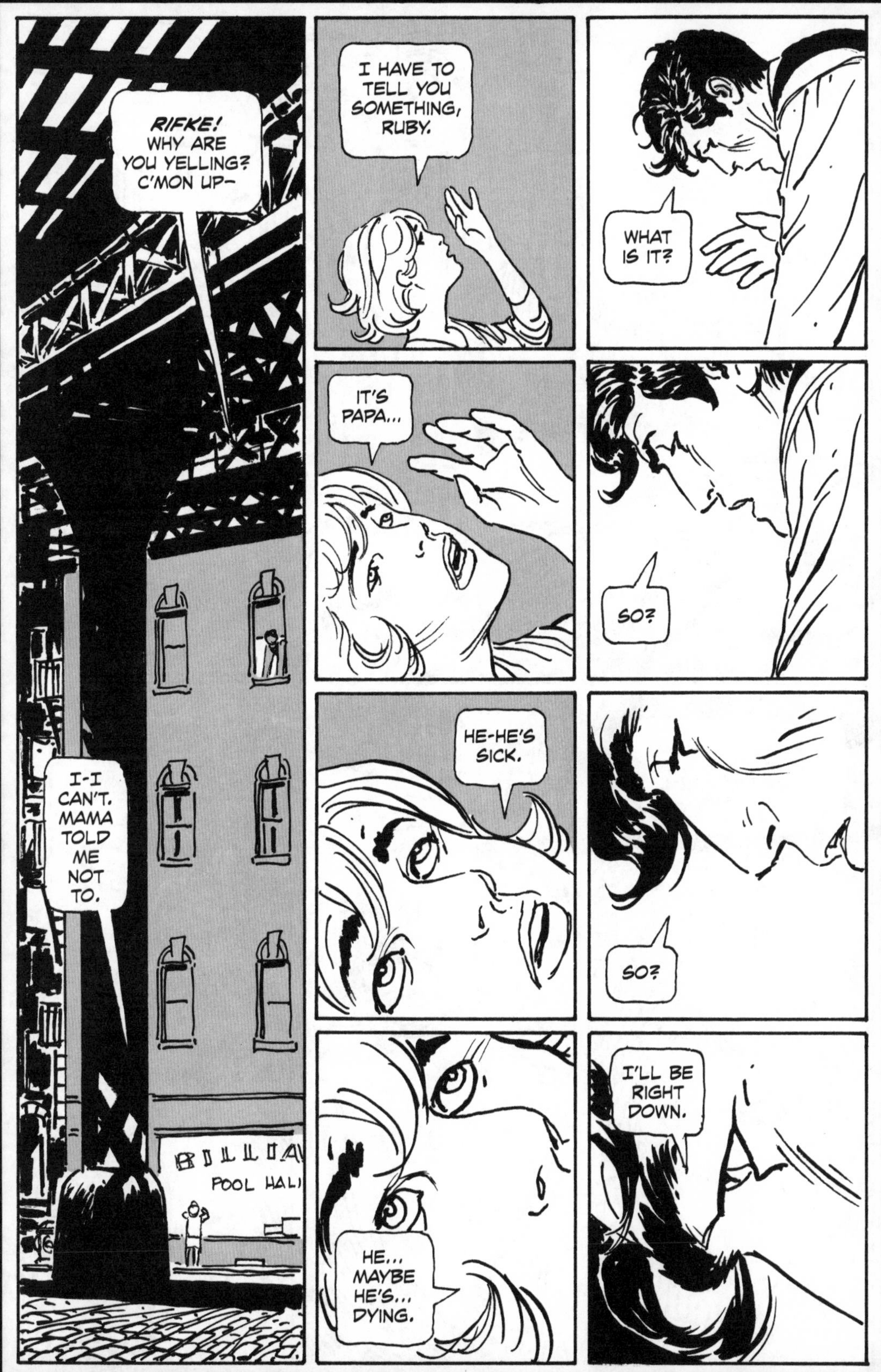
RIFKE! WHY ARE YOU YELLING? C'MON UP—
I-I CAN'T. MAMA TOLD ME NOT TO.
BILLIA
POOL HALL
I HAVE TO TELL YOU SOMETHING, RUBY.
WHAT IS IT?
IT'S PAPA...
SO?
HE-HE'S SICK.
SO?
HE... MAYBE HE'S... DYING.
I'LL BE RIGHT DOWN.

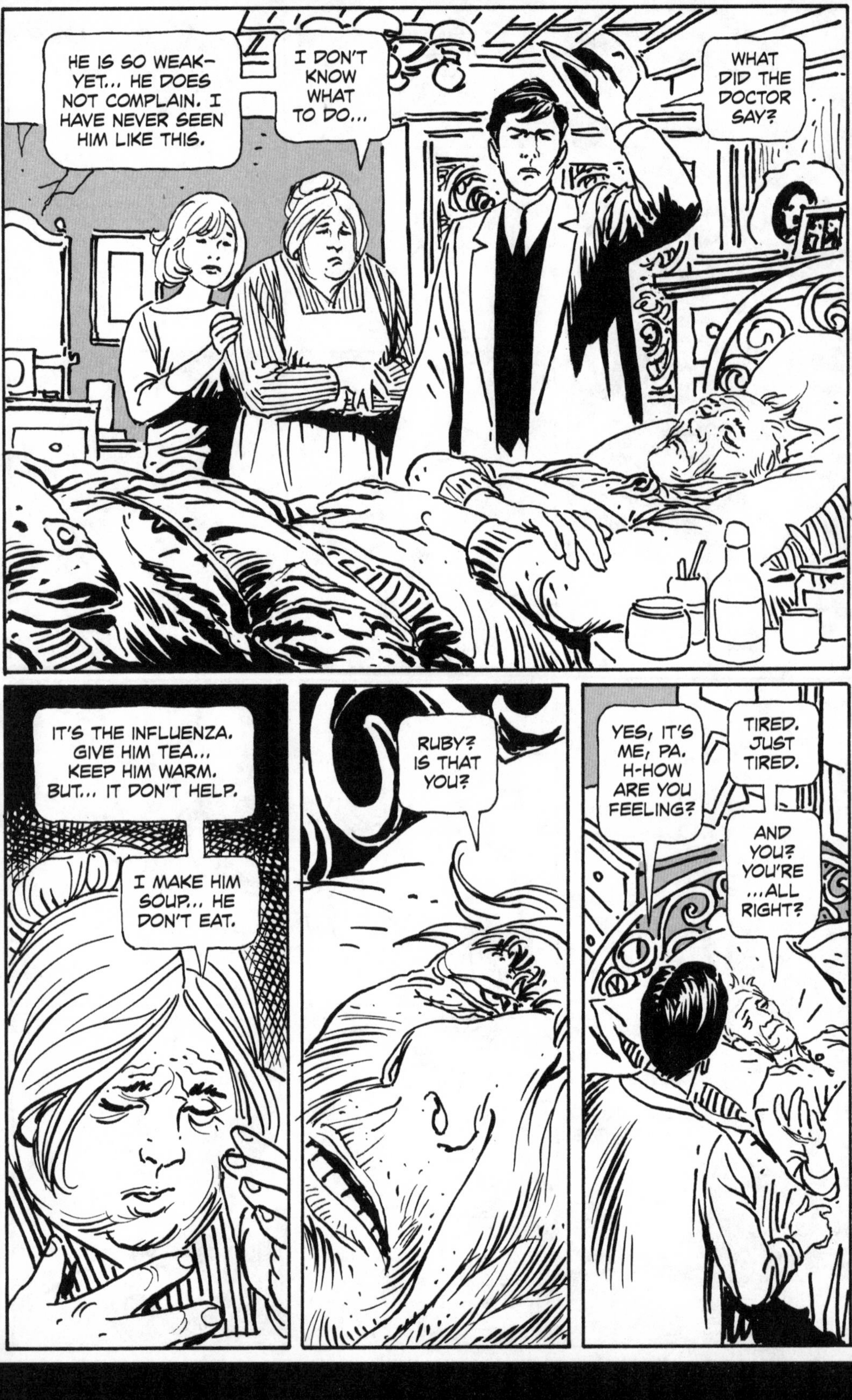
HE IS SO WEAK– YET... HE DOES NOT COMPLAIN. I HAVE NEVER SEEN HIM LIKE THIS.
I DON'T KNOW WHAT TO DO...
WHAT DID THE DOCTOR SAY?
IT'S THE INFLUENZA. GIVE HIM TEA... KEEP HIM WARM. BUT... IT DON'T HELP.
I MAKE HIM SOUP... HE DON'T EAT.
RUBY? IS THAT YOU?
YES, IT'S ME, PA. H-HOW ARE YOU FEELING?
TIRED. JUST TIRED.
AND YOU? YOU'RE ...ALL RIGHT?

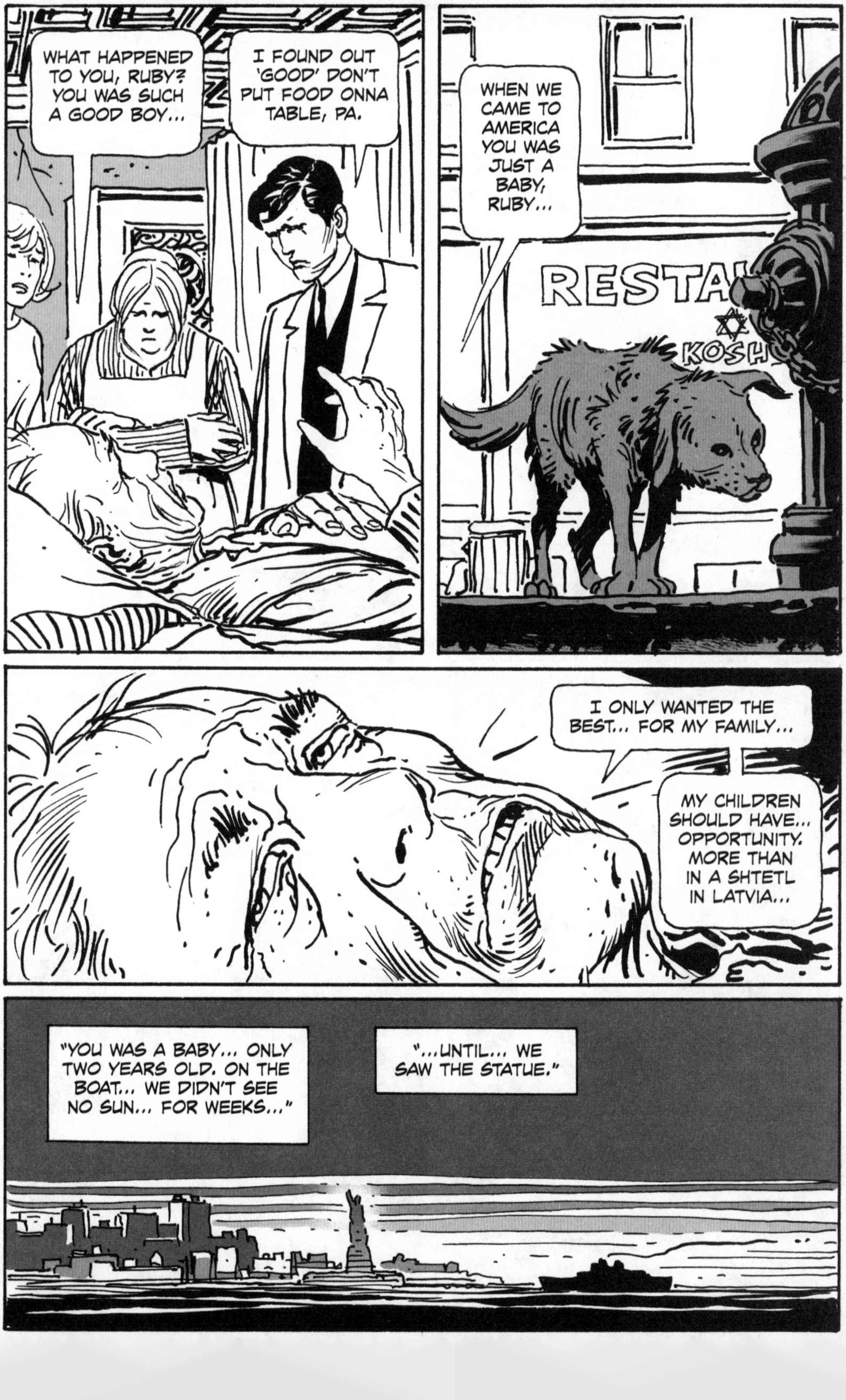
WHAT HAPPENED TO YOU, RUBY? YOU WAS SUCH A GOOD BOY...
I FOUND OUT 'GOOD' DON'T PUT FOOD ONNA TABLE, PA.
WHEN WE CAME TO AMERICA YOU WAS JUST A BABY, RUBY...
RESTA
KOSH
I ONLY WANTED THE BEST... FOR MY FAMILY...
MY CHILDREN SHOULD HAVE... OPPORTUNITY. MORE THAN IN A SHTETL IN LATVIA...
"YOU WAS A BABY... ONLY TWO YEARS OLD. ON THE BOAT... WE DIDN'T SEE NO SUN... FOR WEEKS..."
"...UNTIL... WE SAW THE STATUE."

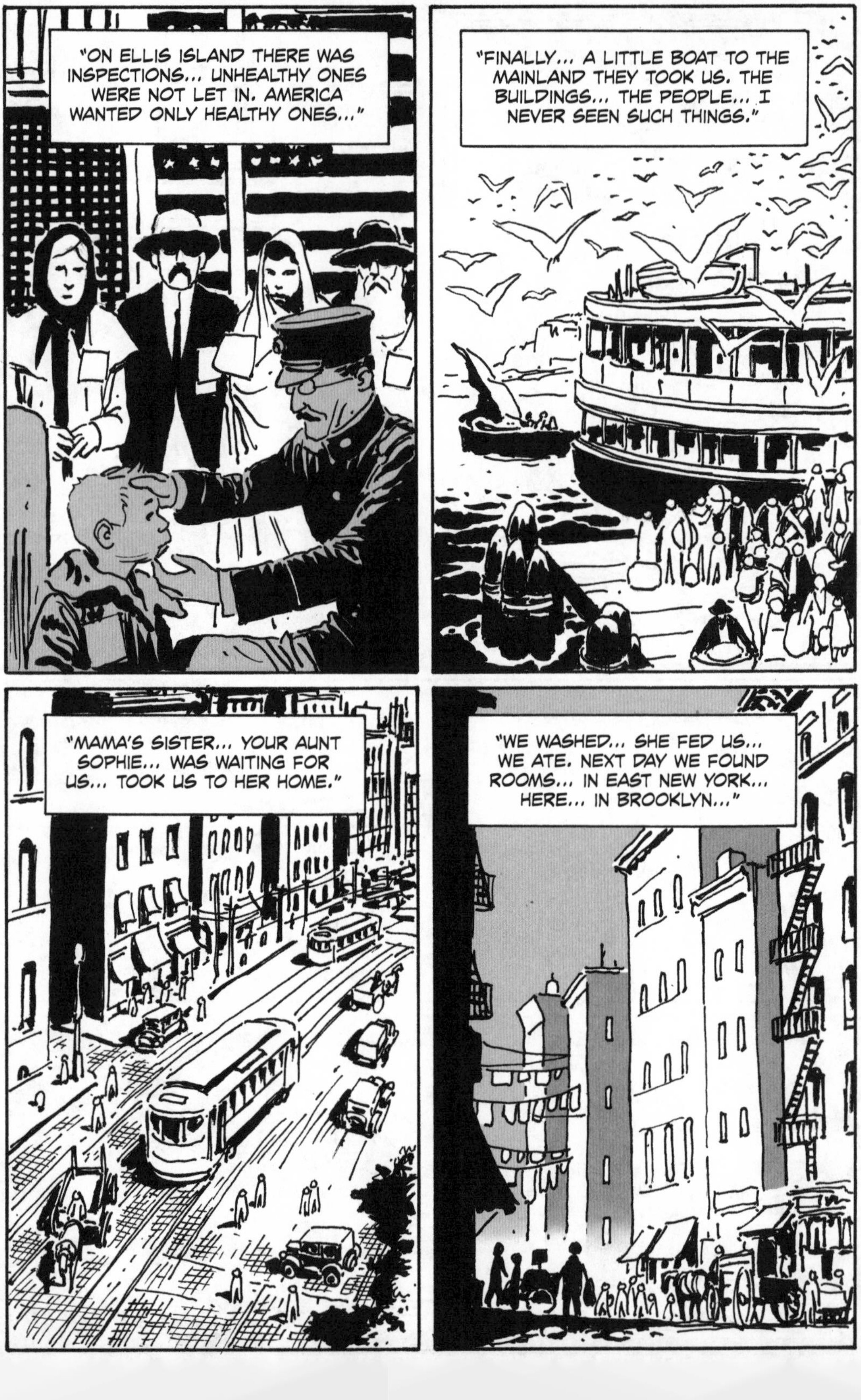
"ON ELLIS ISLAND THERE WAS INSPECTIONS... UNHEALTHY ONES WERE NOT LET IN. AMERICA WANTED ONLY HEALTHY ONES..."
"FINALLY... A LITTLE BOAT TO THE MAINLAND THEY TOOK US. THE BUILDINGS... THE PEOPLE... I NEVER SEEN SUCH THINGS."
"MAMA'S SISTER... YOUR AUNT SOPHIE... WAS WAITING FOR US... TOOK US TO HER HOME."
"WE WASHED... SHE FED US... WE ATE. NEXT DAY WE FOUND ROOMS... IN EAST NEW YORK... HERE... IN BROOKLYN..."

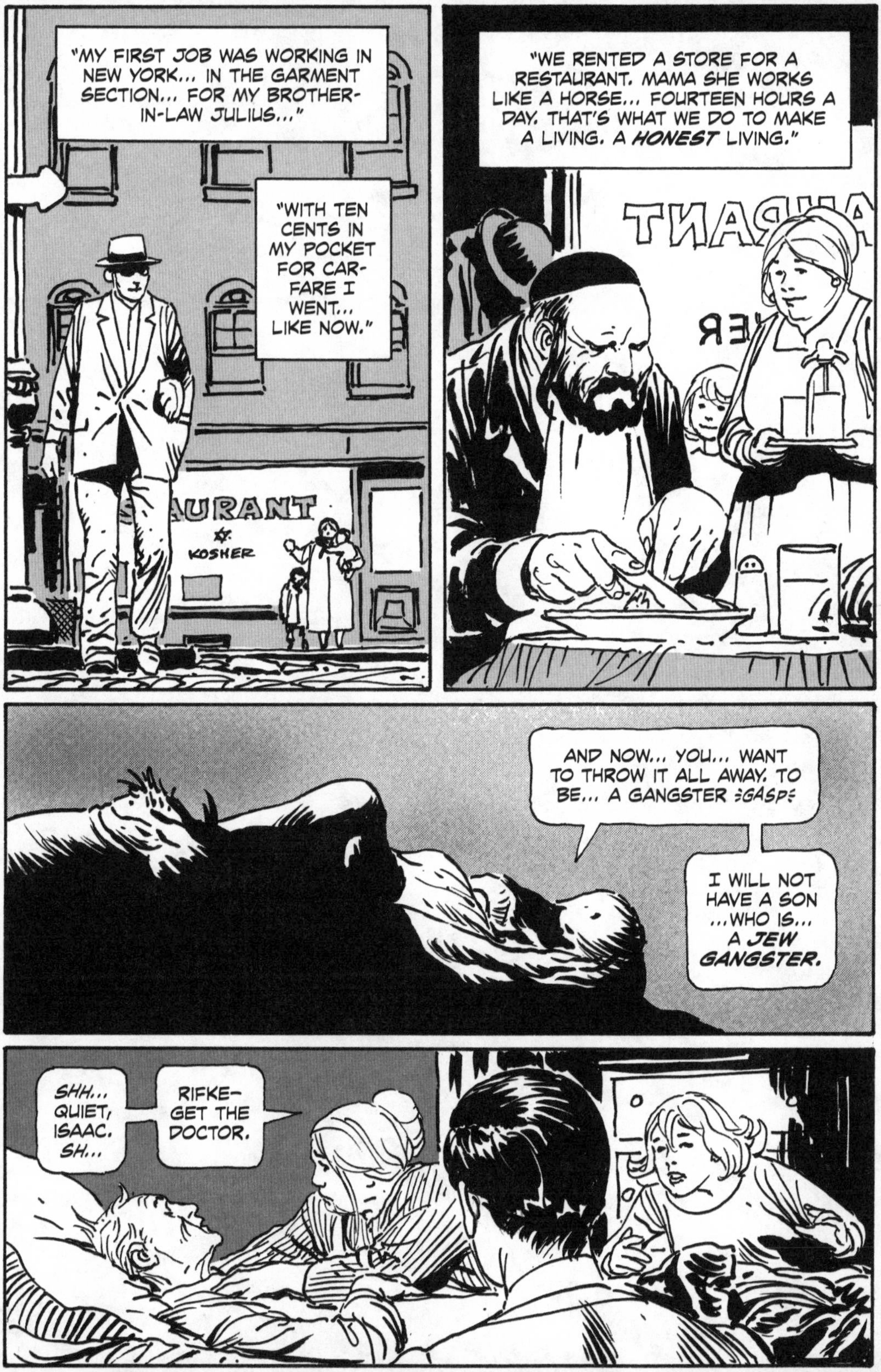
"MY FIRST JOB WAS WORKING IN NEW YORK... IN THE GARMENT SECTION... FOR MY BROTHER-IN-LAW JULIUS..."
"WITH TEN CENTS IN MY POCKET FOR CAR-FARE I WENT... LIKE NOW."
AURANT
KOSHER
"WE RENTED A STORE FOR A RESTAURANT. MAMA SHE WORKS LIKE A HORSE... FOURTEEN HOURS A DAY. THAT'S WHAT WE DO TO MAKE A LIVING. A *HONEST* LIVING."
AND NOW... YOU... WANT TO THROW IT ALL AWAY. TO BE... A GANGSTER *GASP*
I WILL NOT HAVE A SON ...WHO IS... A ***JEW GANGSTER.***
SHH... QUIET, ISAAC. *SH...*
RIFKE-GET THE DOCTOR.

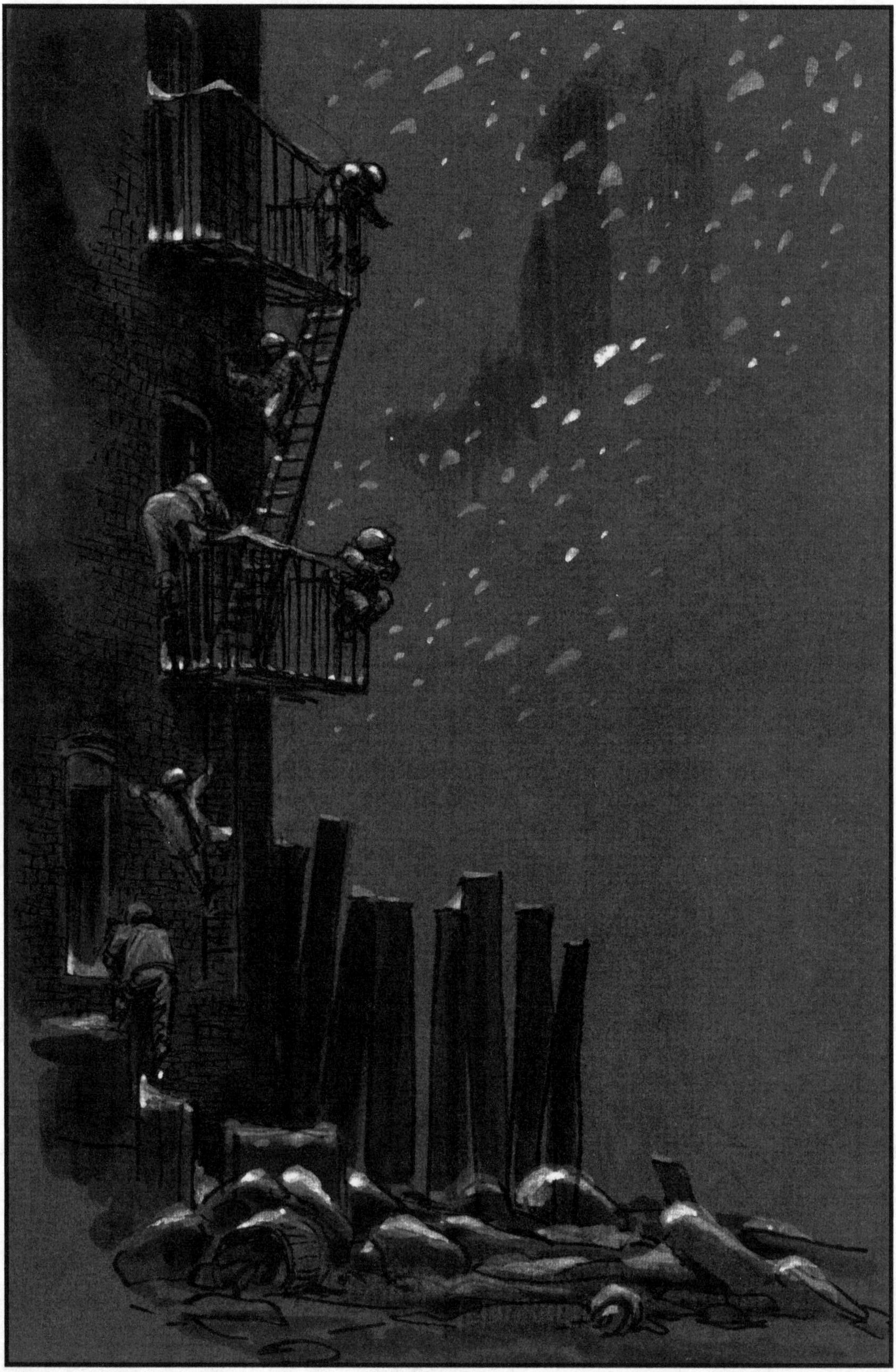

It's Winter

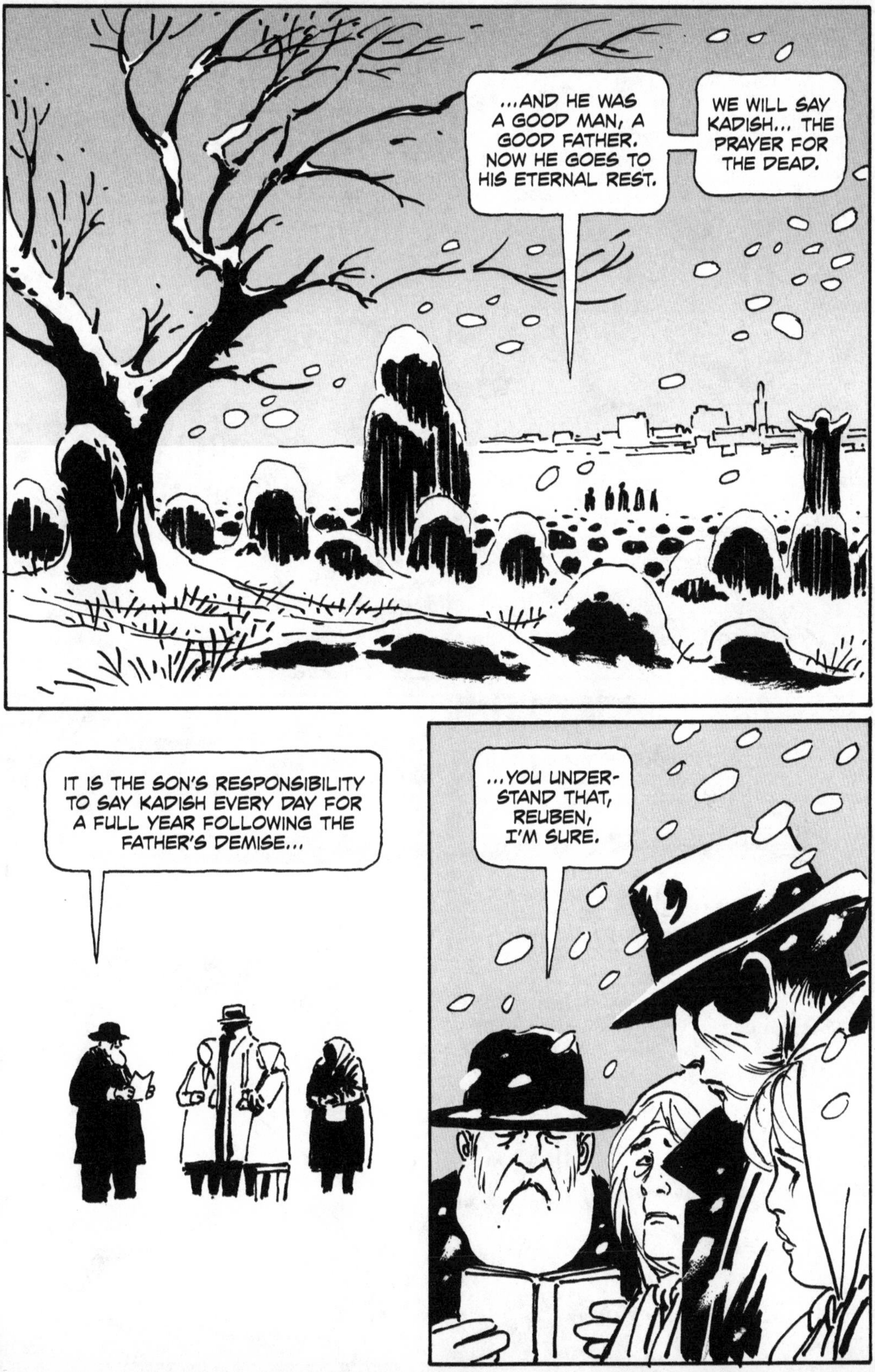
...AND HE WAS A GOOD MAN, A GOOD FATHER. NOW HE GOES TO HIS ETERNAL REST.
WE WILL SAY KADISH... THE PRAYER FOR THE DEAD.
IT IS THE SON'S RESPONSIBILITY TO SAY KADISH EVERY DAY FOR A FULL YEAR FOLLOWING THE FATHER'S DEMISE...
...YOU UNDERSTAND THAT, REUBEN, I'M SURE.

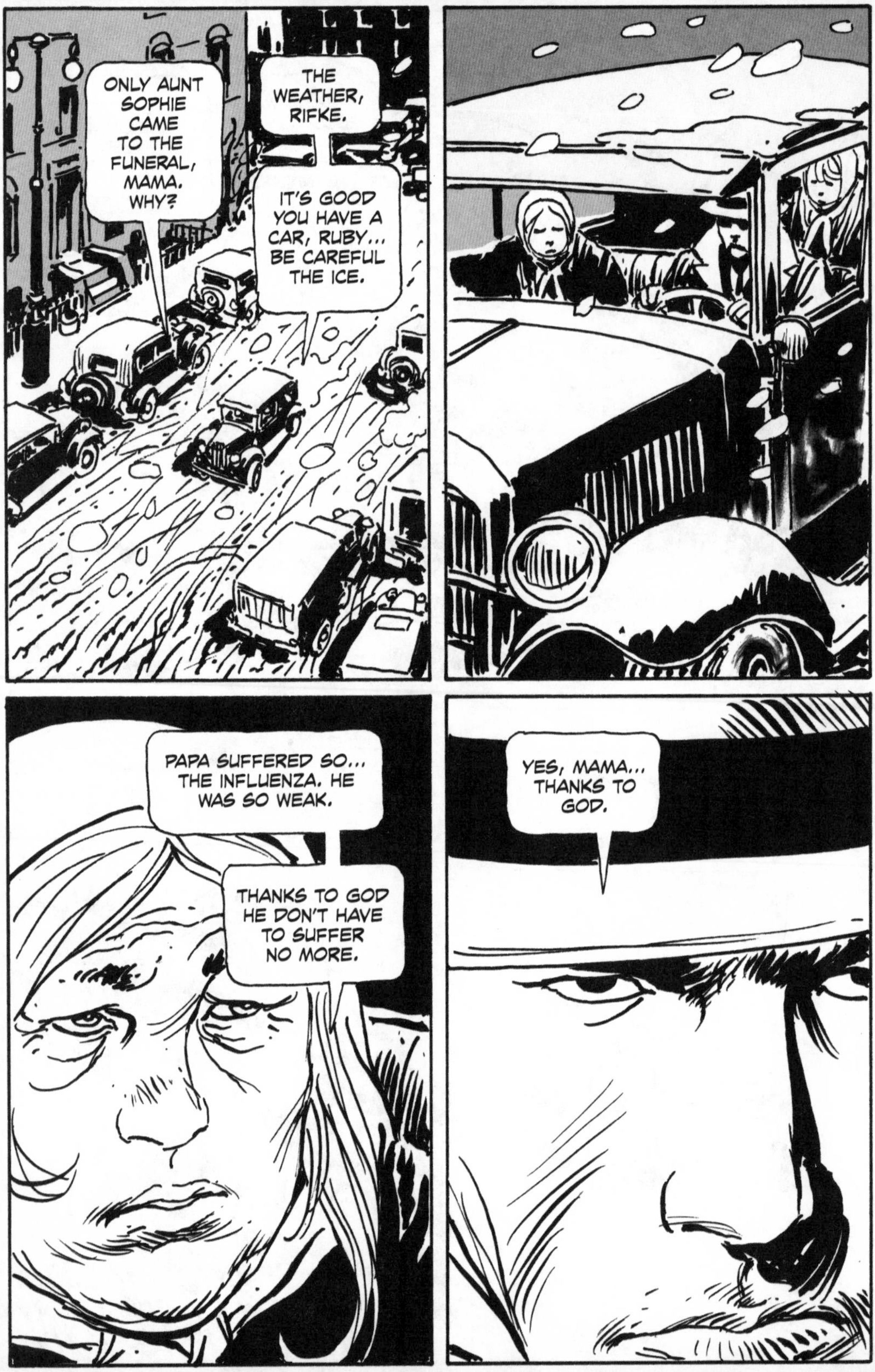
ONLY AUNT SOPHIE CAME TO THE FUNERAL, MAMA. WHY?
THE WEATHER, RIFKE.
IT'S GOOD YOU HAVE A CAR, RUBY... BE CAREFUL THE ICE.
PAPA SUFFERED SO... THE INFLUENZA. HE WAS SO WEAK.
THANKS TO GOD HE DON'T HAVE TO SUFFER NO MORE.
YES, MAMA... THANKS TO GOD.

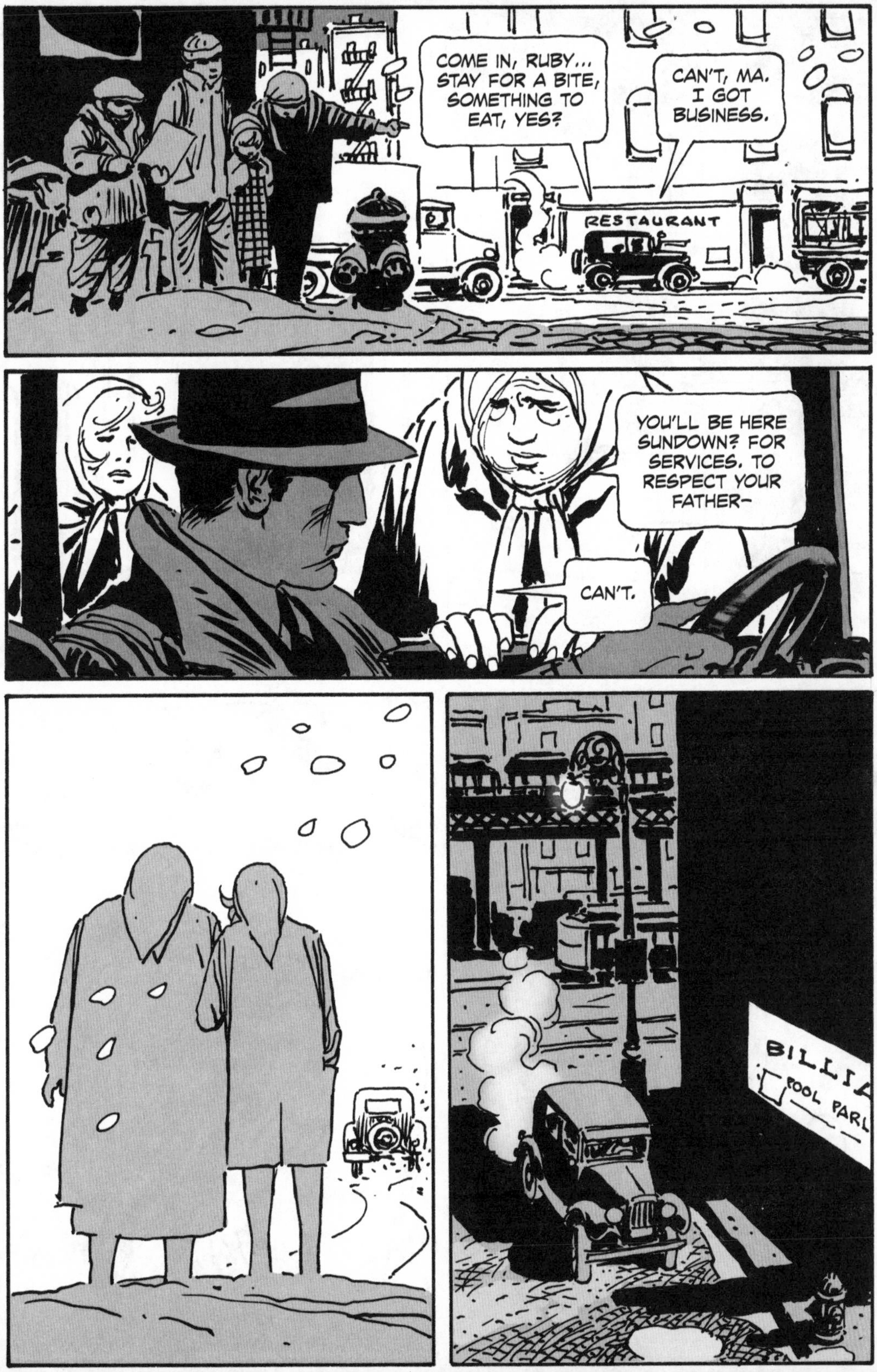
COME IN, RUBY... STAY FOR A BITE, SOMETHING TO EAT, YES?
CAN'T, MA. I GOT BUSINESS.
RESTAURANT
YOU'LL BE HERE SUNDOWN? FOR SERVICES. TO RESPECT YOUR FATHER–
CAN'T.
BILLIA
POOL PARL

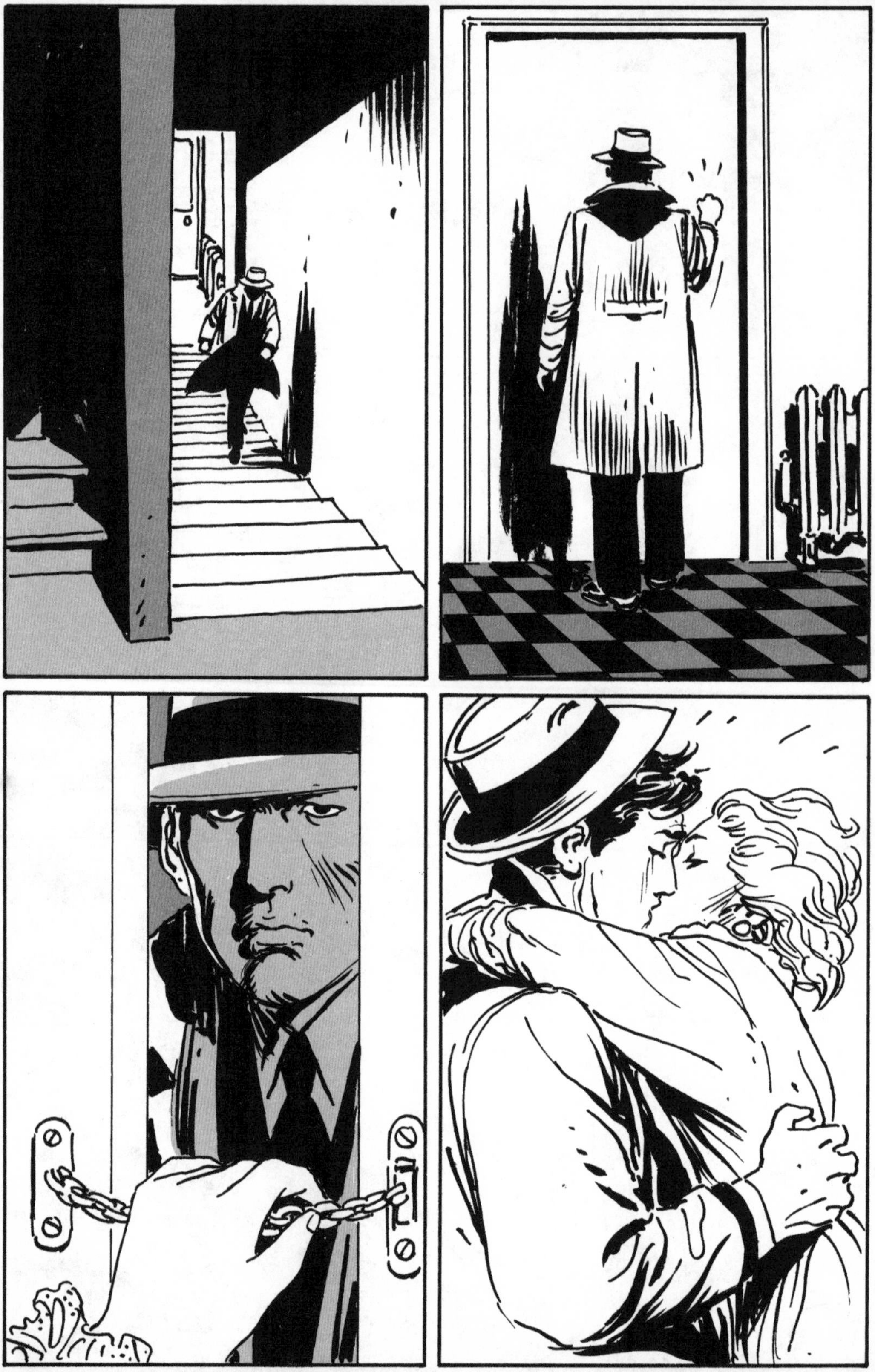

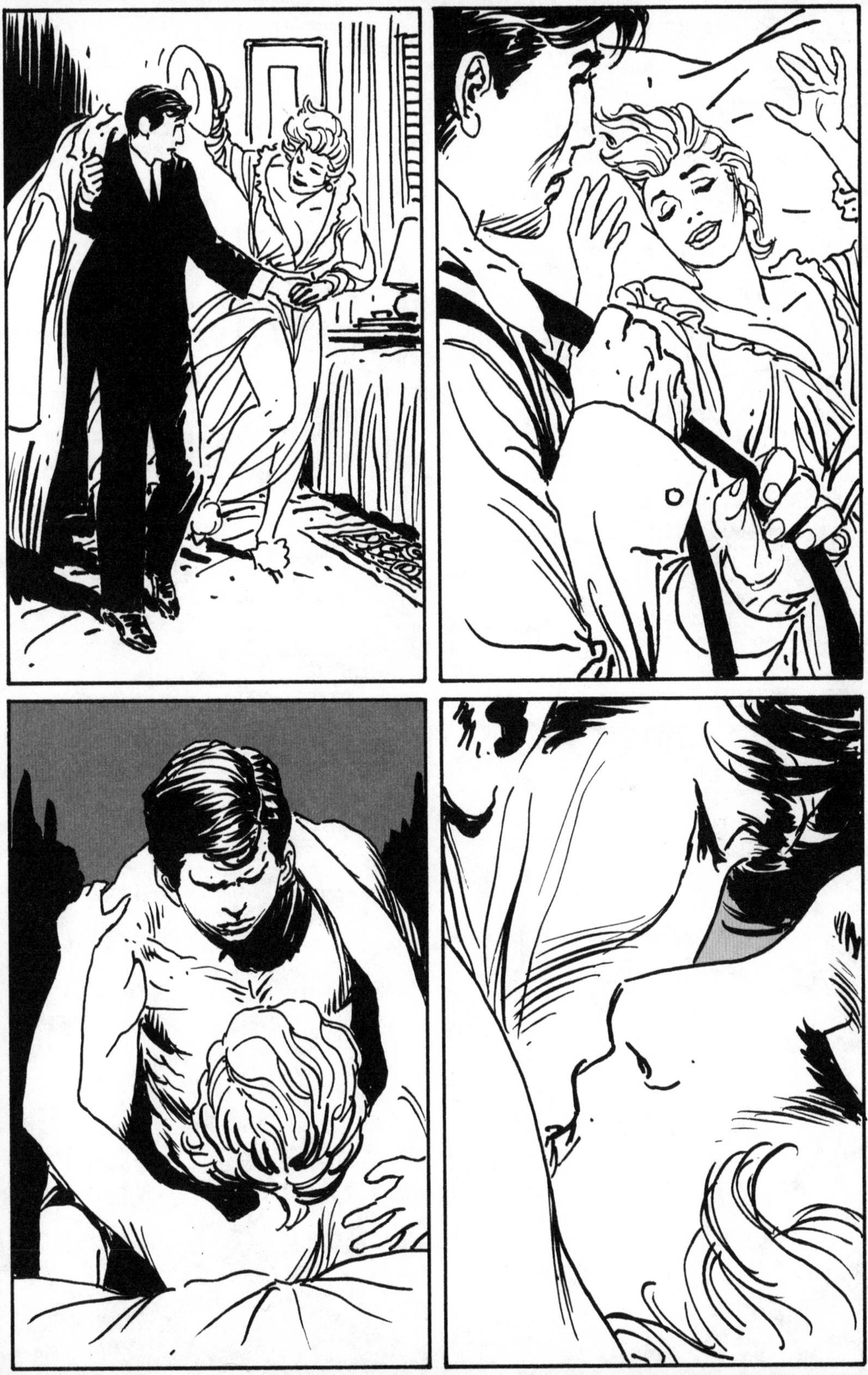

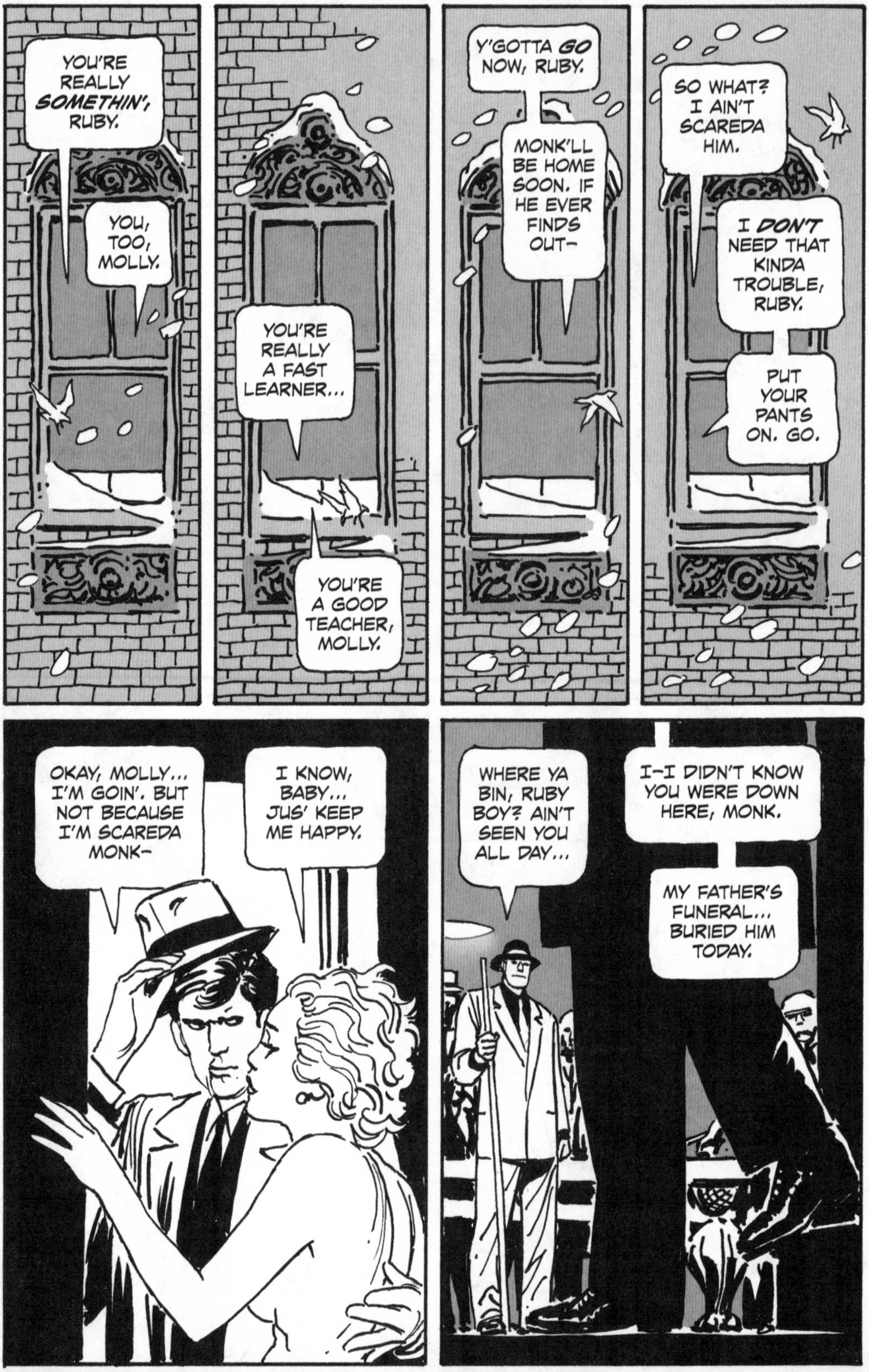
YOU'RE REALLY *SOMETHIN'*, RUBY.
YOU, TOO, MOLLY.
YOU'RE REALLY A FAST LEARNER...
YOU'RE A GOOD TEACHER, MOLLY.
Y'GOTTA *GO* NOW, RUBY.
MONK'LL BE HOME SOON. IF HE EVER FINDS OUT–
SO WHAT? I AIN'T SCAREDA HIM.
I *DON'T* NEED THAT KINDA TROUBLE, RUBY.
PUT YOUR PANTS ON. GO.
OKAY, MOLLY... I'M GOIN'. BUT NOT BECAUSE I'M SCAREDA MONK–
I KNOW, BABY... JUS' KEEP ME HAPPY.
WHERE YA BIN, RUBY BOY? AIN'T SEEN YOU ALL DAY...
I–I DIDN'T KNOW YOU WERE DOWN HERE, MONK.
MY FATHER'S FUNERAL... BURIED HIM TODAY.

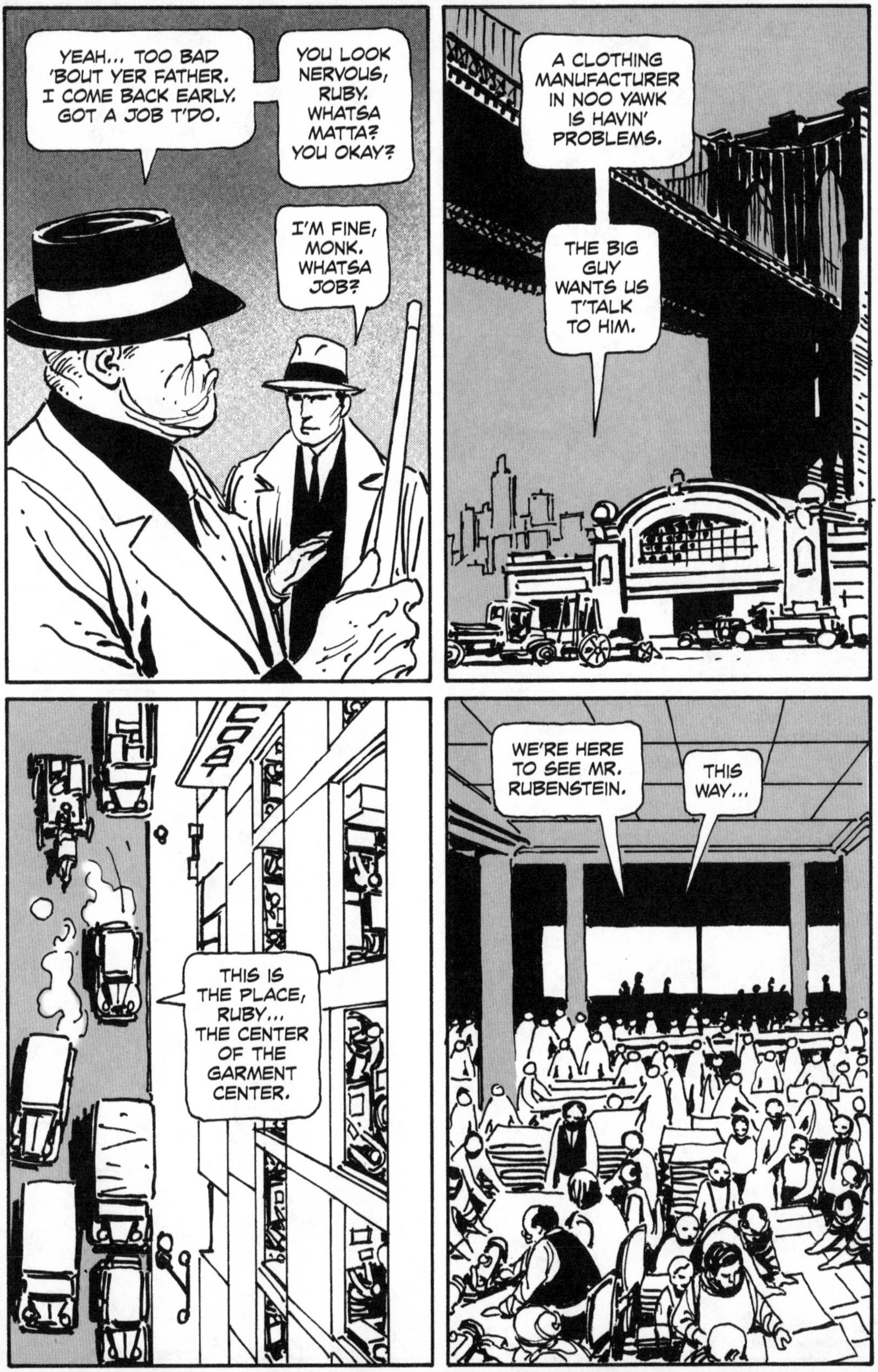
YEAH... TOO BAD 'BOUT YER FATHER. I COME BACK EARLY. GOT A JOB T'DO.
YOU LOOK NERVOUS, RUBY. WHATSA MATTA? YOU OKAY?
I'M FINE, MONK. WHATSA JOB?
A CLOTHING MANUFACTURER IN NOO YAWK IS HAVIN' PROBLEMS.
THE BIG GUY WANTS US T'TALK TO HIM.
THIS IS THE PLACE, RUBY... THE CENTER OF THE GARMENT CENTER.
WE'RE HERE TO SEE MR. RUBENSTEIN.
THIS WAY...

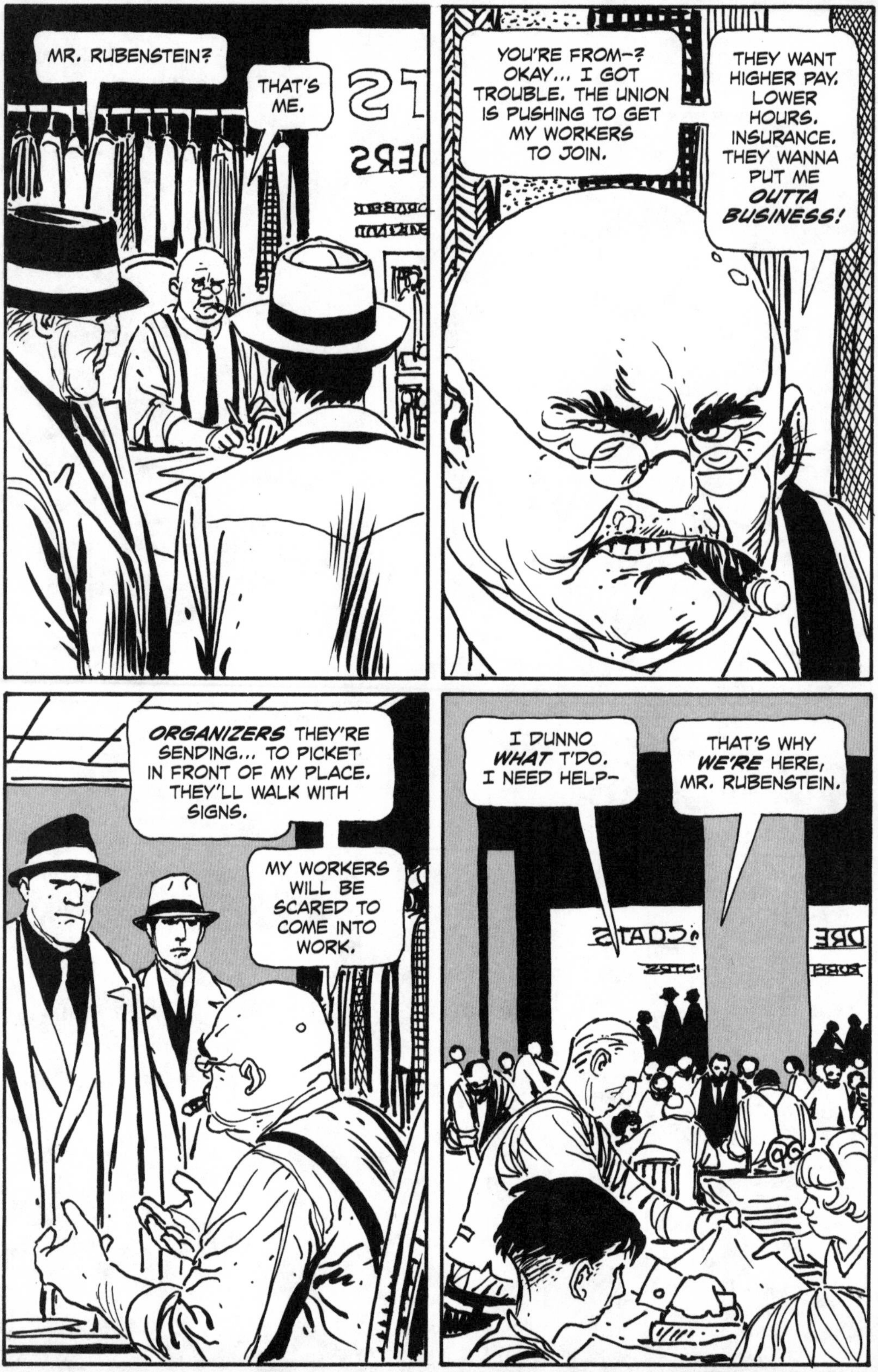
MR. RUBENSTEIN?
THAT'S ME.
YOU'RE FROM--? OKAY... I GOT TROUBLE. THE UNION IS PUSHING TO GET MY WORKERS TO JOIN.
THEY WANT HIGHER PAY. LOWER HOURS. INSURANCE. THEY WANNA PUT ME ***OUTTA BUSINESS!***
ORGANIZERS THEY'RE SENDING... TO PICKET IN FRONT OF MY PLACE. THEY'LL WALK WITH SIGNS.
MY WORKERS WILL BE SCARED TO COME INTO WORK.
I DUNNO ***WHAT*** T'DO. I NEED HELP--
THAT'S WHY ***WE'RE*** HERE, MR. RUBENSTEIN.

DON' WORRY, MR. RUBENSTEIN. ***WE*** WILL SEE TO IT THAT YOU GOT NO PROBLEMS.
YOU GOT OUR FEE?
OF COURSE.
HERE'S YOUR DOWN PAYMENT.
AND THE POLICE? WILL THEY-
THE LESS YOU KNOW THE BETTER FOR YOU. PLEASE... DON'T WORRY.
D'JA SEE THEM WORKERS, RUBY? MOST OF 'EM LOOKED ***STARVED...*** LIKE THEY AIN'T EAT NOTHIN' IN DAYS. KIDS...
MY FATHER WORKED INNA PLACE LIKE THAT, MONK.
KILLED HIM.

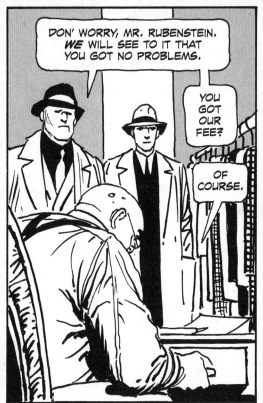

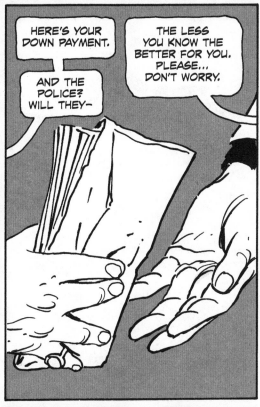

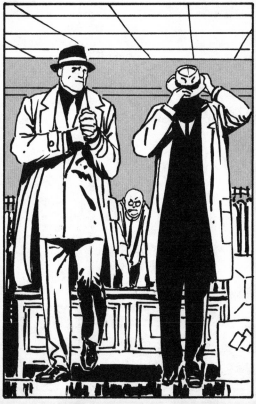

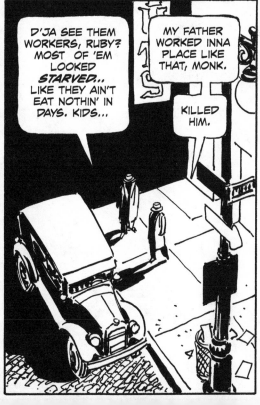

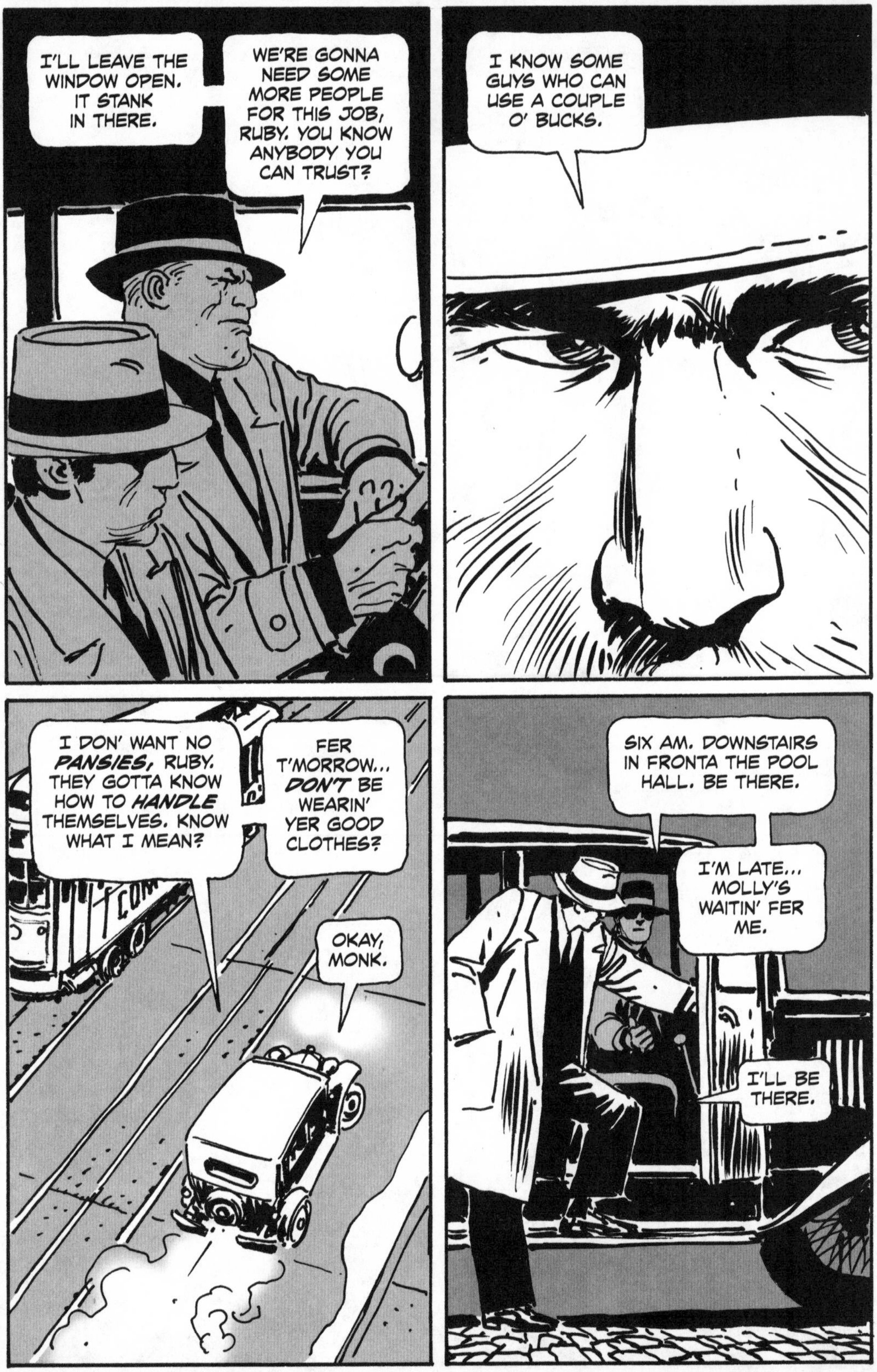
I'LL LEAVE THE WINDOW OPEN. IT STANK IN THERE.
WE'RE GONNA NEED SOME MORE PEOPLE FOR THIS JOB, RUBY. YOU KNOW ANYBODY YOU CAN TRUST?
I KNOW SOME GUYS WHO CAN USE A COUPLE O' BUCKS.
I DON' WANT NO PANSIES, RUBY. THEY GOTTA KNOW HOW TO HANDLE THEMSELVES. KNOW WHAT I MEAN?
FER T'MORROW... DON'T BE WEARIN' YER GOOD CLOTHES?
OKAY, MONK.
SIX AM. DOWNSTAIRS IN FRONTA THE POOL HALL. BE THERE.
I'M LATE... MOLLY'S WAITIN' FER ME.
I'LL BE THERE.

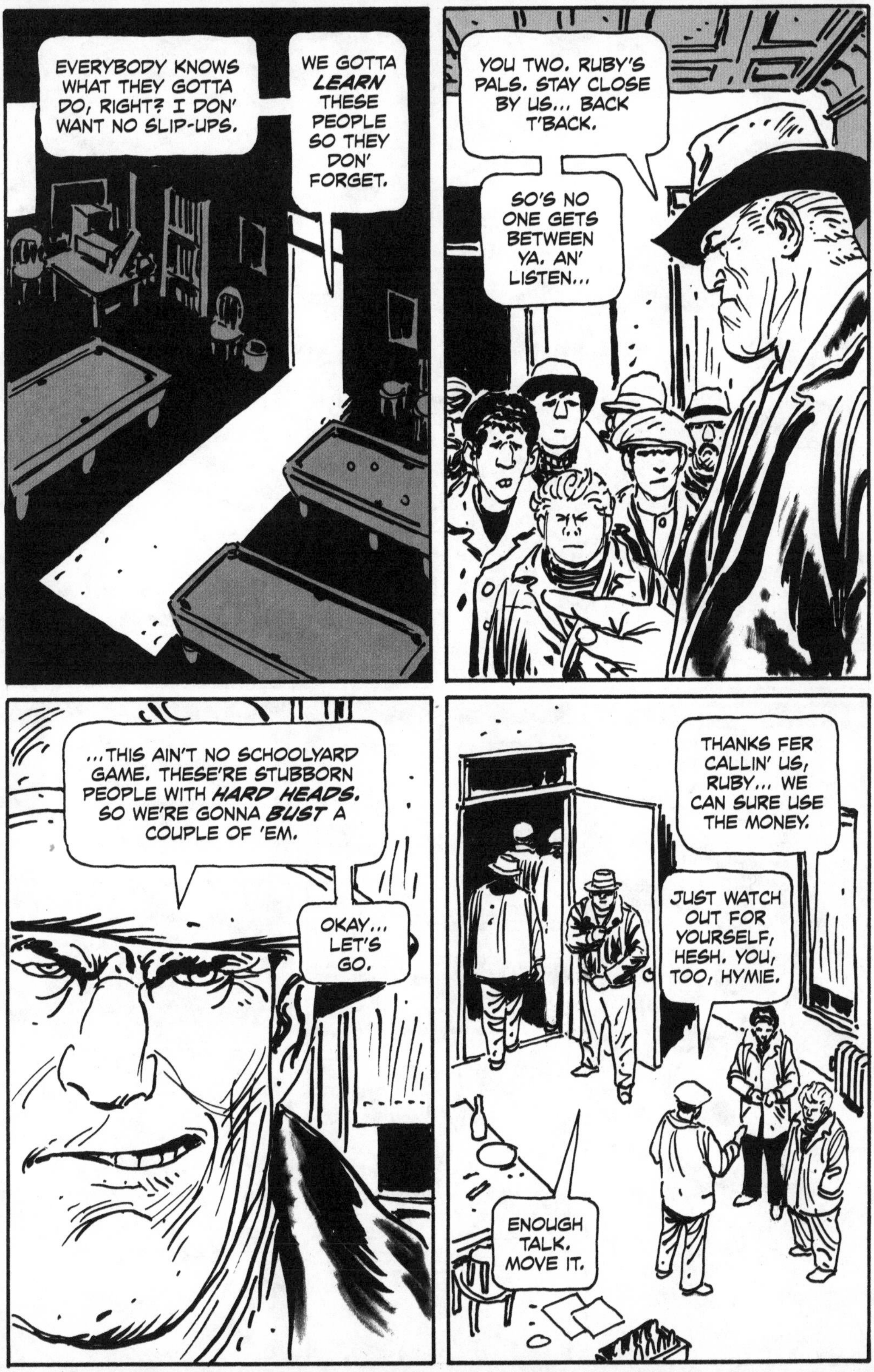
EVERYBODY KNOWS WHAT THEY GOTTA DO, RIGHT? I DON' WANT NO SLIP-UPS.
WE GOTTA LEARN THESE PEOPLE SO THEY DON' FORGET.
YOU TWO. RUBY'S PALS. STAY CLOSE BY US... BACK T'BACK.
SO'S NO ONE GETS BETWEEN YA. AN' LISTEN...
...THIS AIN'T NO SCHOOLYARD GAME. THESE'RE STUBBORN PEOPLE WITH HARD HEADS. SO WE'RE GONNA BUST A COUPLE OF 'EM.
OKAY... LET'S GO.
THANKS FER CALLIN' US, RUBY... WE CAN SURE USE THE MONEY.
JUST WATCH OUT FOR YOURSELF, HESH. YOU, TOO, HYMIE.
ENOUGH TALK. MOVE IT.

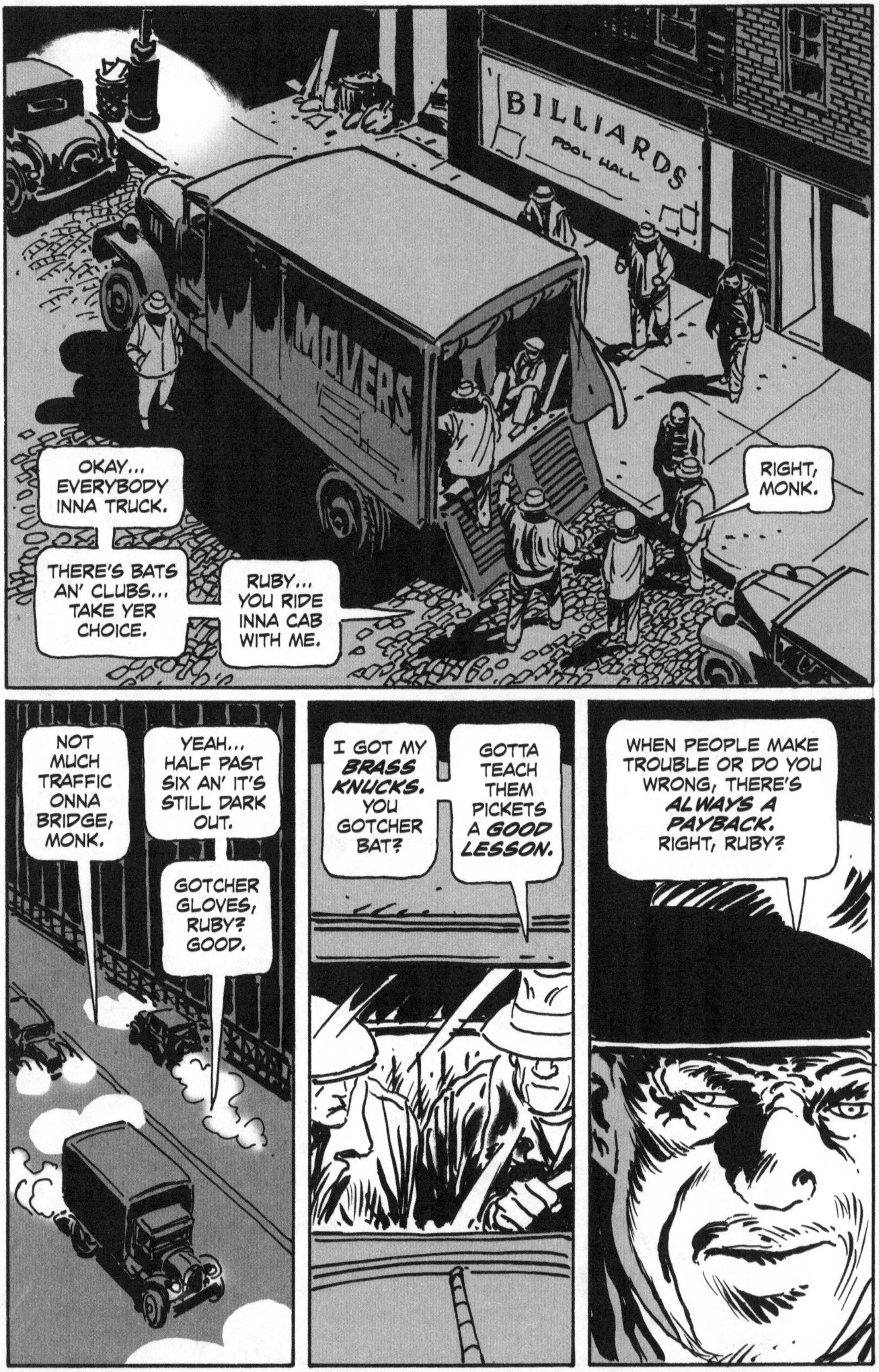
BILLIARDS
POOL HALL
MOVERS
OKAY... EVERYBODY INNA TRUCK.
THERE'S BATS AN' CLUBS... TAKE YER CHOICE.
RUBY... YOU RIDE INNA CAB WITH ME.
RIGHT, MONK.
NOT MUCH TRAFFIC ONNA BRIDGE, MONK.
YEAH... HALF PAST SIX AN' IT'S STILL DARK OUT.
GOTCHER GLOVES, RUBY? GOOD.
I GOT MY ***BRASS KNUCKS.*** YOU GOTCHER BAT?
GOTTA TEACH THEM PICKETS A ***GOOD LESSON.***
WHEN PEOPLE MAKE TROUBLE OR DO YOU WRONG, THERE'S ***ALWAYS A PAYBACK.*** RIGHT, RUBY?

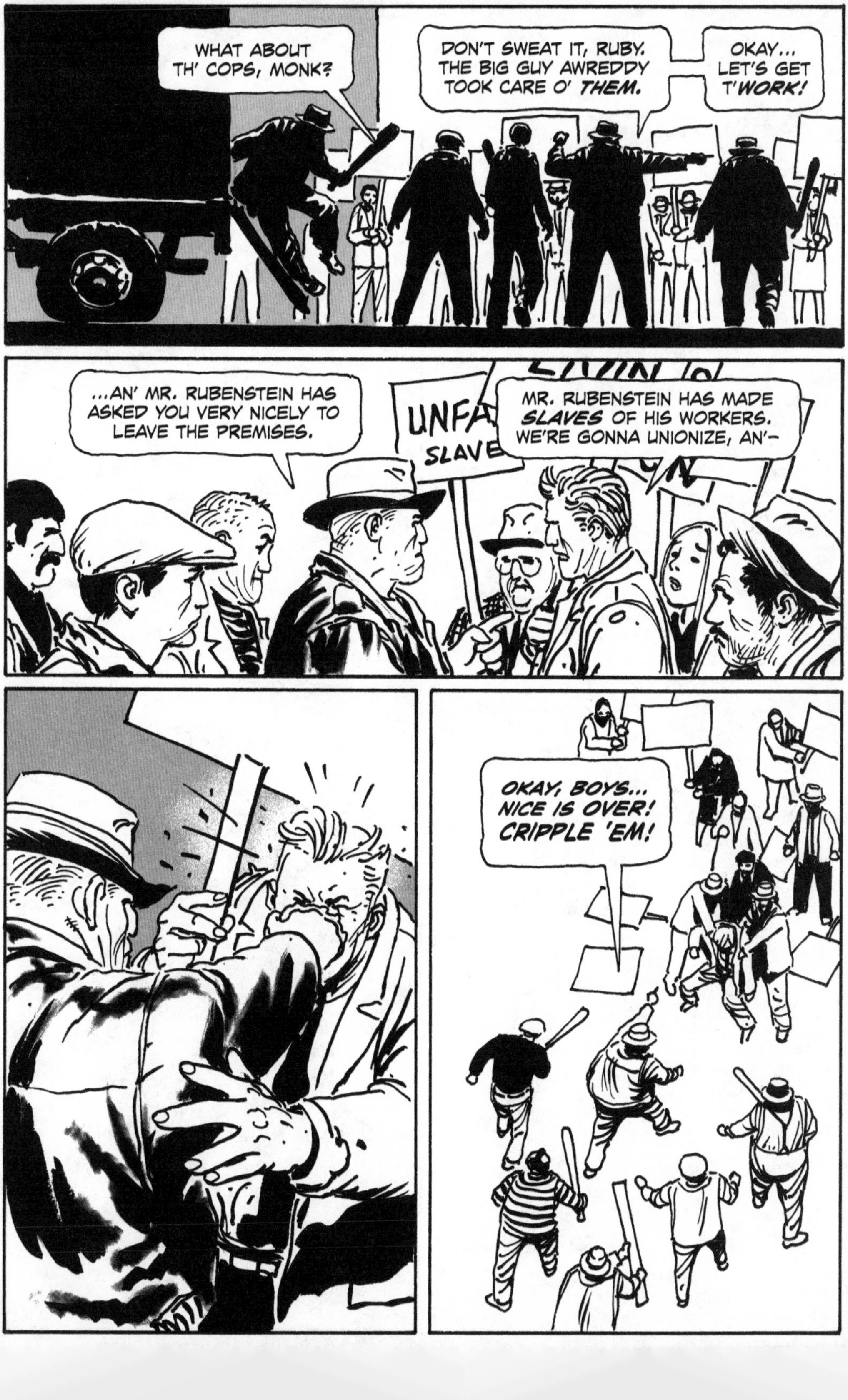
WHAT ABOUT TH' COPS, MONK?
DON'T SWEAT IT, RUBY. THE BIG GUY AWREDDY TOOK CARE O' THEM.
OKAY... LET'S GET T'WORK!
...AN' MR. RUBENSTEIN HAS ASKED YOU VERY NICELY TO LEAVE THE PREMISES.
MR. RUBENSTEIN HAS MADE SLAVES OF HIS WORKERS. WE'RE GONNA UNIONIZE, AN'—
OKAY, BOYS... NICE IS OVER! CRIPPLE 'EM!

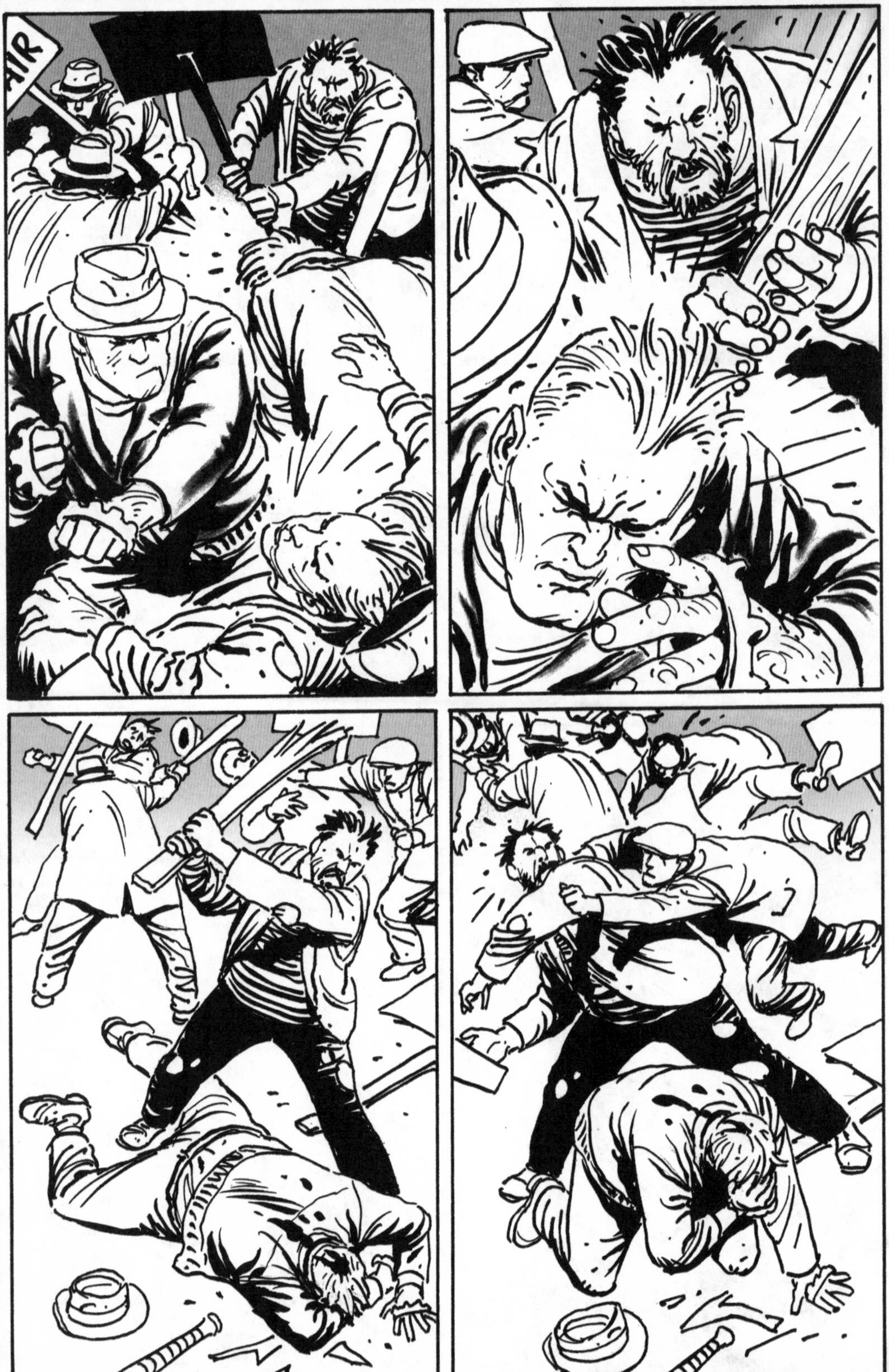
AIR

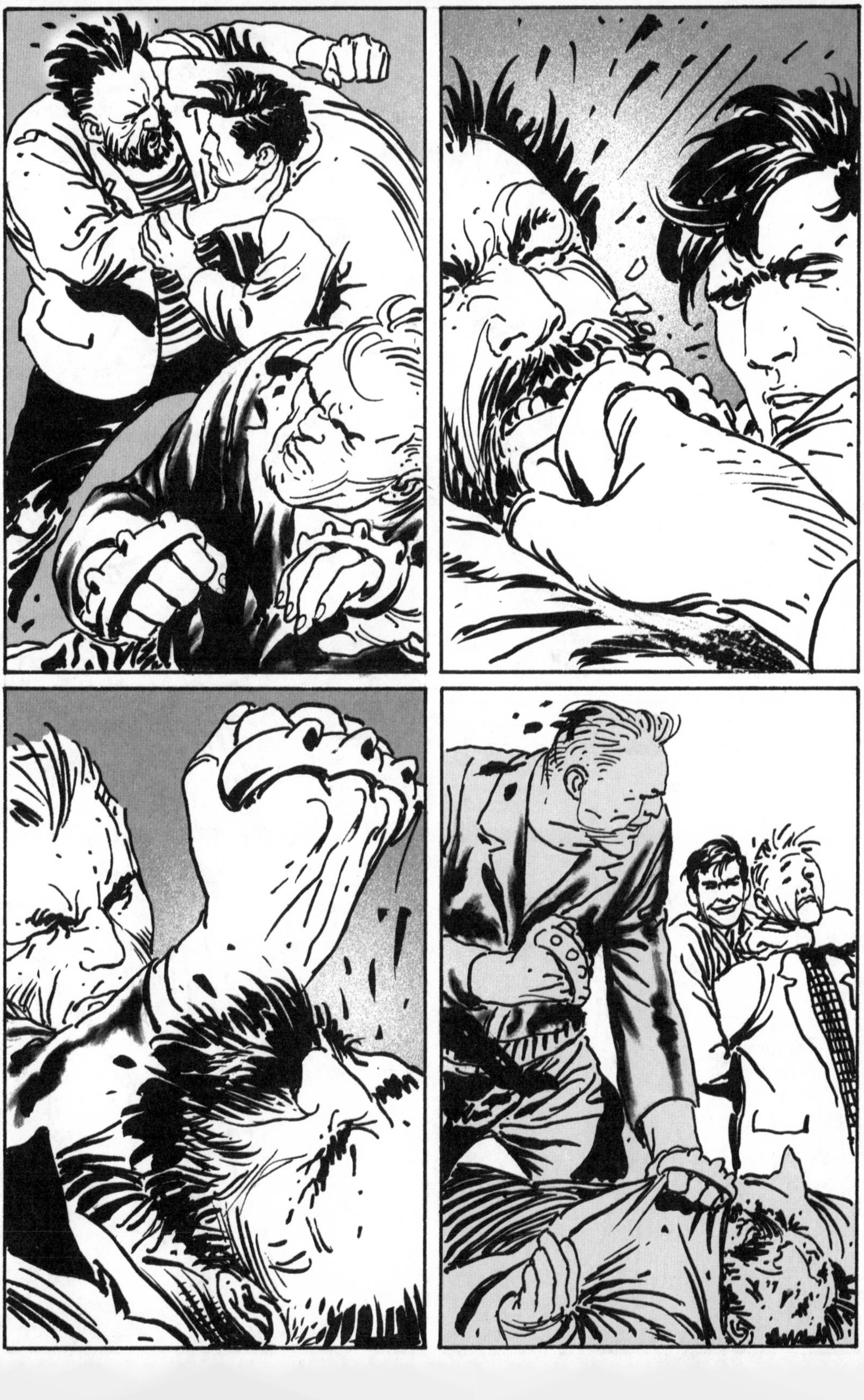

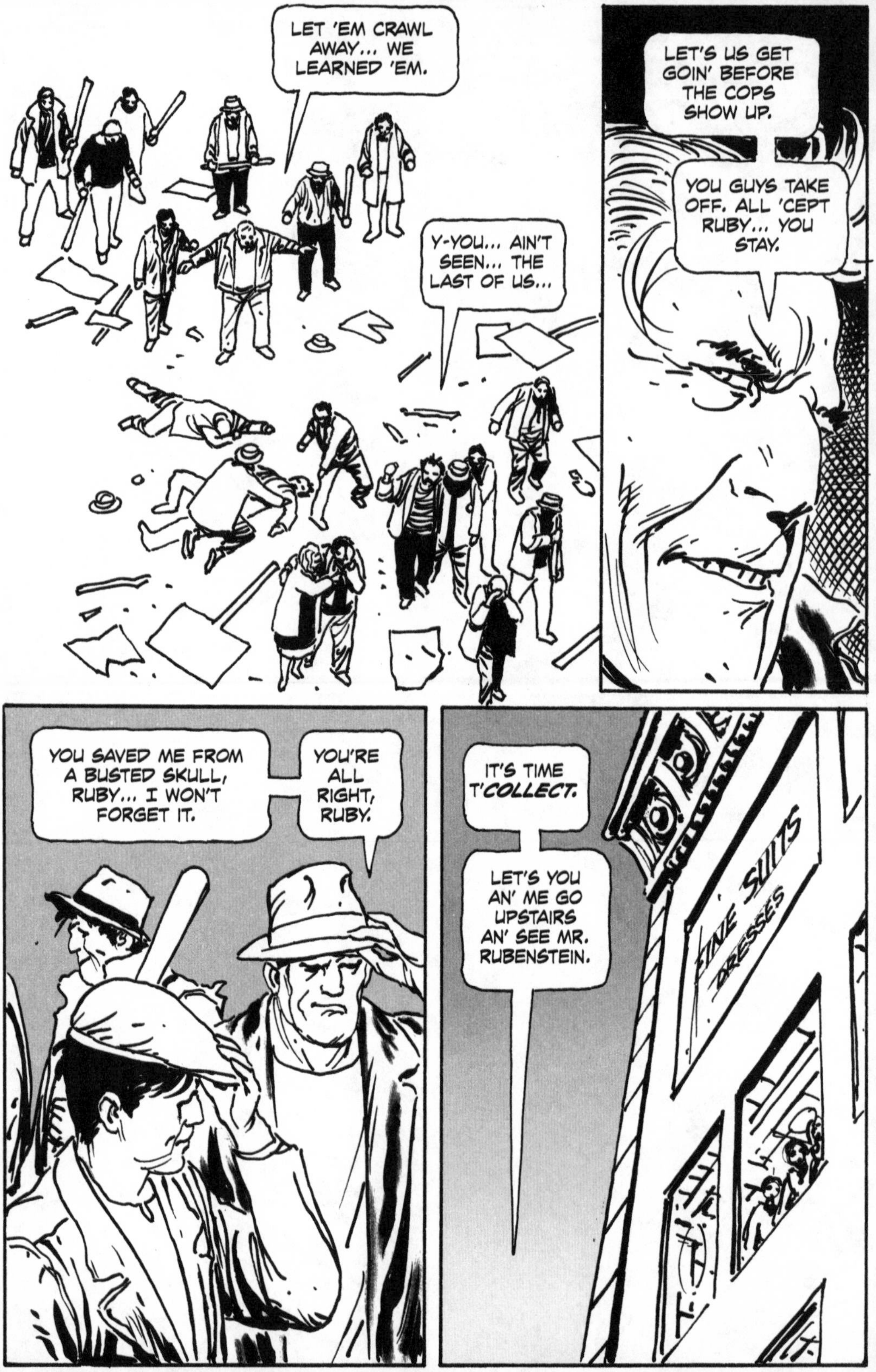

LET 'EM CRAWL AWAY... WE LEARNED 'EM.
Y-YOU... AIN'T SEEN... THE LAST OF US...
LET'S US GET GOIN' BEFORE THE COPS SHOW UP.
YOU GUYS TAKE OFF. ALL 'CEPT RUBY... YOU STAY.
YOU SAVED ME FROM A BUSTED SKULL, RUBY... I WON'T FORGET IT.
YOU'RE ALL RIGHT, RUBY.
IT'S TIME T'COLLECT.
LET'S YOU AN' ME GO UPSTAIRS AN' SEE MR. RUBENSTEIN.
FINE SUITS
DRESSES

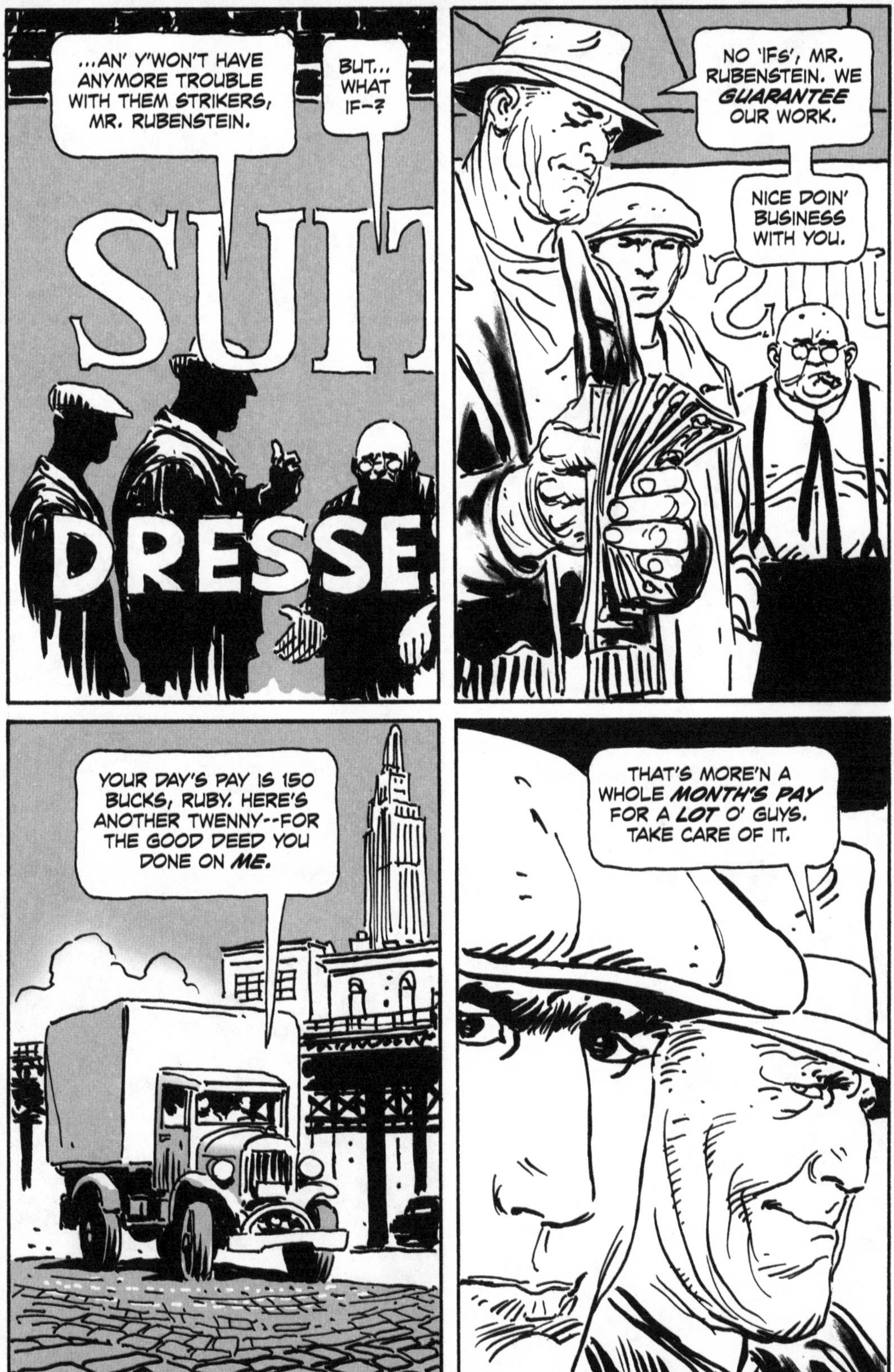
...AN' Y'WON'T HAVE ANYMORE TROUBLE WITH THEM STRIKERS, MR. RUBENSTEIN.
BUT... WHAT IF--?
SUIT
DRESSE
NO 'IFs', MR. RUBENSTEIN. WE GUARANTEE OUR WORK.
NICE DOIN' BUSINESS WITH YOU.
YOUR DAY'S PAY IS 150 BUCKS, RUBY. HERE'S ANOTHER TWENNY--FOR THE GOOD DEED YOU DONE ON ME.
THAT'S MORE'N A WHOLE MONTH'S PAY FOR A LOT O' GUYS. TAKE CARE OF IT.

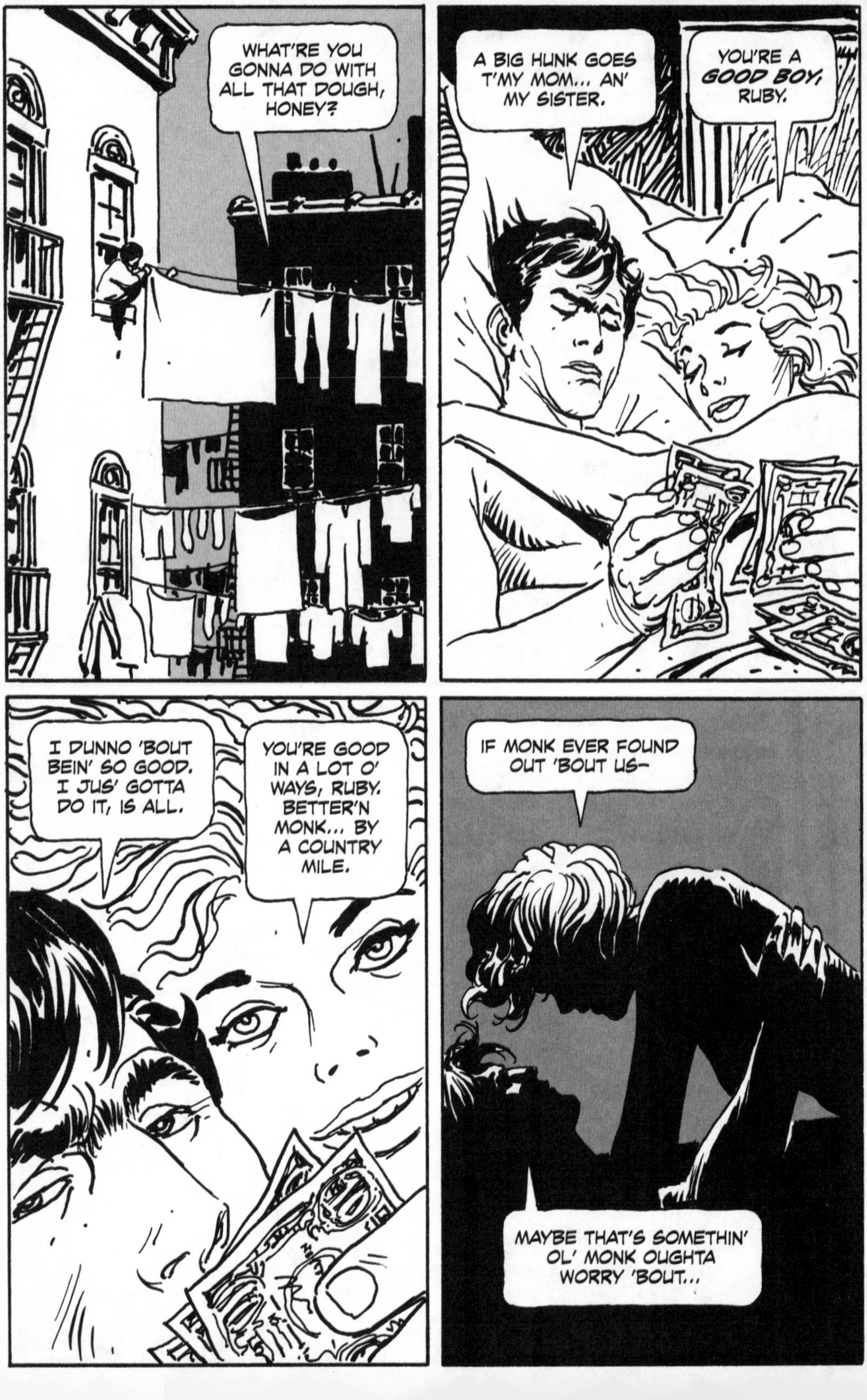
WHAT'RE YOU GONNA DO WITH ALL THAT DOUGH, HONEY?
A BIG HUNK GOES T'MY MOM... AN' MY SISTER.
YOU'RE A GOOD BOY, RUBY.
I DUNNO 'BOUT BEIN' SO GOOD. I JUS' GOTTA DO IT, IS ALL.
YOU'RE GOOD IN A LOT O' WAYS, RUBY. BETTER'N MONK... BY A COUNTRY MILE.
IF MONK EVER FOUND OUT 'BOUT US--
MAYBE THAT'S SOMETHIN' OL' MONK OUGHTA WORRY 'BOUT...

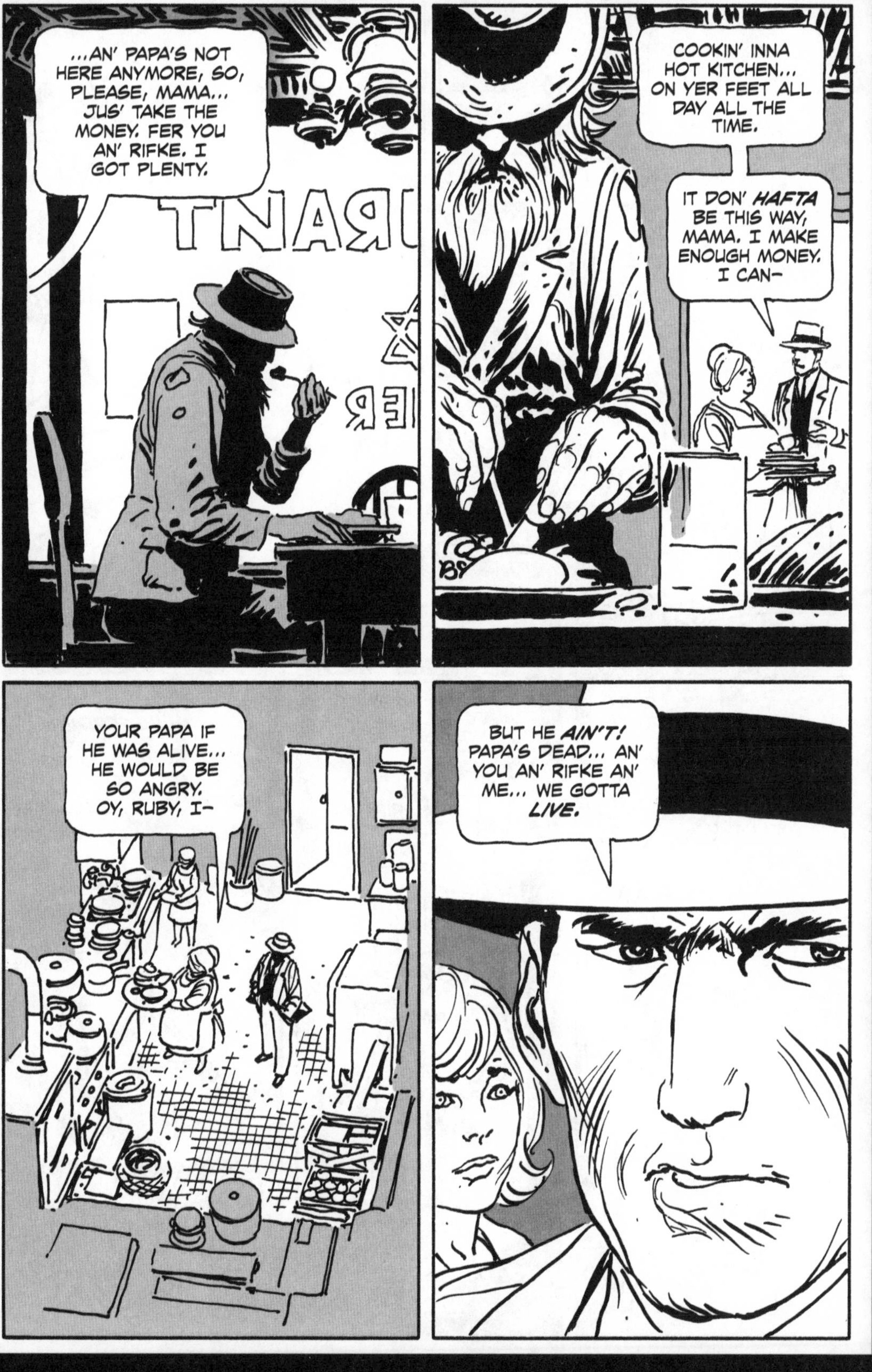
...AN' PAPA'S NOT HERE ANYMORE, SO, PLEASE, MAMA... JUS' TAKE THE MONEY. FER YOU AN' RIFKE. I GOT PLENTY.
COOKIN' INNA HOT KITCHEN... ON YER FEET ALL DAY ALL THE TIME.
IT DON' HAFTA BE THIS WAY, MAMA. I MAKE ENOUGH MONEY. I CAN-
YOUR PAPA IF HE WAS ALIVE... HE WOULD BE SO ANGRY. OY, RUBY, I-
BUT HE AIN'T! PAPA'S DEAD... AN' YOU AN' RIFKE AN' ME... WE GOTTA LIVE.

PLEASE, MAMA... JUS' TAKE THE MONEY. PUT IT AWAY... OR *THROW* IT AWAY.

FOR RIFKE.

NOW I GOT WORK, RUBY.

MR. COHEN IS WAITING FOR HIS DESSERT.

IT'S HARD FOR MAMA, RUBY. SHE'S MIXED UP. YOU AND PAPA...

YEAH, RIFKE... WELL... YOU KEEP AN EYE ON HER.

TAKE CARE OF YOUR-SELF, RUBY.

IF YOU NEED ME FOR *ANY-THING*, YOU KNOW WHERE I AM.

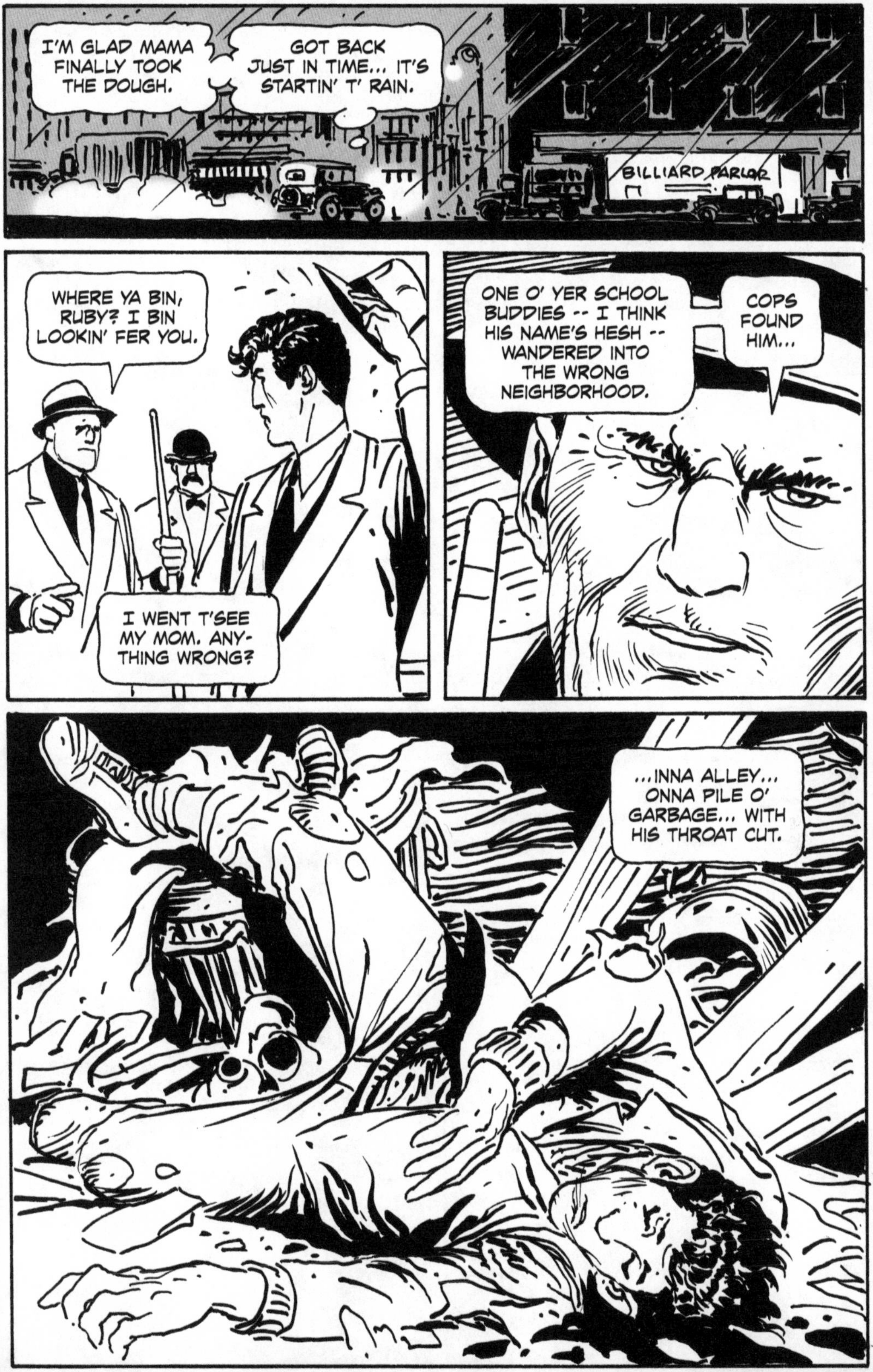
I'M GLAD MAMA FINALLY TOOK THE DOUGH.
GOT BACK JUST IN TIME... IT'S STARTIN' T' RAIN.
BILLIARD PARLOR
WHERE YA BIN, RUBY? I BIN LOOKIN' FER YOU.
I WENT T'SEE MY MOM. ANY-THING WRONG?
ONE O' YER SCHOOL BUDDIES -- I THINK HIS NAME'S HESH -- WANDERED INTO THE WRONG NEIGHBORHOOD.
COPS FOUND HIM...
...INNA ALLEY... ONNA PILE O' GARBAGE... WITH HIS THROAT CUT.

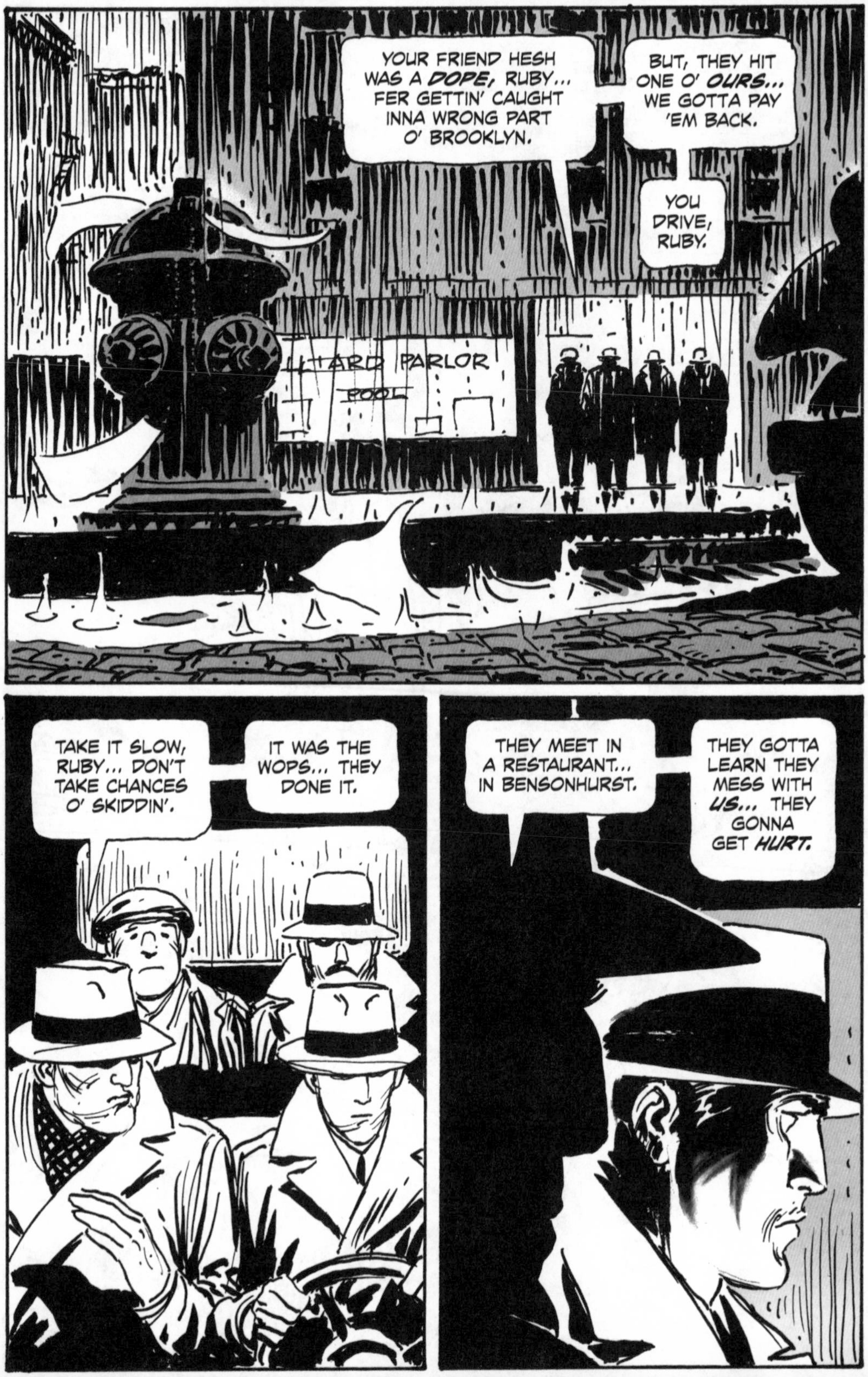
YOUR FRIEND HESH WAS A DOPE, RUBY... FER GETTIN' CAUGHT INNA WRONG PART O' BROOKLYN.
BUT, THEY HIT ONE O' OURS... WE GOTTA PAY 'EM BACK.
YOU DRIVE, RUBY.
...ARD PARLOR
POOL
TAKE IT SLOW, RUBY... DON'T TAKE CHANCES O' SKIDDIN'.
IT WAS THE WOPS... THEY DONE IT.
THEY MEET IN A RESTAURANT... IN BENSONHURST.
THEY GOTTA LEARN THEY MESS WITH US... THEY GONNA GET HURT.

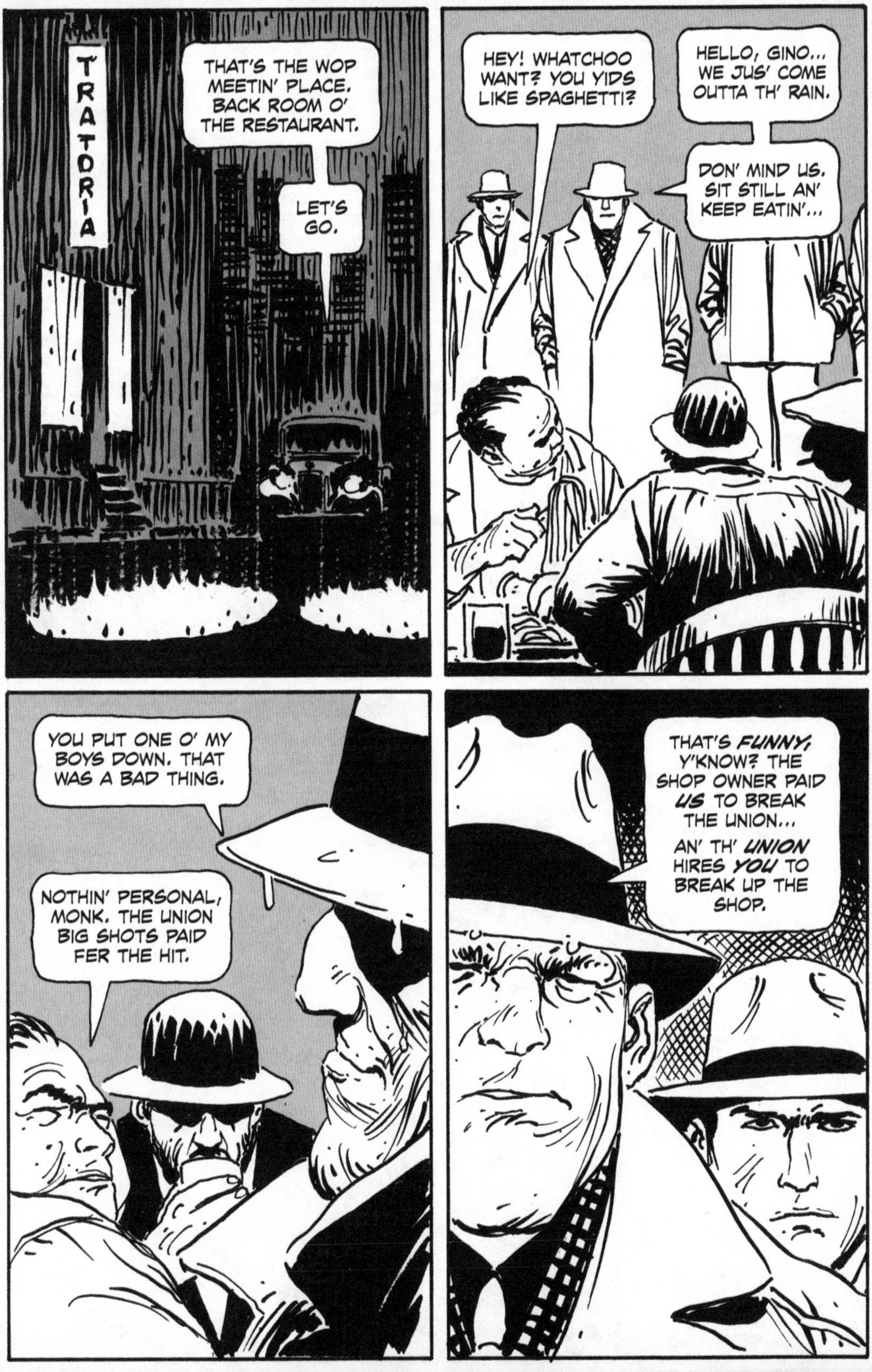
TRATORIA
THAT'S THE WOP MEETIN' PLACE. BACK ROOM O' THE RESTAURANT.
LET'S GO.
HEY! WHATCHOO WANT? YOU YIDS LIKE SPAGHETTI?
HELLO, GINO... WE JUS' COME OUTTA TH' RAIN.
DON' MIND US. SIT STILL AN' KEEP EATIN'...
YOU PUT ONE O' MY BOYS DOWN. THAT WAS A BAD THING.
NOTHIN' PERSONAL, MONK. THE UNION BIG SHOTS PAID FER THE HIT.
THAT'S FUNNY, Y'KNOW? THE SHOP OWNER PAID US TO BREAK THE UNION...
AN' TH' UNION HIRES YOU TO BREAK UP THE SHOP.

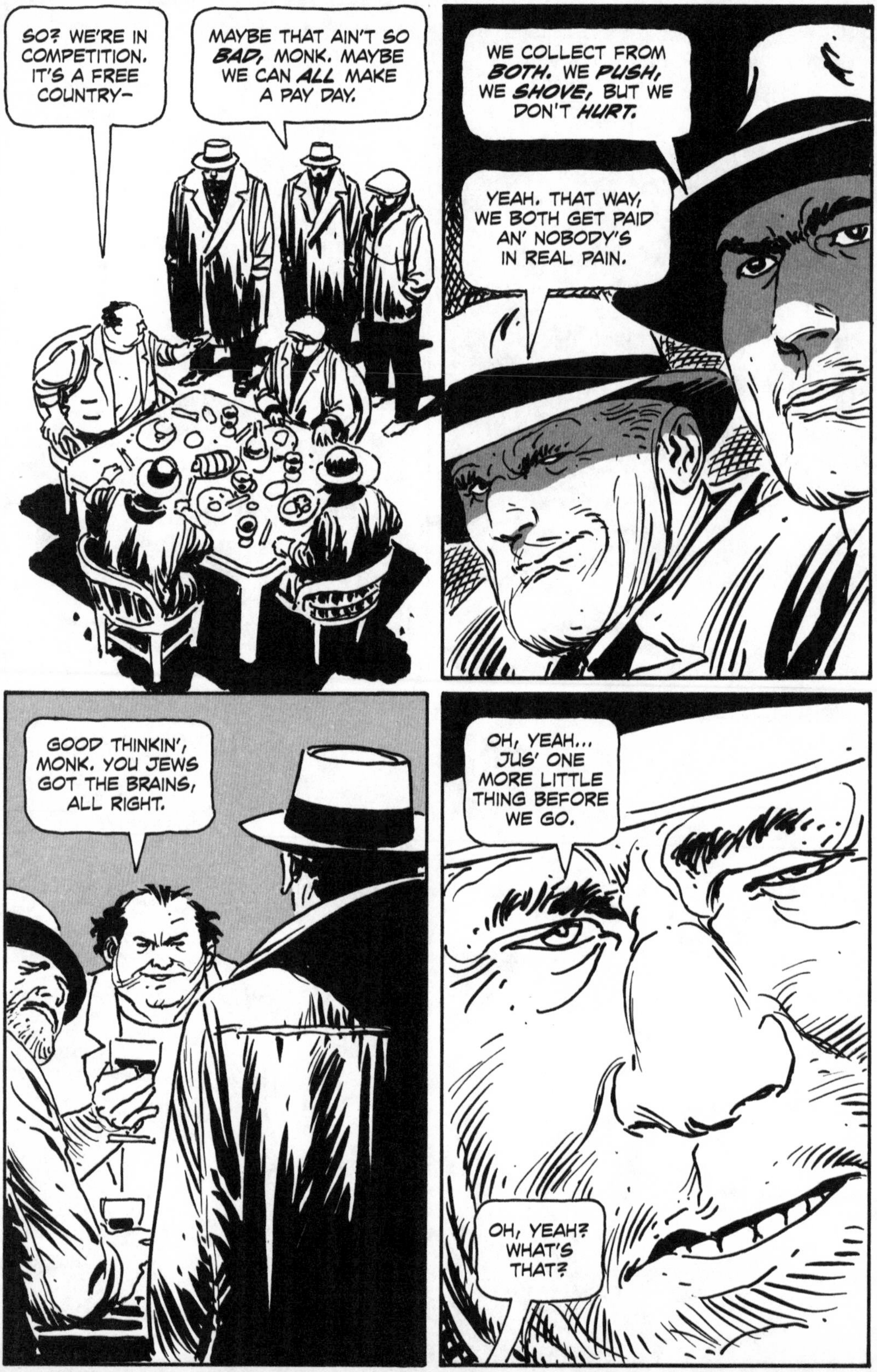
SO? WE'RE IN COMPETITION. IT'S A FREE COUNTRY–
MAYBE THAT AIN'T SO BAD, MONK. MAYBE WE CAN ALL MAKE A PAY DAY.
WE COLLECT FROM BOTH. WE PUSH, WE SHOVE, BUT WE DON'T HURT.
YEAH. THAT WAY, WE BOTH GET PAID AN' NOBODY'S IN REAL PAIN.
GOOD THINKIN', MONK. YOU JEWS GOT THE BRAINS, ALL RIGHT.
OH, YEAH... JUS' ONE MORE LITTLE THING BEFORE WE GO.
OH, YEAH? WHAT'S THAT?

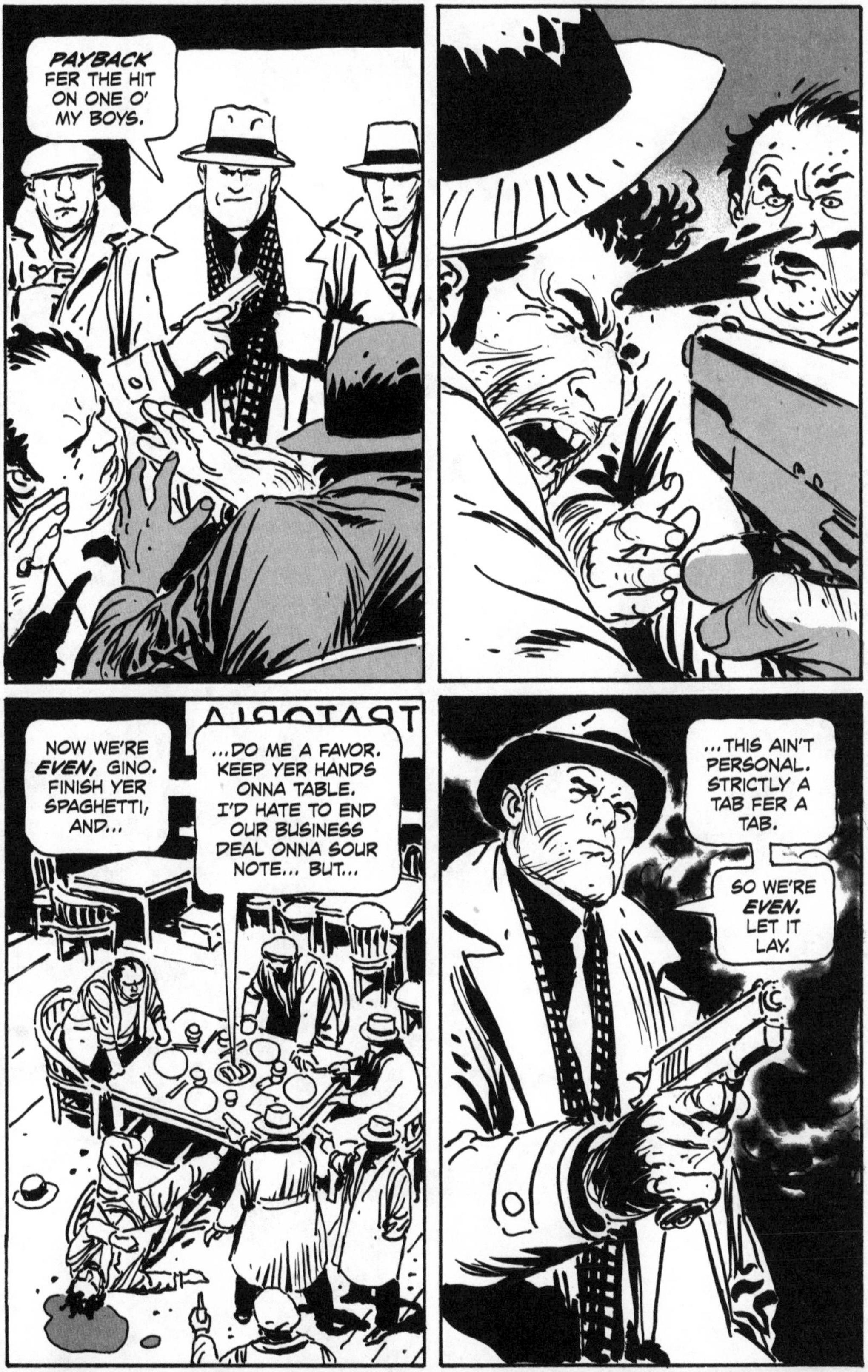
PAYBACK FER THE HIT ON ONE O' MY BOYS.
NOW WE'RE EVEN, GINO. FINISH YER SPAGHETTI, AND...
...DO ME A FAVOR. KEEP YER HANDS ONNA TABLE. I'D HATE TO END OUR BUSINESS DEAL ONNA SOUR NOTE... BUT...
...THIS AIN'T PERSONAL. STRICTLY A TAB FER A TAB.
SO WE'RE EVEN. LET IT LAY.

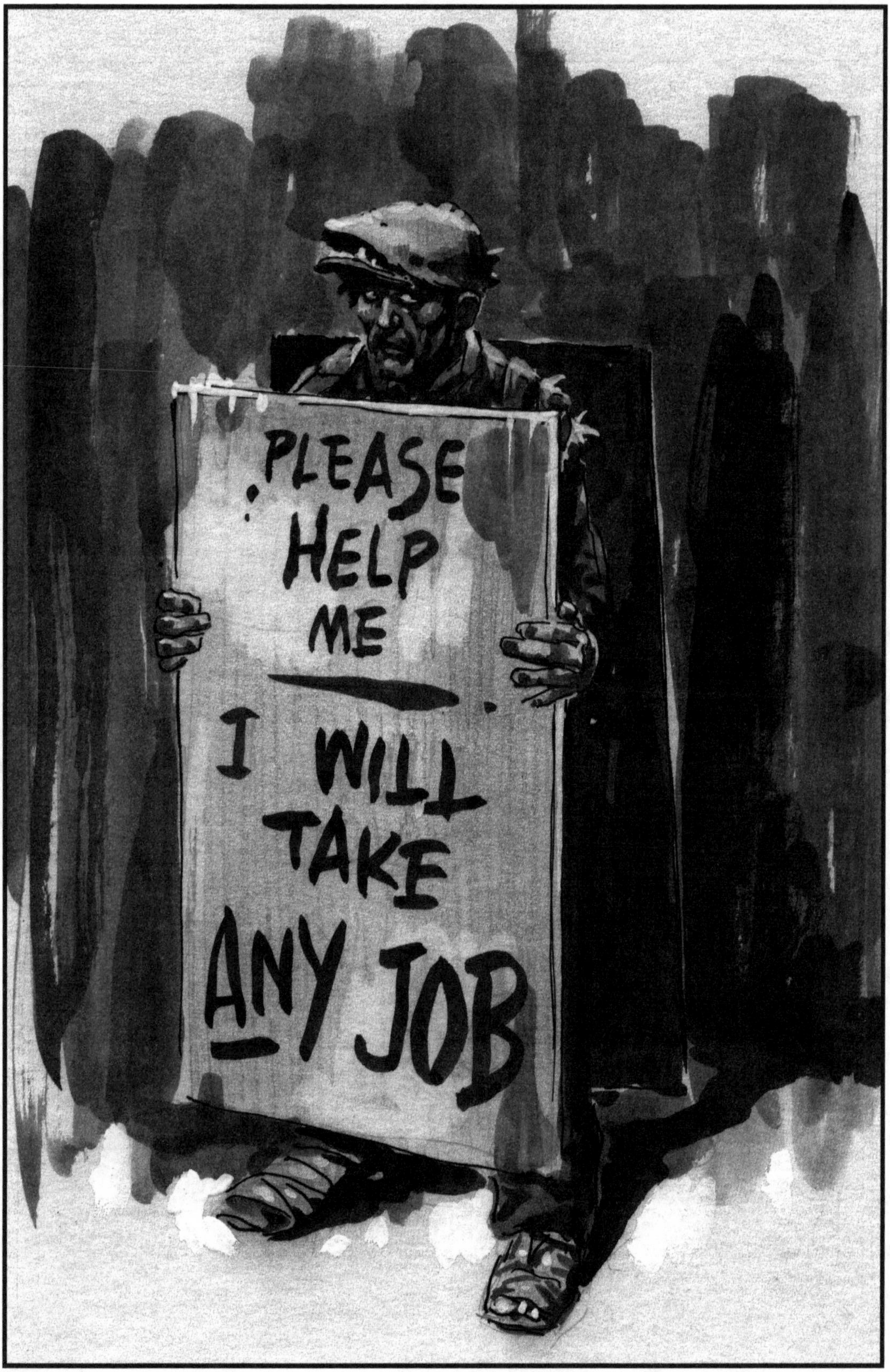
PLEASE
HELP
ME
I WILL
TAKE
ANY JOB

The Depression

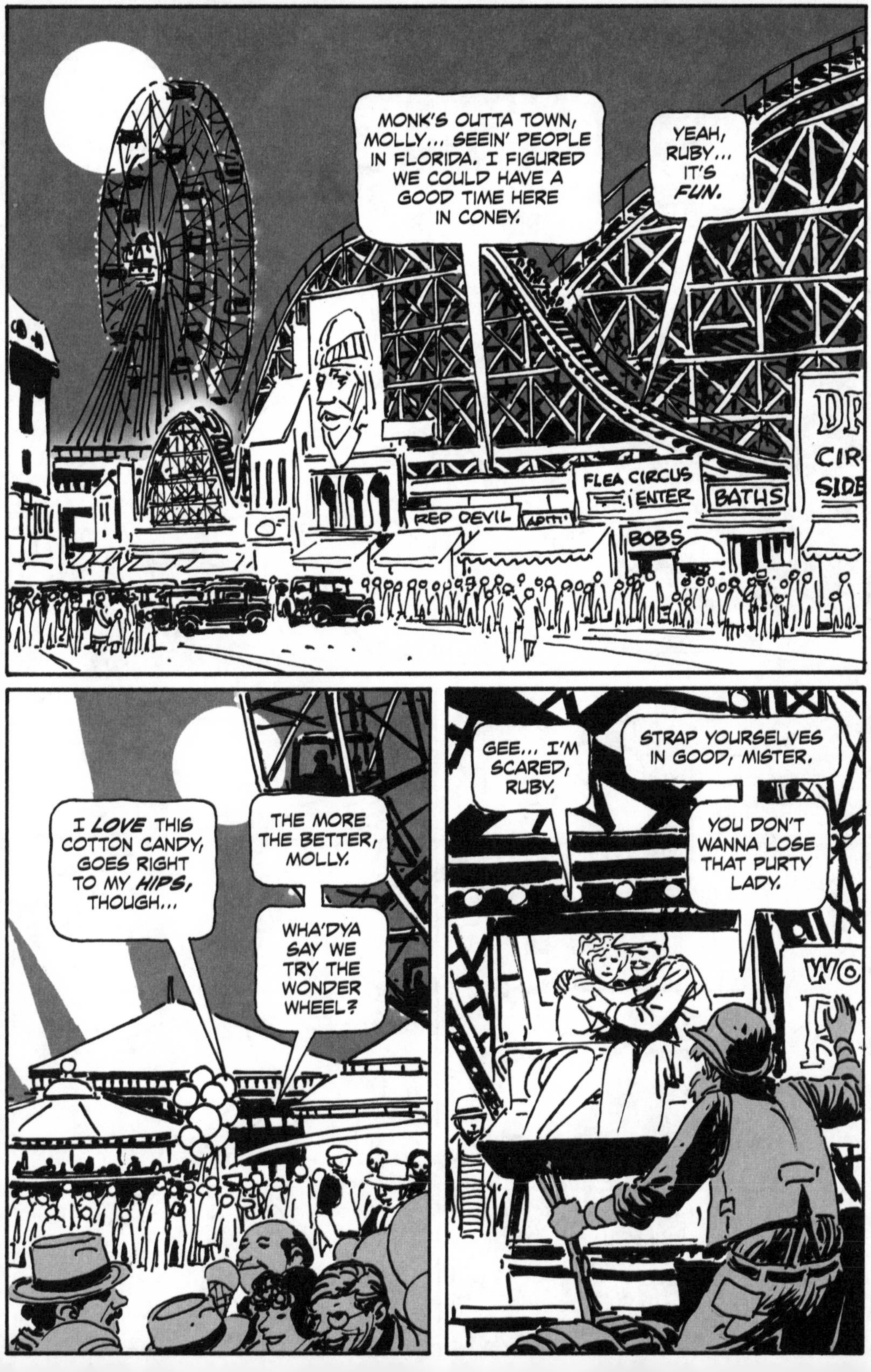
MONK'S OUTTA TOWN, MOLLY... SEEIN' PEOPLE IN FLORIDA. I FIGURED WE COULD HAVE A GOOD TIME HERE IN CONEY.
YEAH, RUBY... IT'S *FUN.*
FLEA CIRCUS
ENTER
BATHS
RED DEVIL
BOBS
I *LOVE* THIS COTTON CANDY, GOES RIGHT TO MY *HIPS,* THOUGH...
THE MORE THE BETTER, MOLLY.
WHA'DYA SAY WE TRY THE WONDER WHEEL?
GEE... I'M SCARED, RUBY.
STRAP YOURSELVES IN GOOD, MISTER.
YOU DON'T WANNA LOSE THAT PURTY LADY.

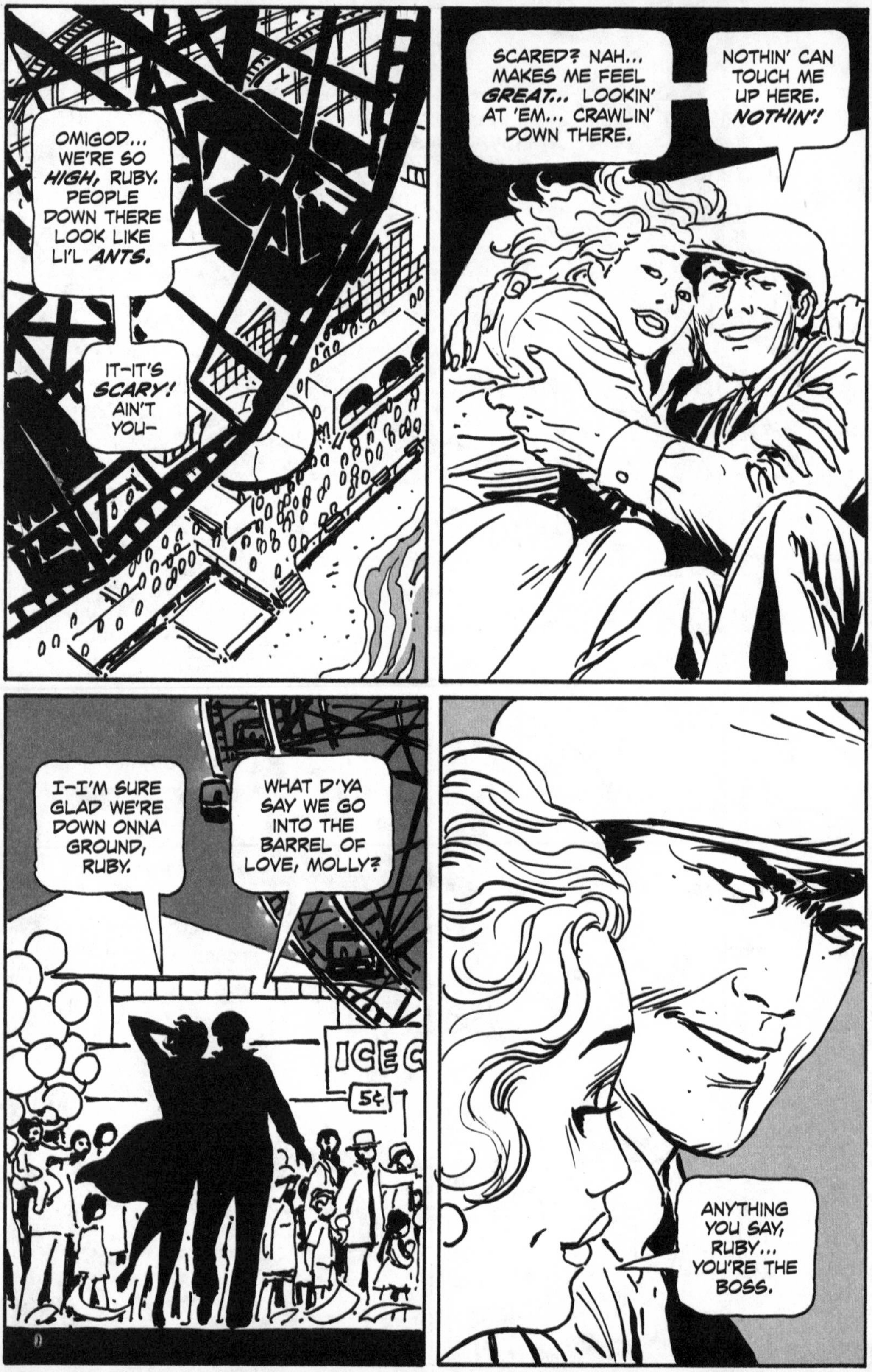
OMIGOD... WE'RE SO HIGH, RUBY. PEOPLE DOWN THERE LOOK LIKE LI'L ANTS.
IT-IT'S SCARY! AIN'T YOU-
SCARED? NAH... MAKES ME FEEL GREAT... LOOKIN' AT 'EM... CRAWLIN' DOWN THERE.
NOTHIN' CAN TOUCH ME UP HERE. NOTHIN'!
I-I'M SURE GLAD WE'RE DOWN ONNA GROUND, RUBY.
WHAT D'YA SAY WE GO INTO THE BARREL OF LOVE, MOLLY?
ICE C
5¢
ANYTHING YOU SAY, RUBY... YOU'RE THE BOSS.

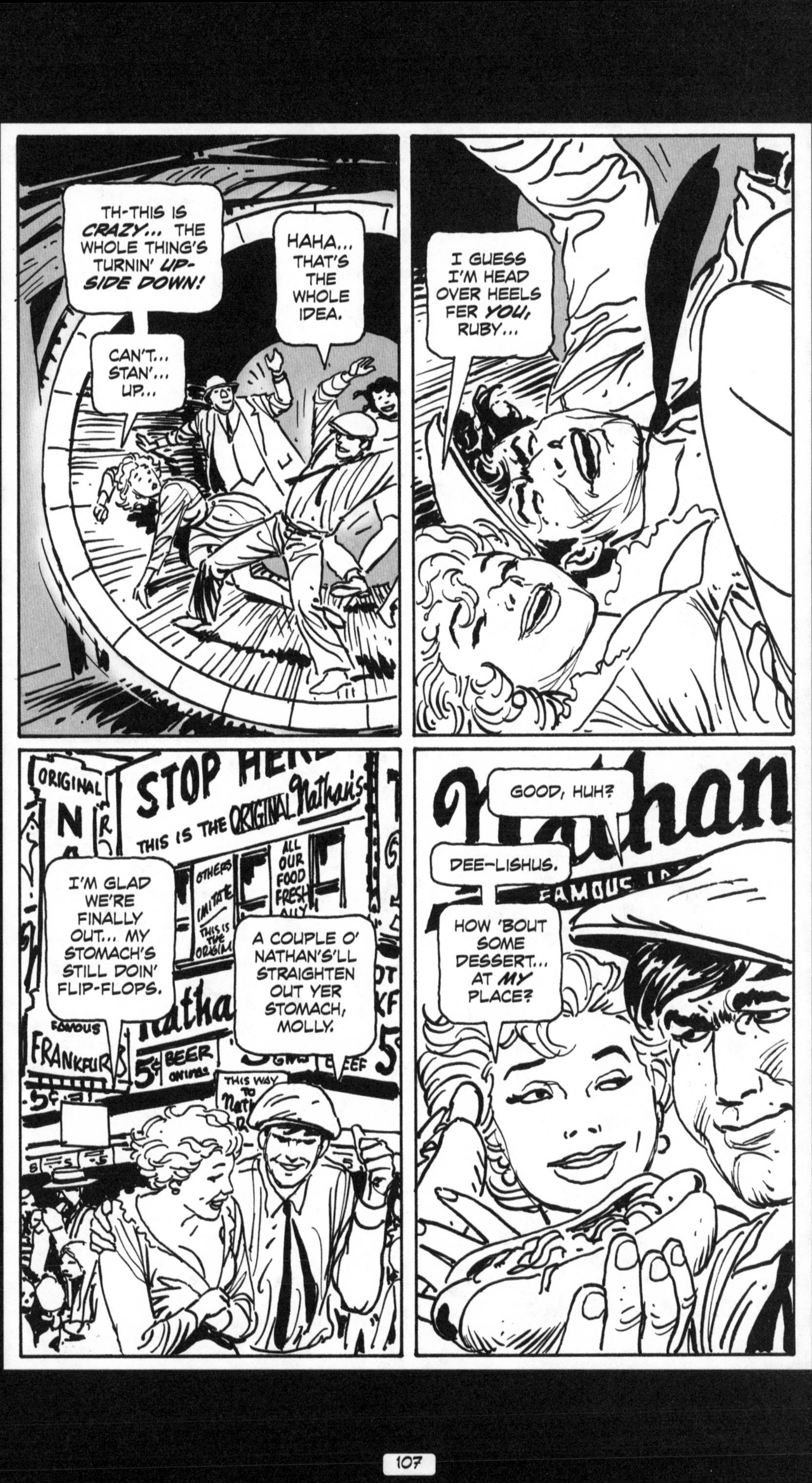

TH-THIS IS CRAZY... THE WHOLE THING'S TURNIN' UP-SIDE DOWN!
CAN'T... STAN'... UP...
HAHA... THAT'S THE WHOLE IDEA.
I GUESS I'M HEAD OVER HEELS FER YOU, RUBY...
ORIGINAL
STOP HER
THIS IS THE ORIGINAL Nathan's
ALL OUR FOOD FRESH
OTHERS IMITATE
I'M GLAD WE'RE FINALLY OUT... MY STOMACH'S STILL DOIN' FLIP-FLOPS.
A COUPLE O' NATHAN'S'LL STRAIGHTEN OUT YER STOMACH, MOLLY.
FAMOUS
FRANKFUR
5¢ BEER
THIS WAY TO
GOOD, HUH?
DEE-LISHUS.
HOW 'BOUT SOME DESSERT... AT MY PLACE?

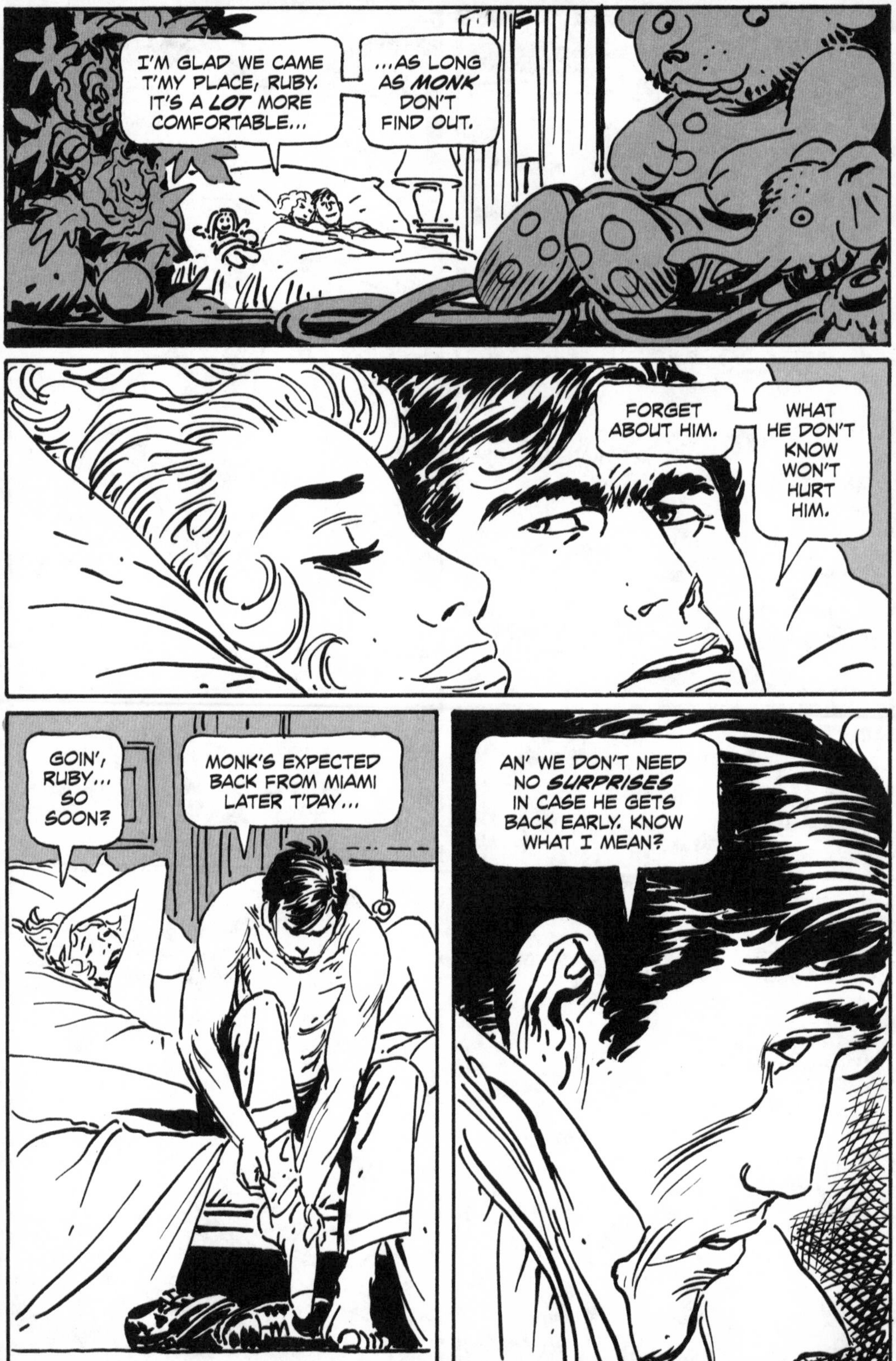
I'M GLAD WE CAME T'MY PLACE, RUBY. IT'S A *LOT* MORE COMFORTABLE...
...AS LONG AS *MONK* DON'T FIND OUT.
FORGET ABOUT HIM.
WHAT HE DON'T KNOW WON'T HURT HIM.
GOIN', RUBY... SO SOON?
MONK'S EXPECTED BACK FROM MIAMI LATER T'DAY...
AN' WE DON'T NEED NO *SURPRISES* IN CASE HE GETS BACK EARLY. KNOW WHAT I MEAN?

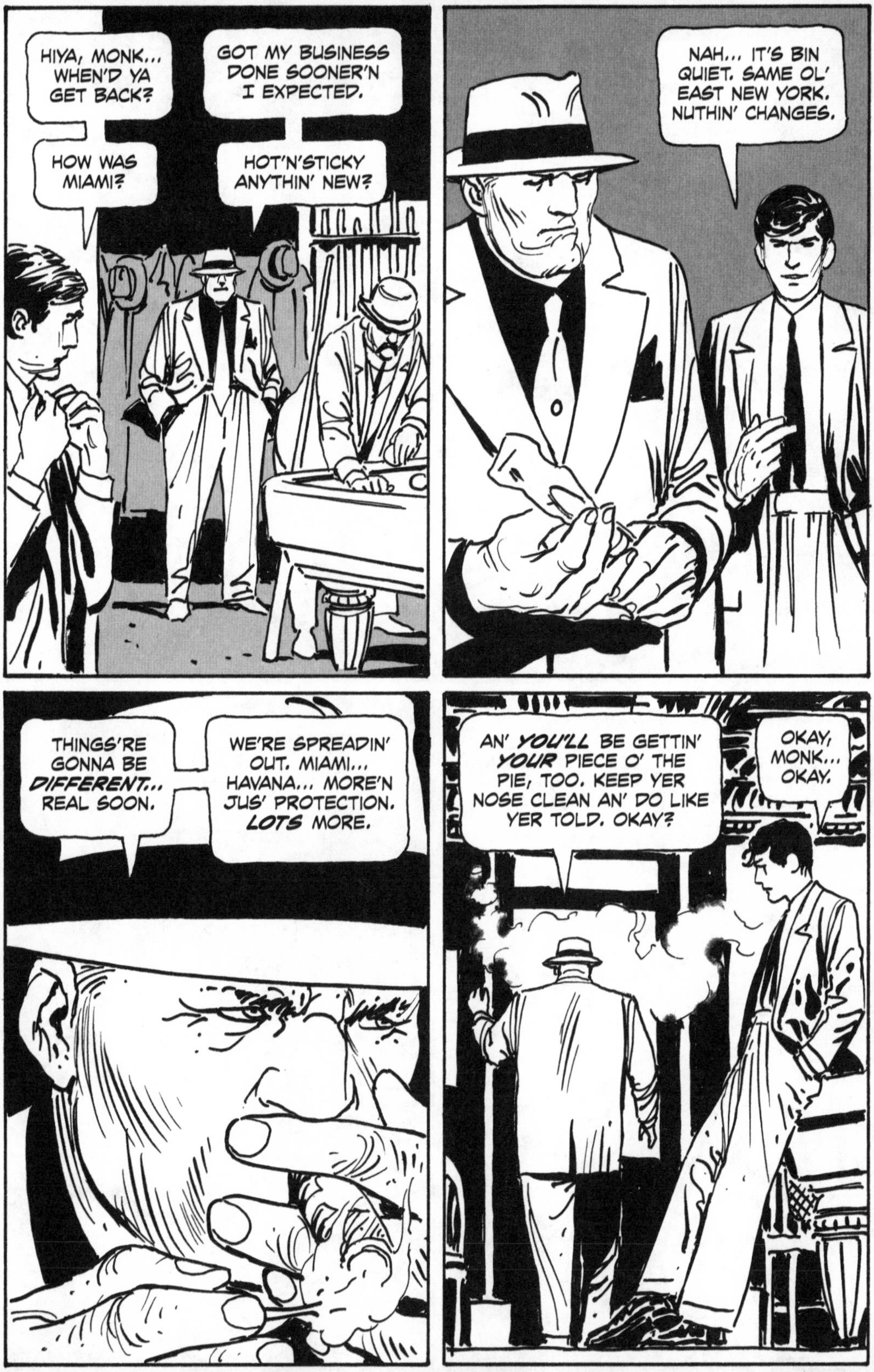
HIYA, MONK... WHEN'D YA GET BACK?
GOT MY BUSINESS DONE SOONER'N I EXPECTED.
HOW WAS MIAMI?
HOT'N'STICKY ANYTHIN' NEW?
NAH... IT'S BIN QUIET. SAME OL' EAST NEW YORK. NUTHIN' CHANGES.
THINGS'RE GONNA BE *DIFFERENT*... REAL SOON.
WE'RE SPREADIN' OUT. MIAMI... HAVANA... MORE'N JUS' PROTECTION. *LOTS* MORE.
AN' *YOU'LL* BE GETTIN' *YOUR* PIECE O' THE PIE, TOO. KEEP YER NOSE CLEAN AN' DO LIKE YER TOLD. OKAY?
OKAY, MONK... OKAY.

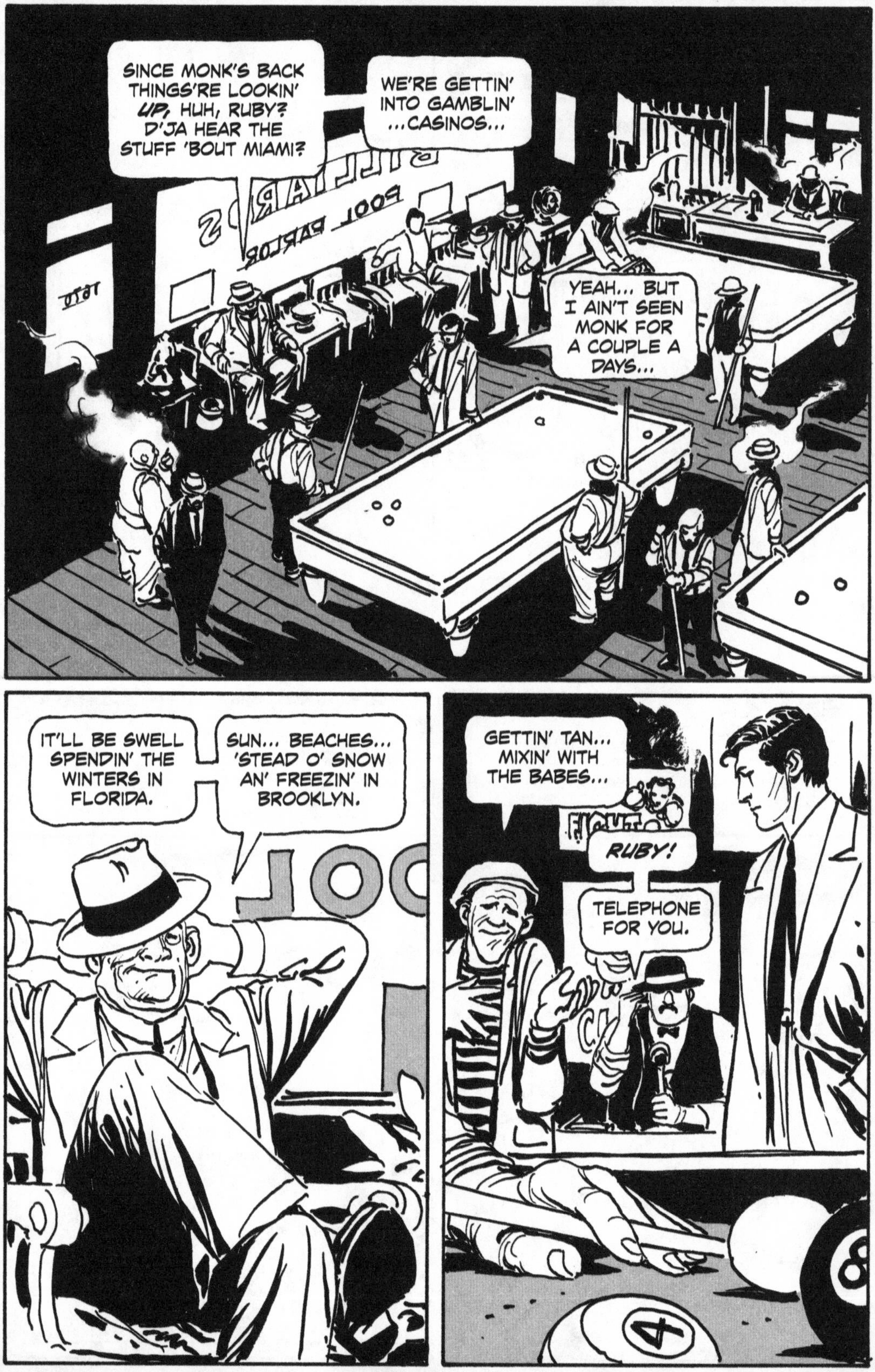
SINCE MONK'S BACK THINGS'RE LOOKIN' *UP*, HUH, RUBY? D'JA HEAR THE STUFF 'BOUT MIAMI?
WE'RE GETTIN' INTO GAMBLIN' ...CASINOS...
YEAH... BUT I AIN'T SEEN MONK FOR A COUPLE A DAYS...
IT'LL BE SWELL SPENDIN' THE WINTERS IN FLORIDA.
SUN... BEACHES... 'STEAD O' SNOW AN' FREEZIN' IN BROOKLYN.
GETTIN' TAN... MIXIN' WITH THE BABES...
RUBY!
TELEPHONE FOR YOU.

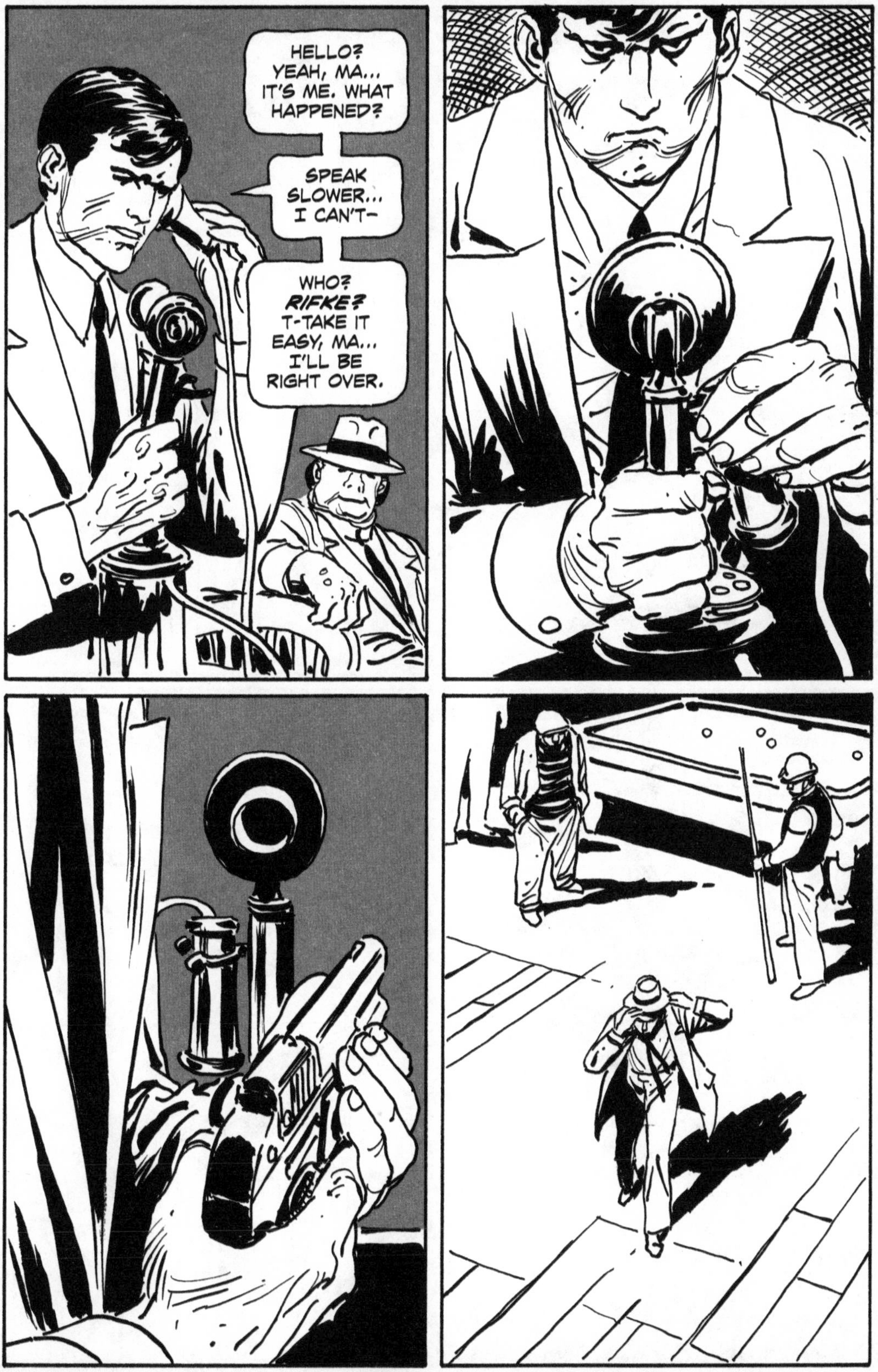
HELLO? YEAH, MA... IT'S ME. WHAT HAPPENED?
SPEAK SLOWER... I CAN'T—
WHO? ***RIFKE?*** T-TAKE IT EASY, MA... I'LL BE RIGHT OVER.

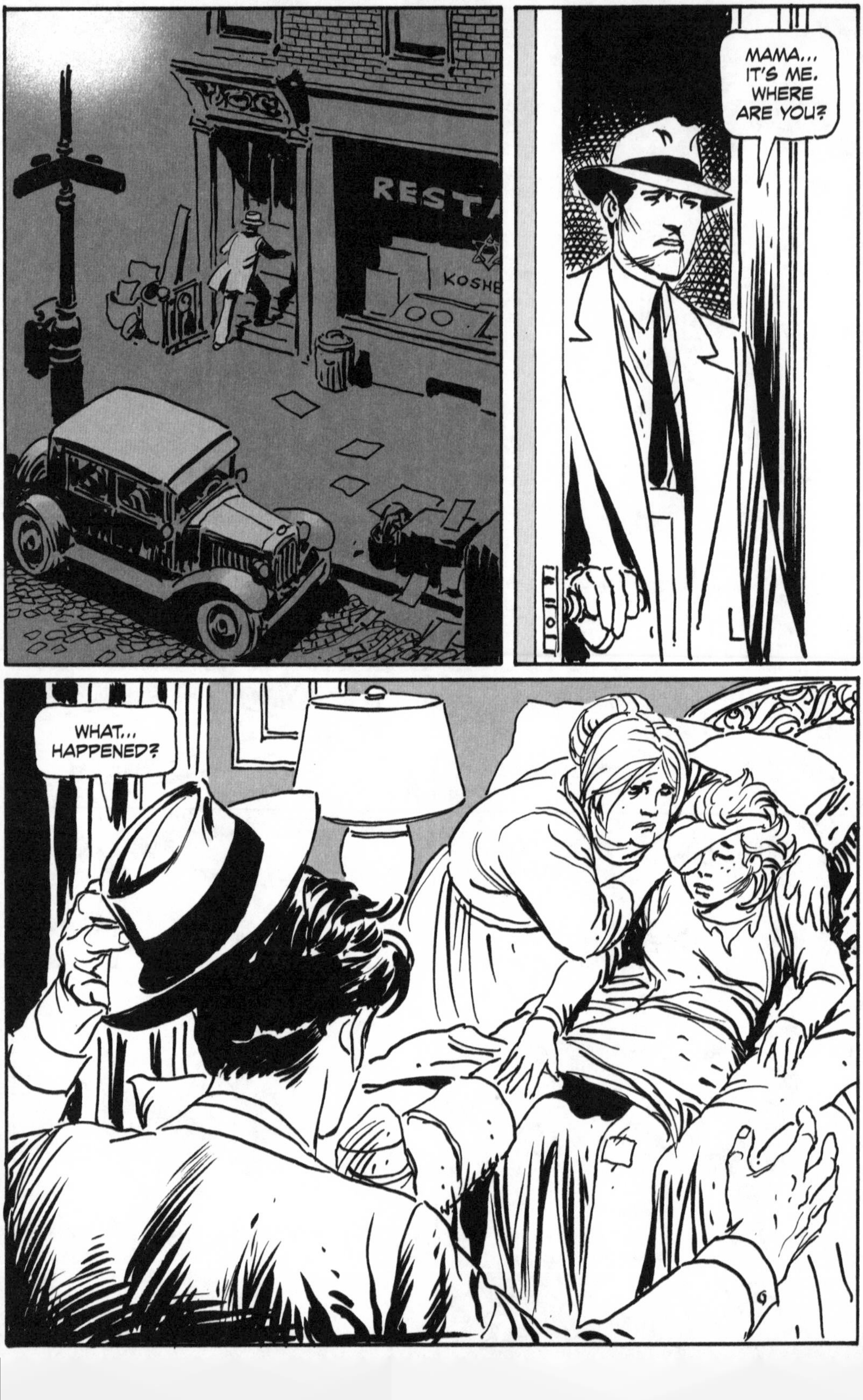
MAMA... IT'S ME. WHERE ARE YOU?
WHAT... HAPPENED?

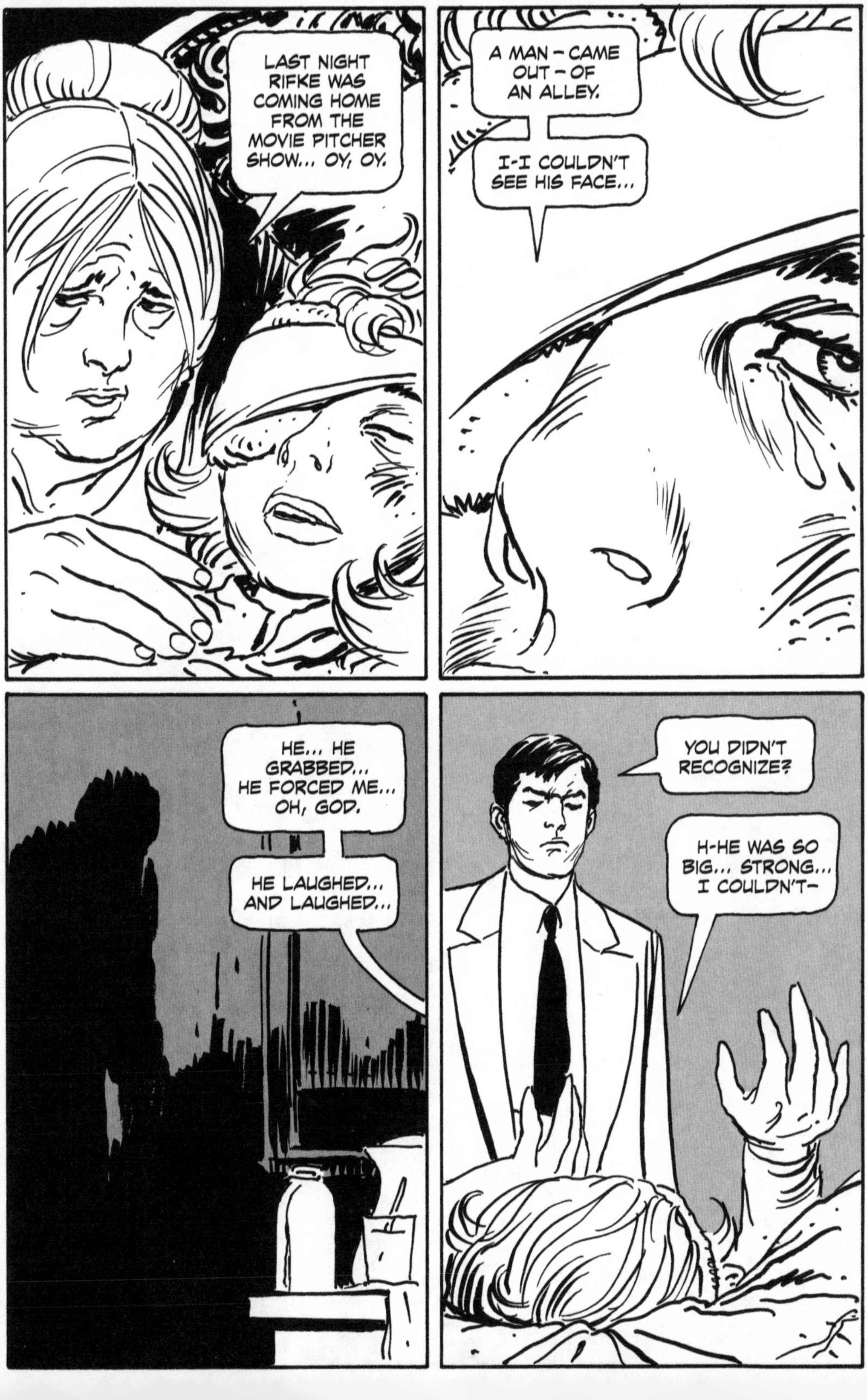
LAST NIGHT RIFKE WAS COMING HOME FROM THE MOVIE PITCHER SHOW... OY, OY.
A MAN—CAME OUT—OF AN ALLEY.
I-I COULDN'T SEE HIS FACE...
HE... HE GRABBED... HE FORCED ME... OH, GOD.
HE LAUGHED... AND LAUGHED...
YOU DIDN'T RECOGNIZE?
H-HE WAS SO BIG... STRONG... I COULDN'T-

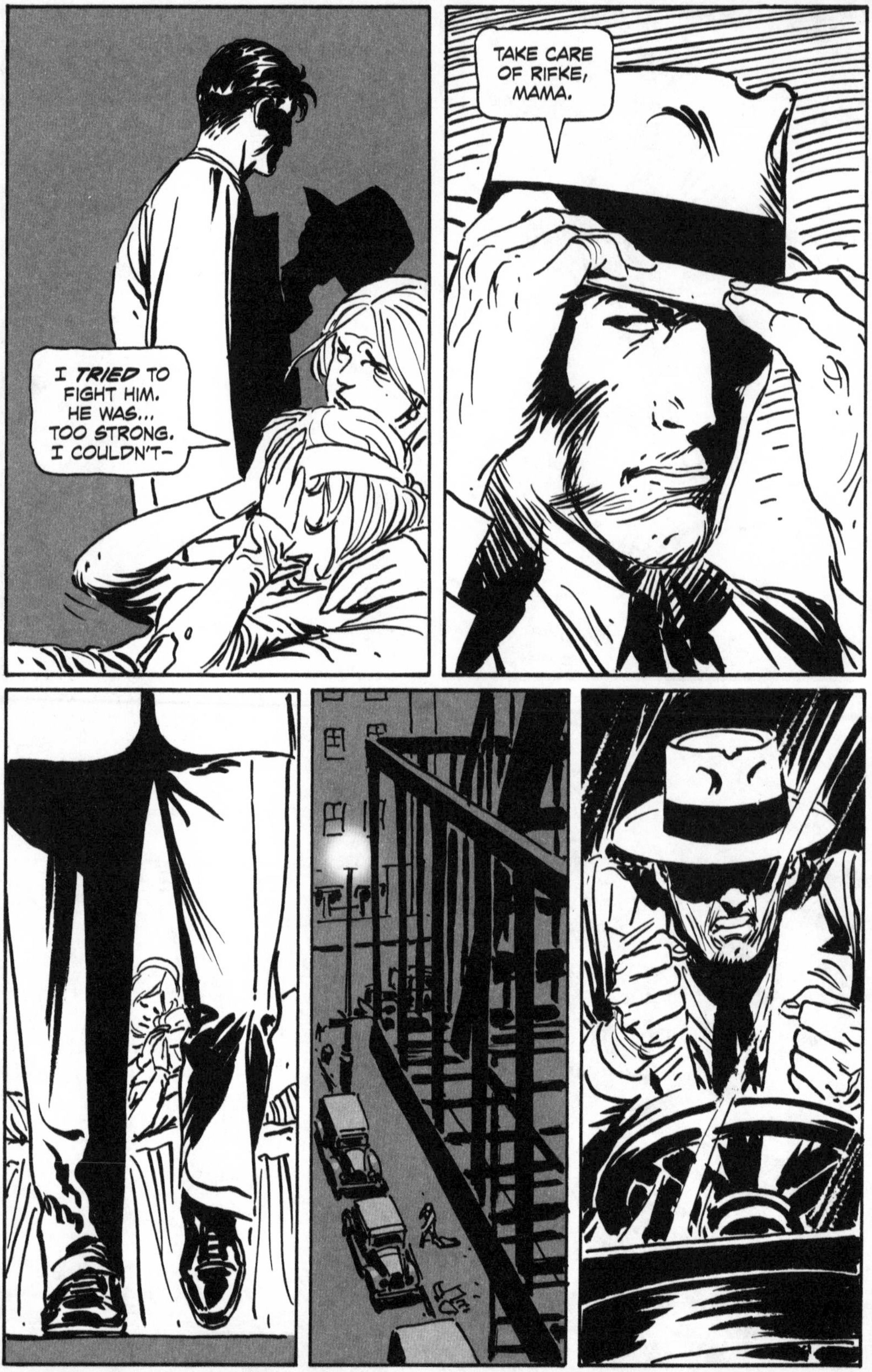
I TRIED TO FIGHT HIM. HE WAS... TOO STRONG. I COULDN'T-
TAKE CARE OF RIFKE, MAMA.

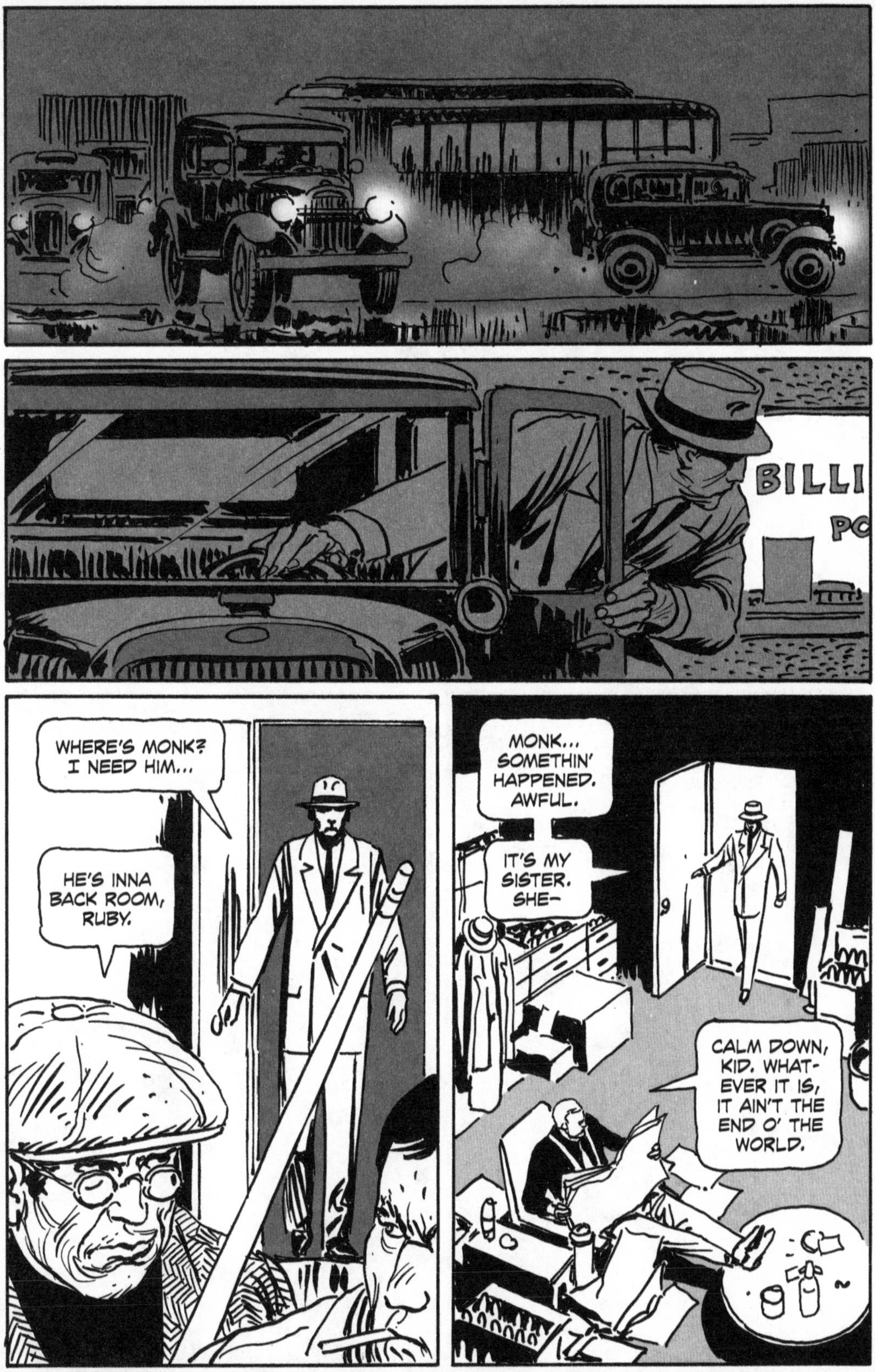
BILLI
PC
WHERE'S MONK? I NEED HIM...
HE'S INNA BACK ROOM, RUBY.
MONK... SOMETHIN' HAPPENED. AWFUL.
IT'S MY SISTER. SHE–
CALM DOWN, KID. WHAT-EVER IT IS, IT AIN'T THE END O' THE WORLD.

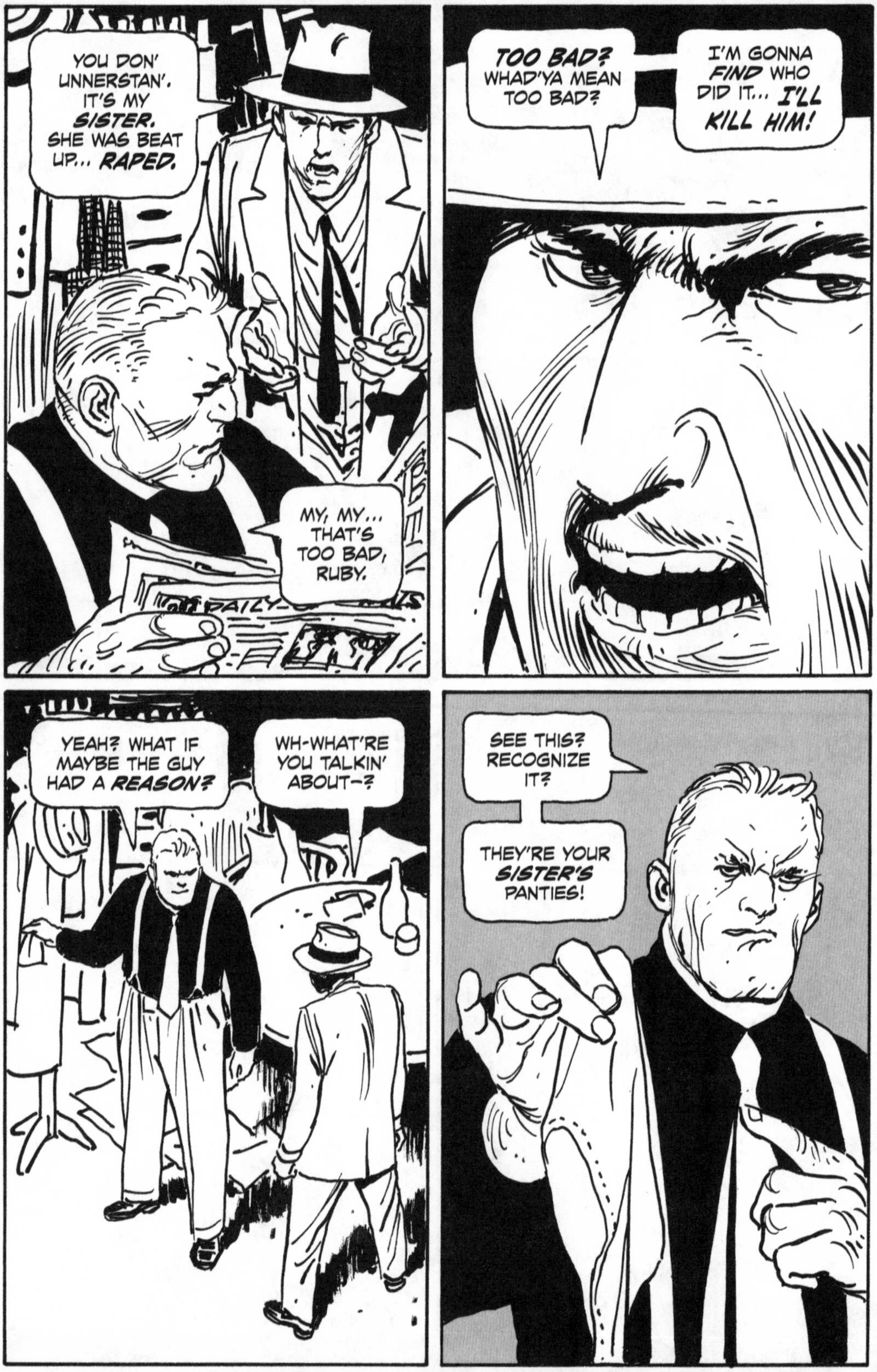
YOU DON' UNNERSTAN'. IT'S MY SISTER. SHE WAS BEAT UP... RAPED.
MY, MY... THAT'S TOO BAD, RUBY.
DAILY
TOO BAD? WHAD'YA MEAN TOO BAD?
I'M GONNA FIND WHO DID IT... I'LL KILL HIM!
YEAH? WHAT IF MAYBE THE GUY HAD A REASON?
WH-WHAT'RE YOU TALKIN' ABOUT--?
SEE THIS? RECOGNIZE IT?
THEY'RE YOUR SISTER'S PANTIES!

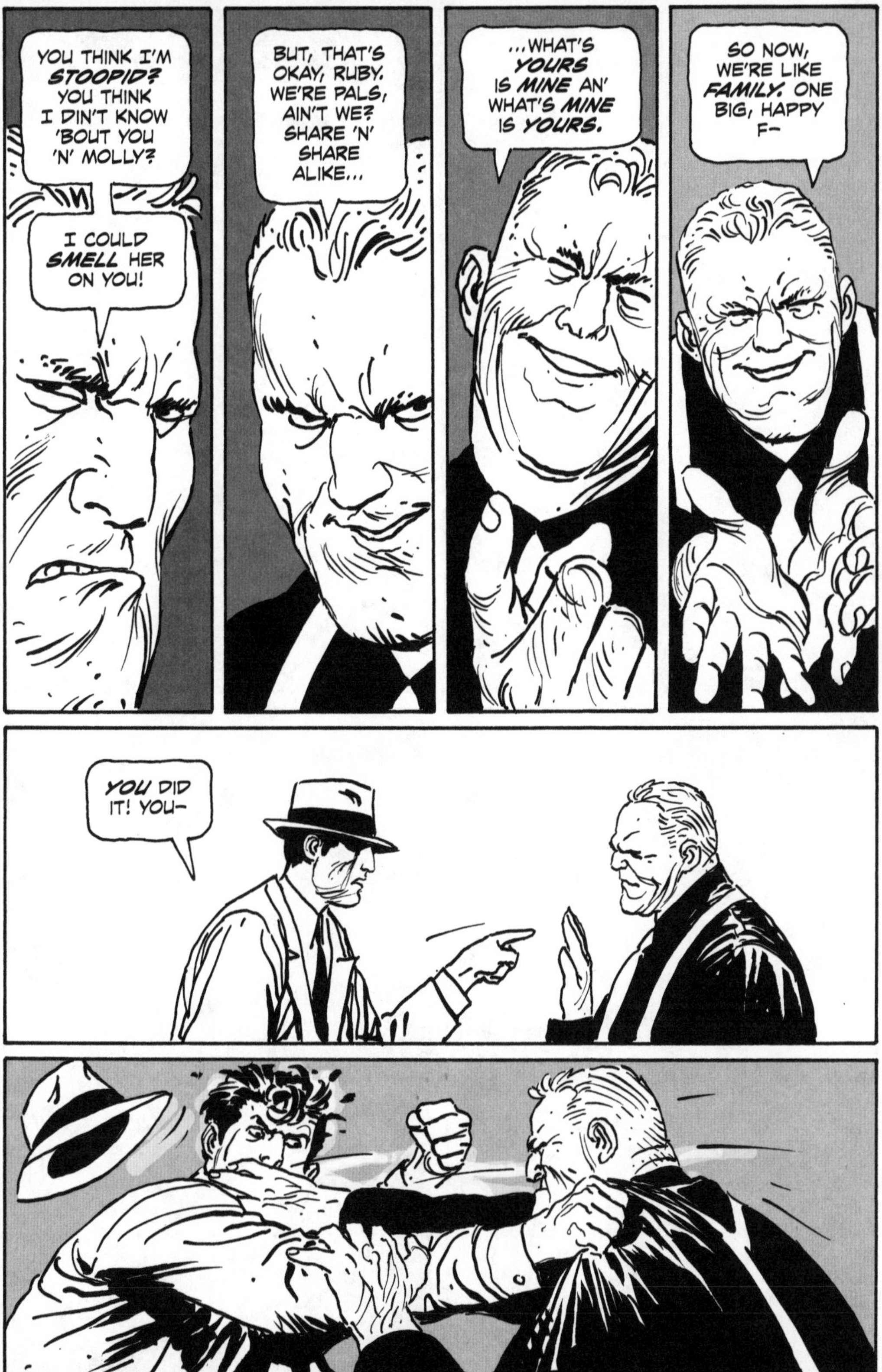
YOU THINK I'M STOOPID? YOU THINK I DIN'T KNOW 'BOUT YOU 'N' MOLLY?
I COULD SMELL HER ON YOU!
BUT, THAT'S OKAY, RUBY. WE'RE PALS, AIN'T WE? SHARE 'N' SHARE ALIKE...
...WHAT'S YOURS IS MINE AN' WHAT'S MINE IS YOURS.
SO NOW, WE'RE LIKE FAMILY. ONE BIG, HAPPY F–
YOU DID IT! YOU–

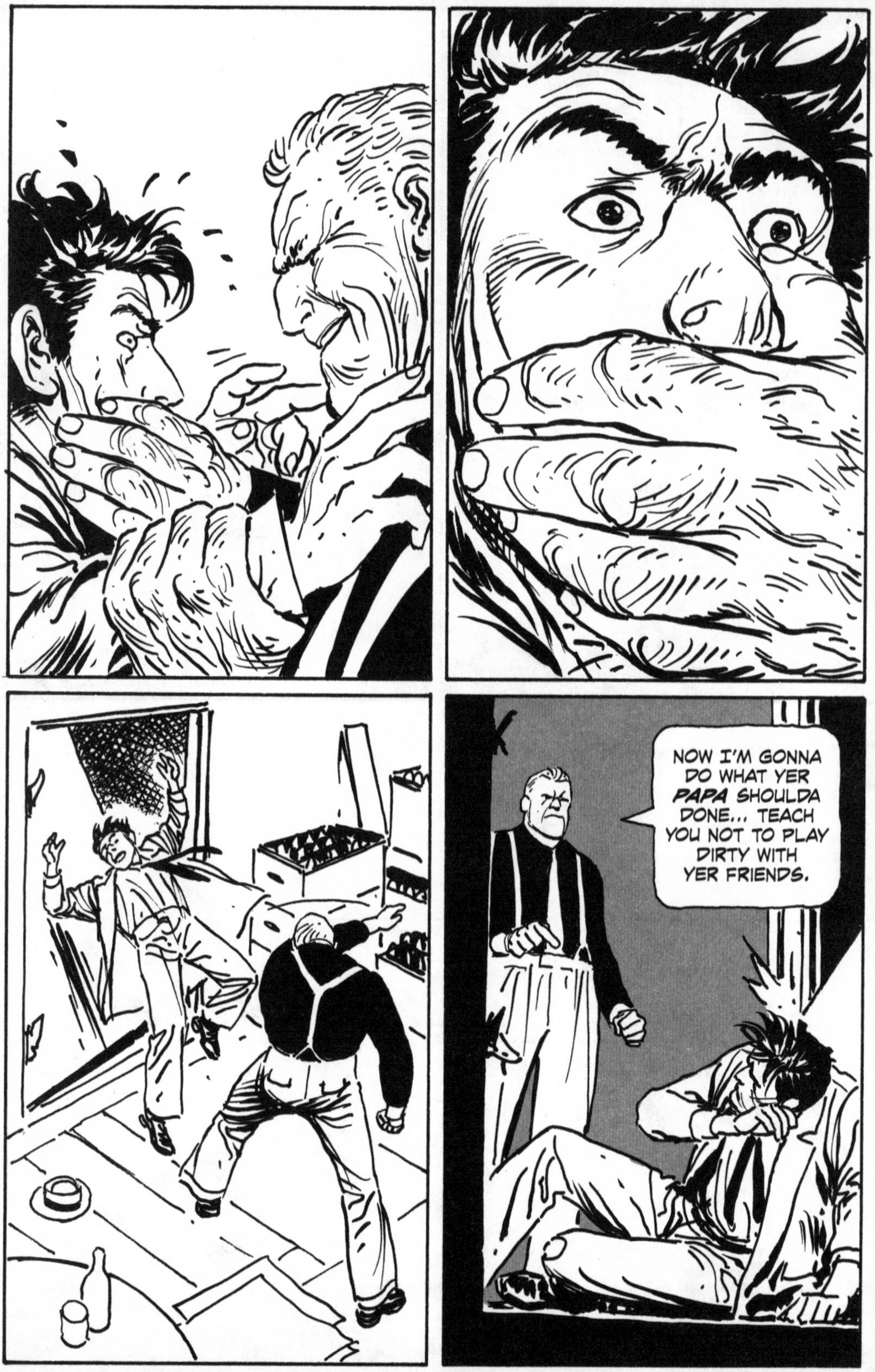
NOW I'M GONNA DO WHAT YER *PAPA* SHOULDA DONE... TEACH YOU NOT TO PLAY DIRTY WITH YER FRIENDS.

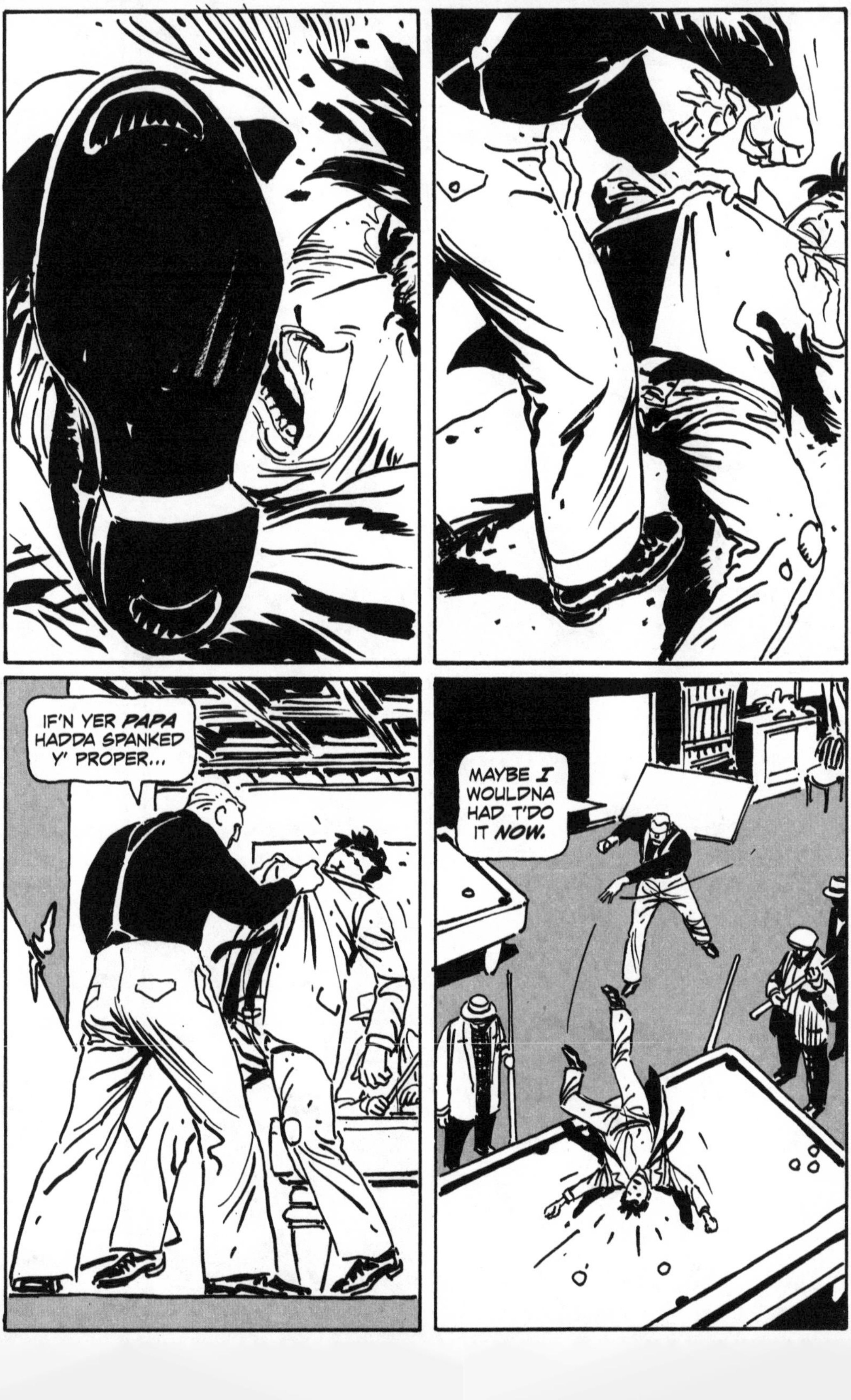
IF'N YER *PAPA* HADDA SPANKED Y' PROPER...
MAYBE *I* WOULDNA HAD T'DO IT *NOW.*

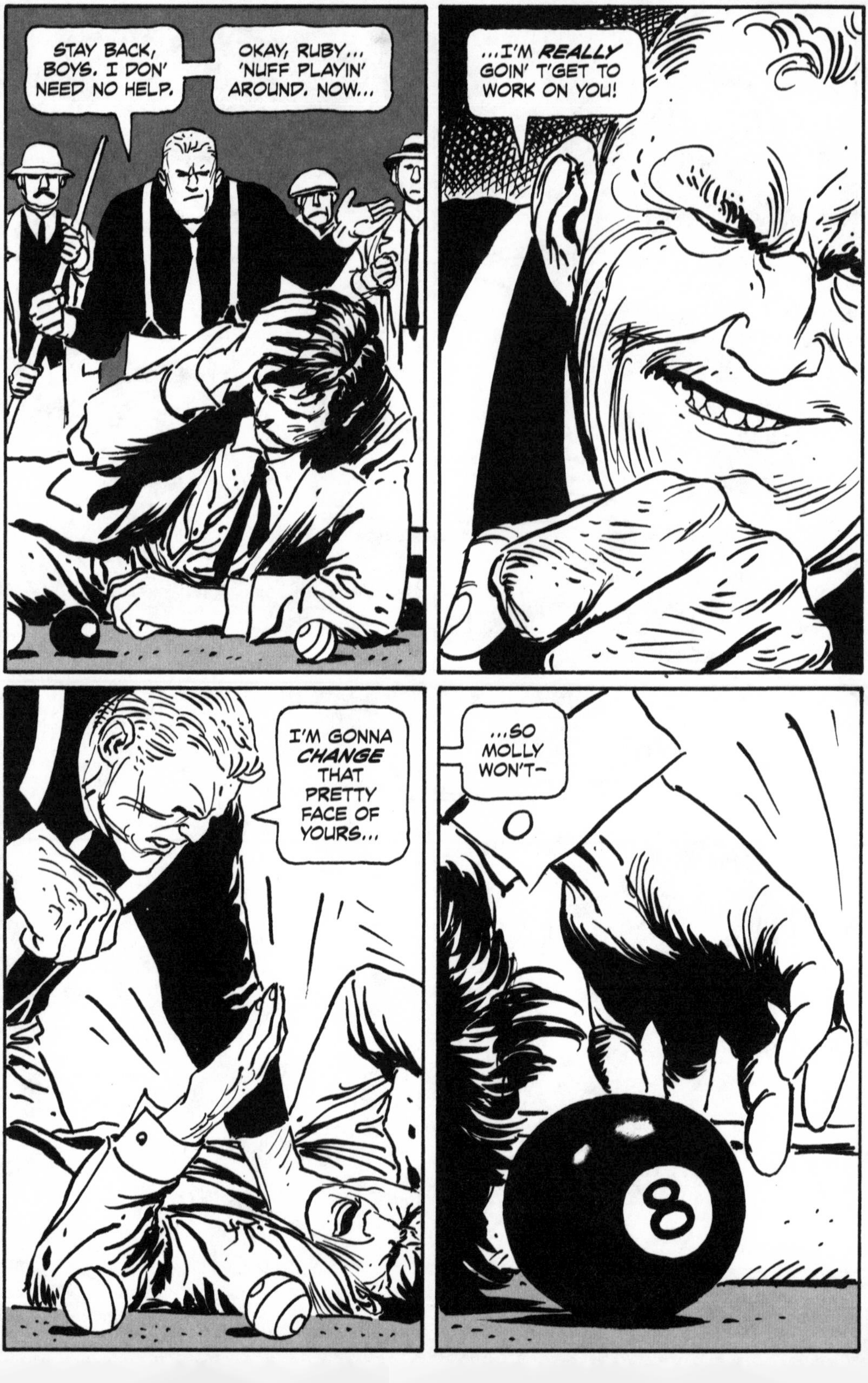
STAY BACK, BOYS. I DON' NEED NO HELP.
OKAY, RUBY... 'NUFF PLAYIN' AROUND. NOW...
...I'M REALLY GOIN' T'GET TO WORK ON YOU!
I'M GONNA CHANGE THAT PRETTY FACE OF YOURS...
...SO MOLLY WON'T-
8

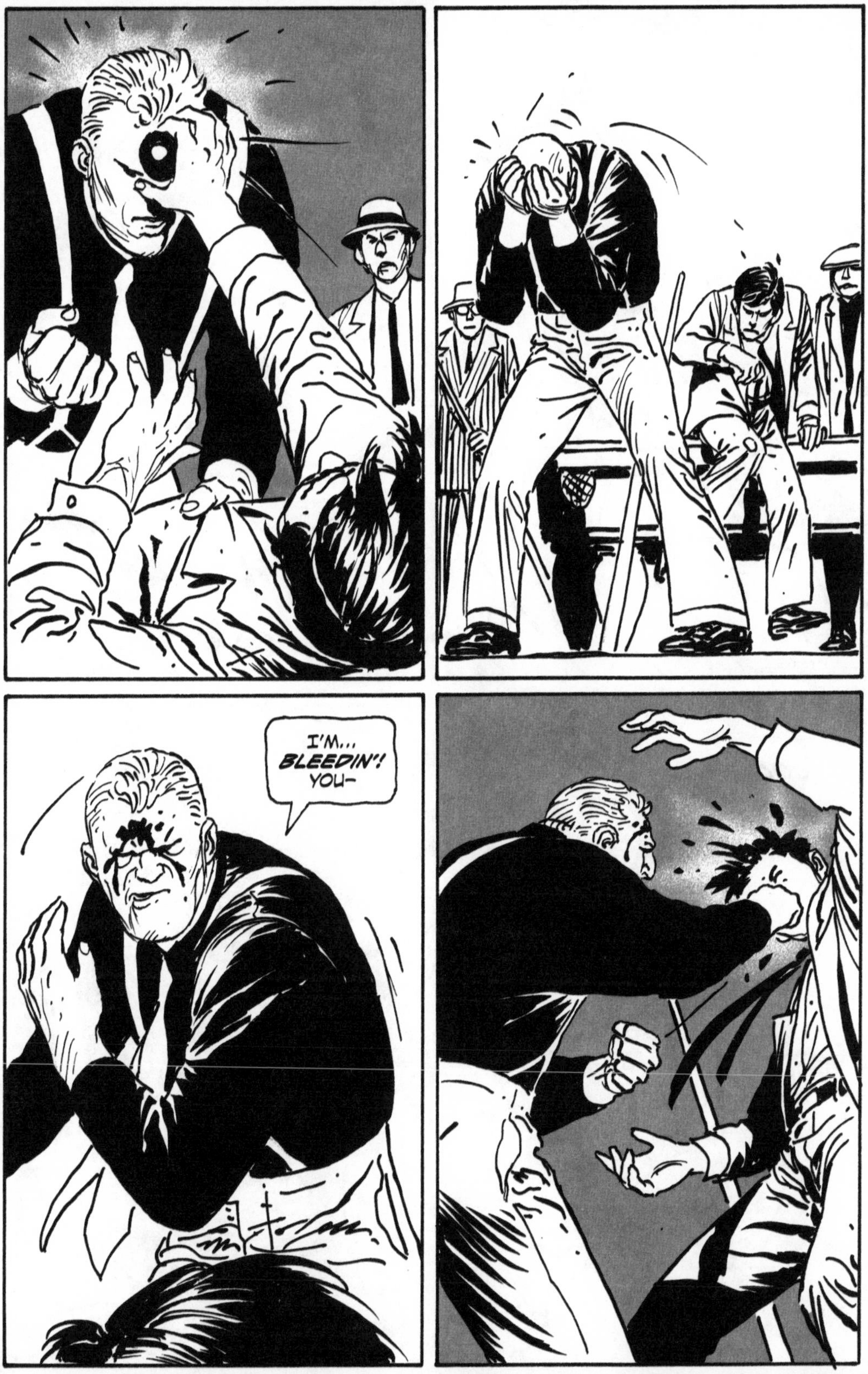
I'M... BLEEDIN'! YOU-

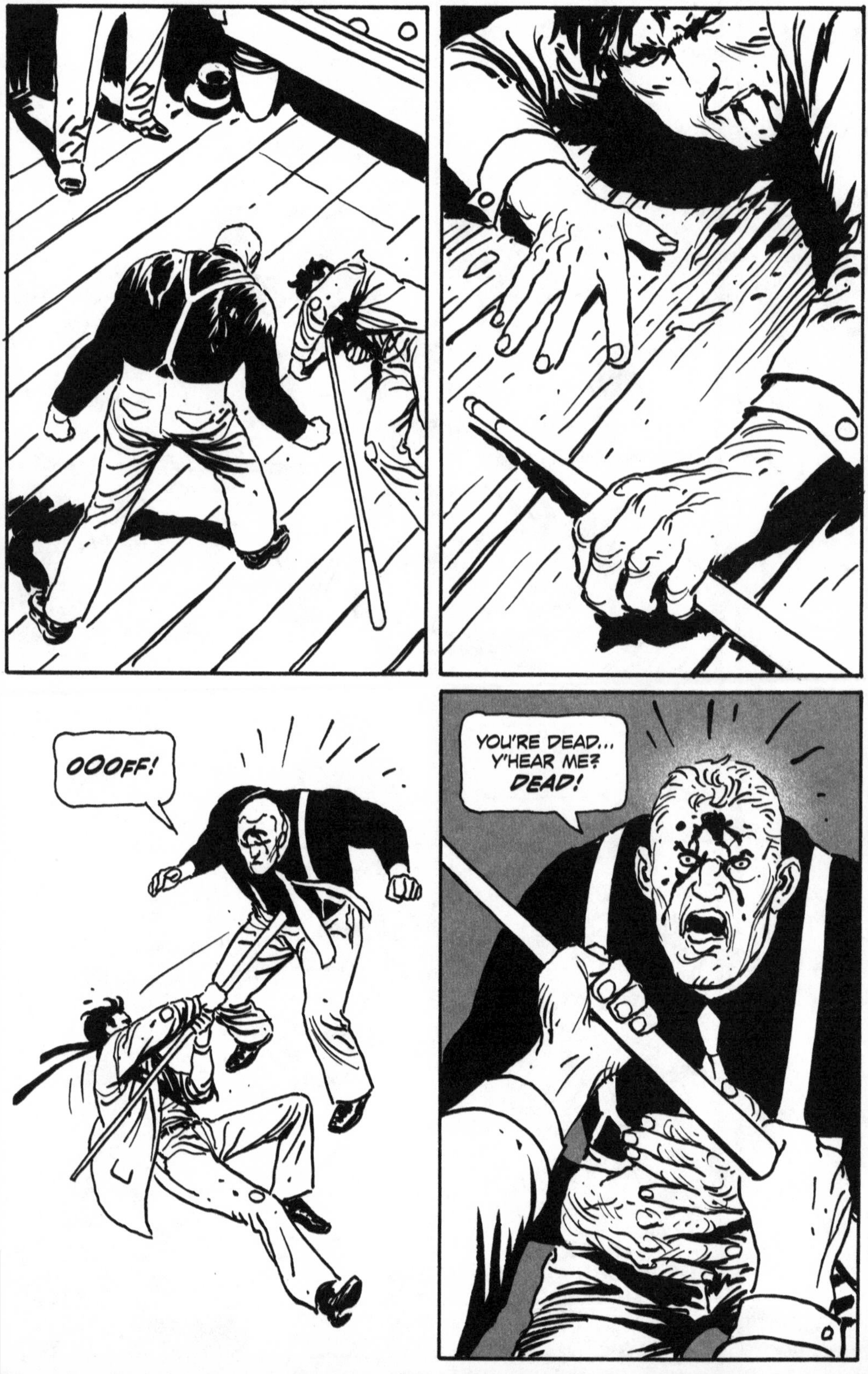
OOOFF!
YOU'RE DEAD... Y'HEAR ME? DEAD!

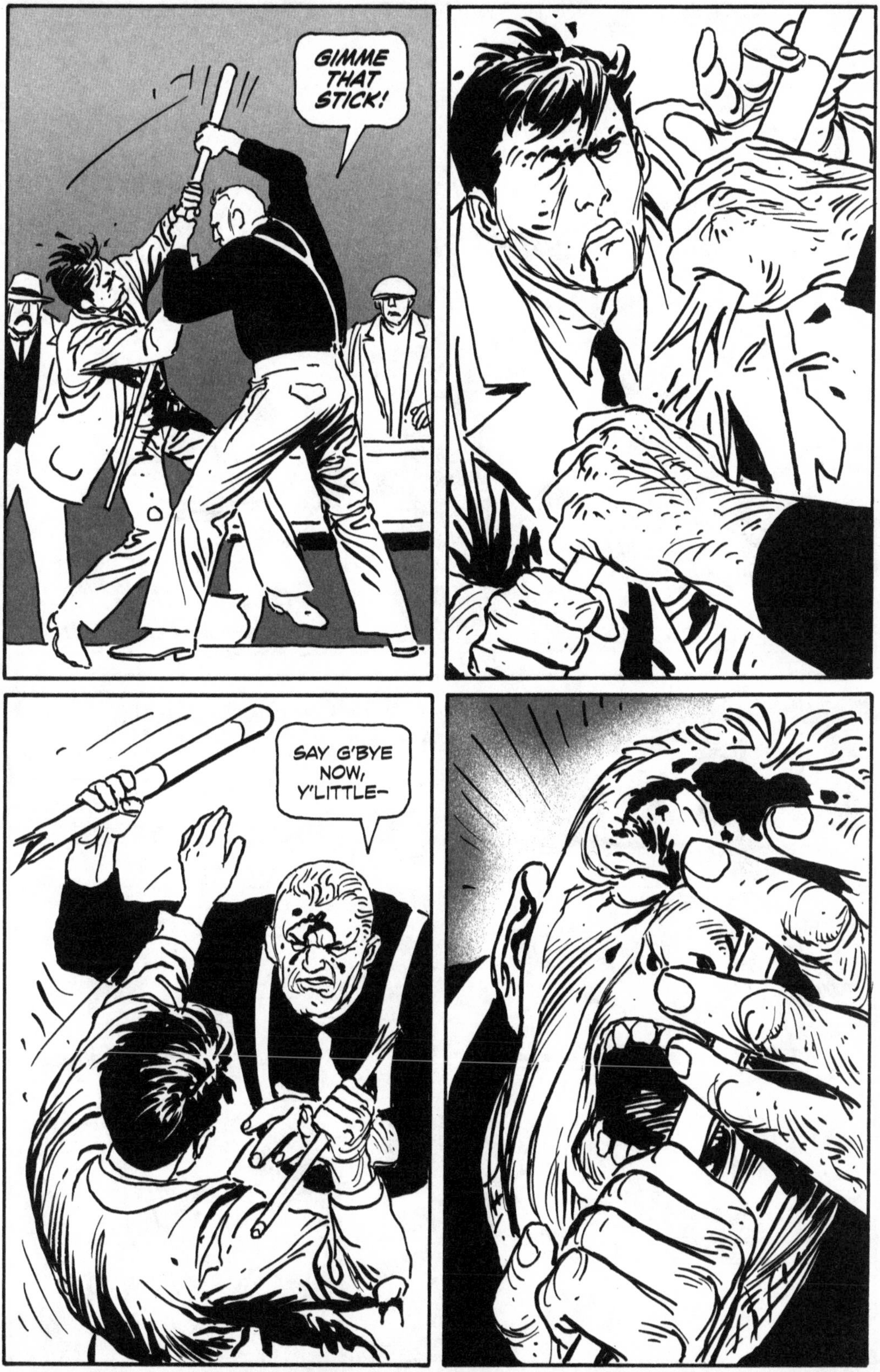
GIMME THAT STICK!
SAY G'BYE NOW, Y'LITTLE-

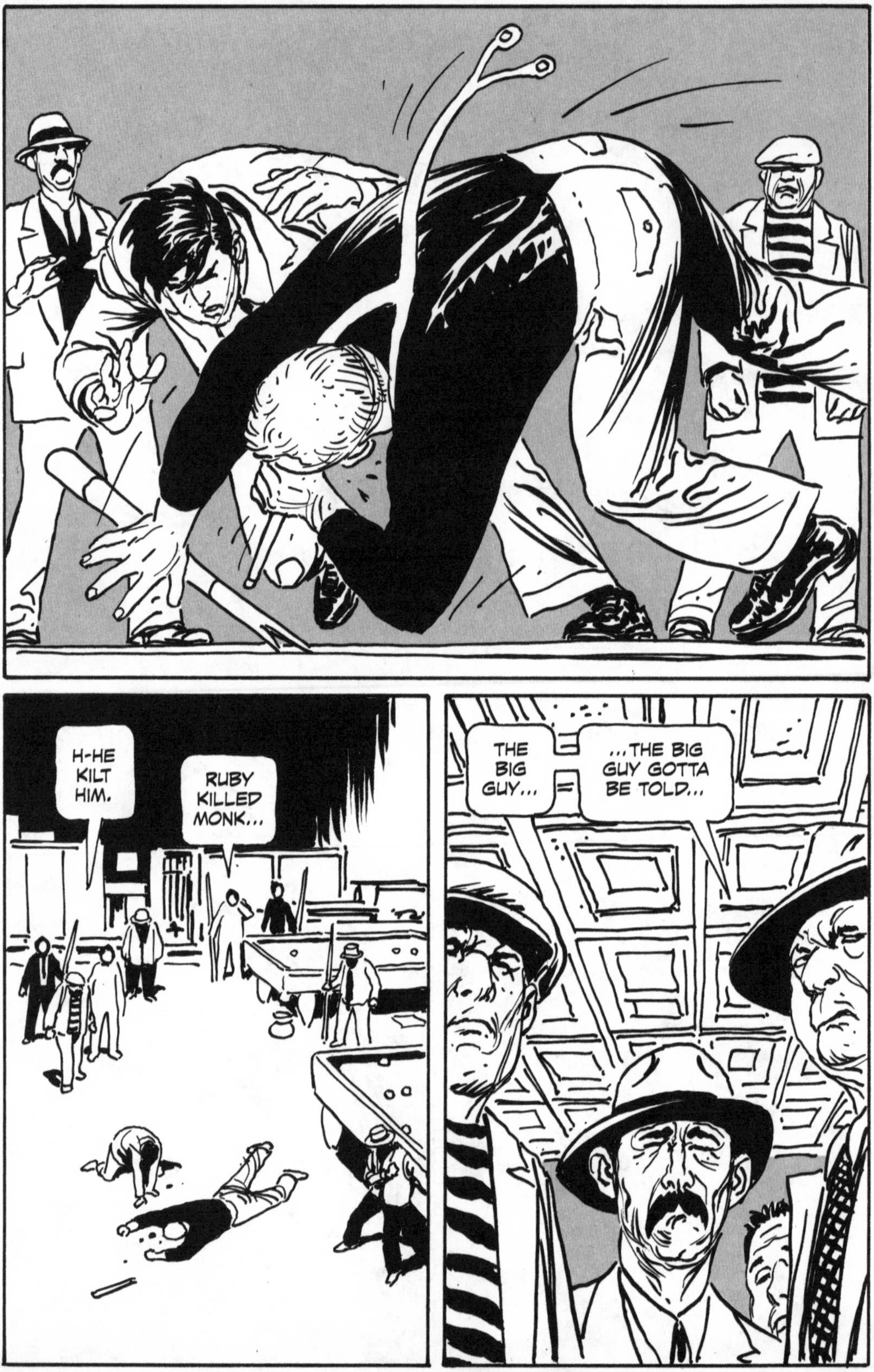
H-HE KILT HIM.
RUBY KILLED MONK...
THE BIG GUY...
...THE BIG GUY GOTTA BE TOLD...

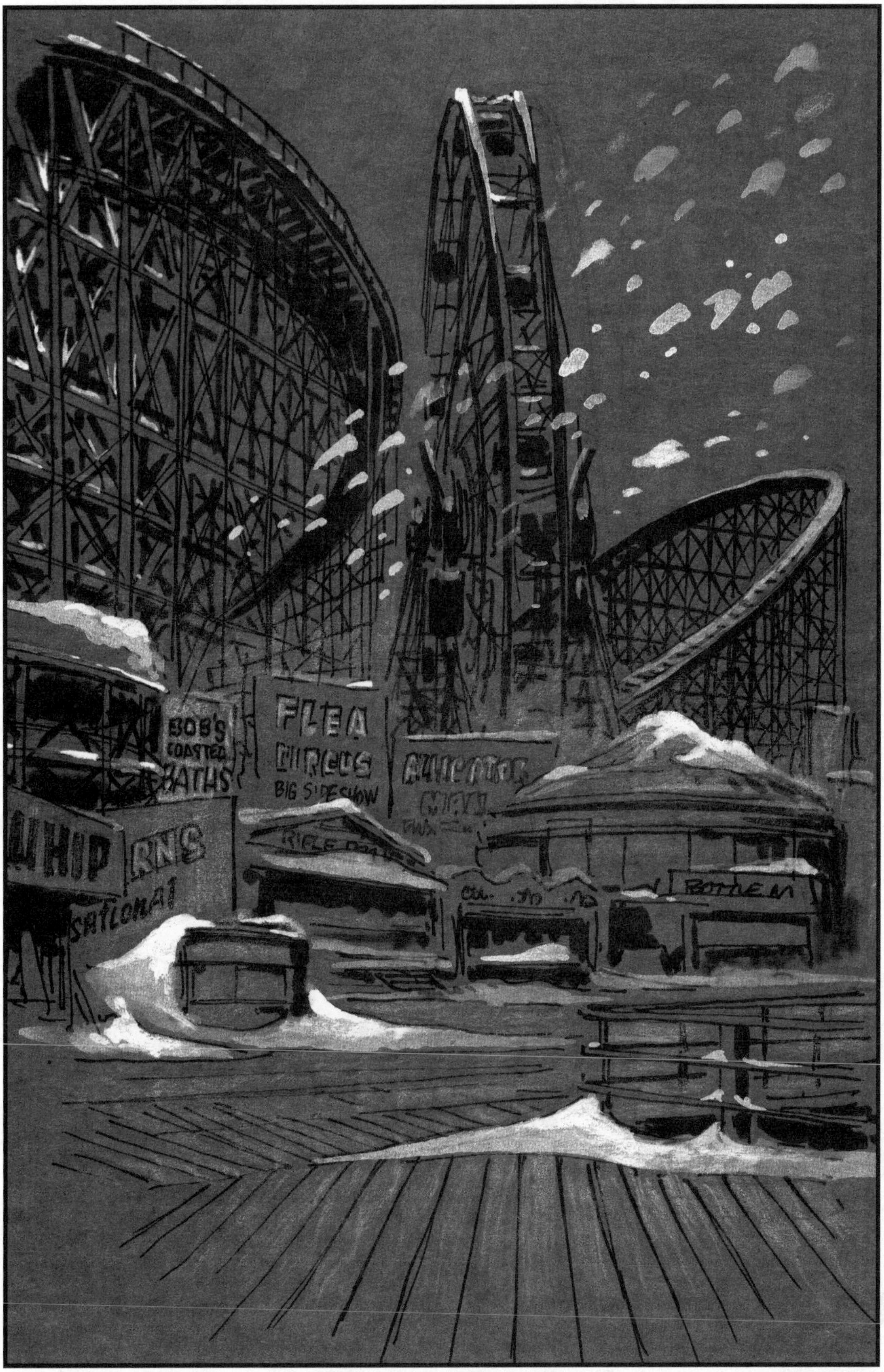
BOB'S
BATHS
FLEA
BIG SIDESHOW
WHIP

Coney in Winter

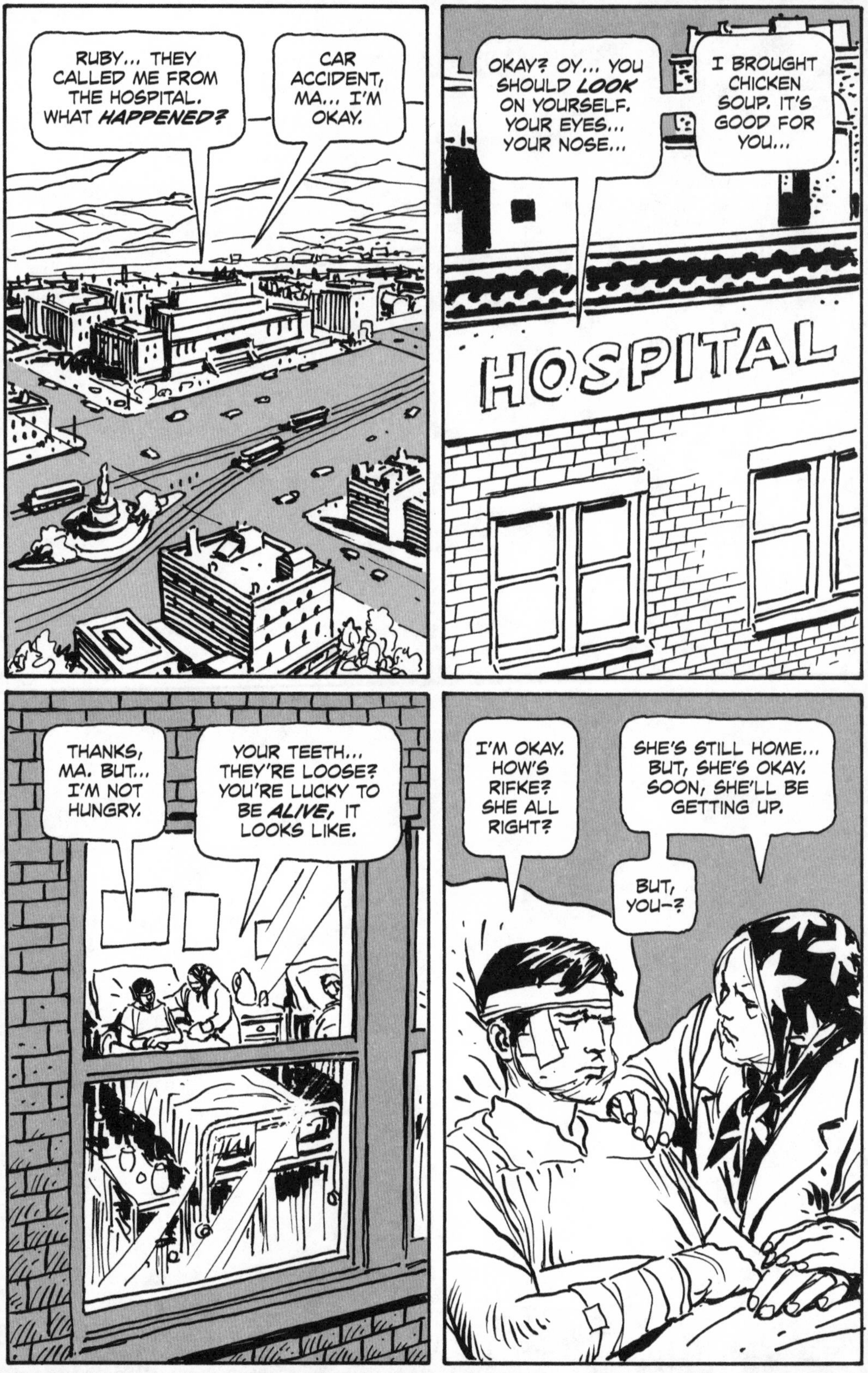
RUBY... THEY CALLED ME FROM THE HOSPITAL. WHAT HAPPENED?
CAR ACCIDENT, MA... I'M OKAY.
OKAY? OY... YOU SHOULD LOOK ON YOURSELF. YOUR EYES... YOUR NOSE...
I BROUGHT CHICKEN SOUP. IT'S GOOD FOR YOU...
HOSPITAL
THANKS, MA. BUT... I'M NOT HUNGRY.
YOUR TEETH... THEY'RE LOOSE? YOU'RE LUCKY TO BE ALIVE, IT LOOKS LIKE.
I'M OKAY. HOW'S RIFKE? SHE ALL RIGHT?
SHE'S STILL HOME... BUT, SHE'S OKAY. SOON, SHE'LL BE GETTING UP.
BUT, YOU--?

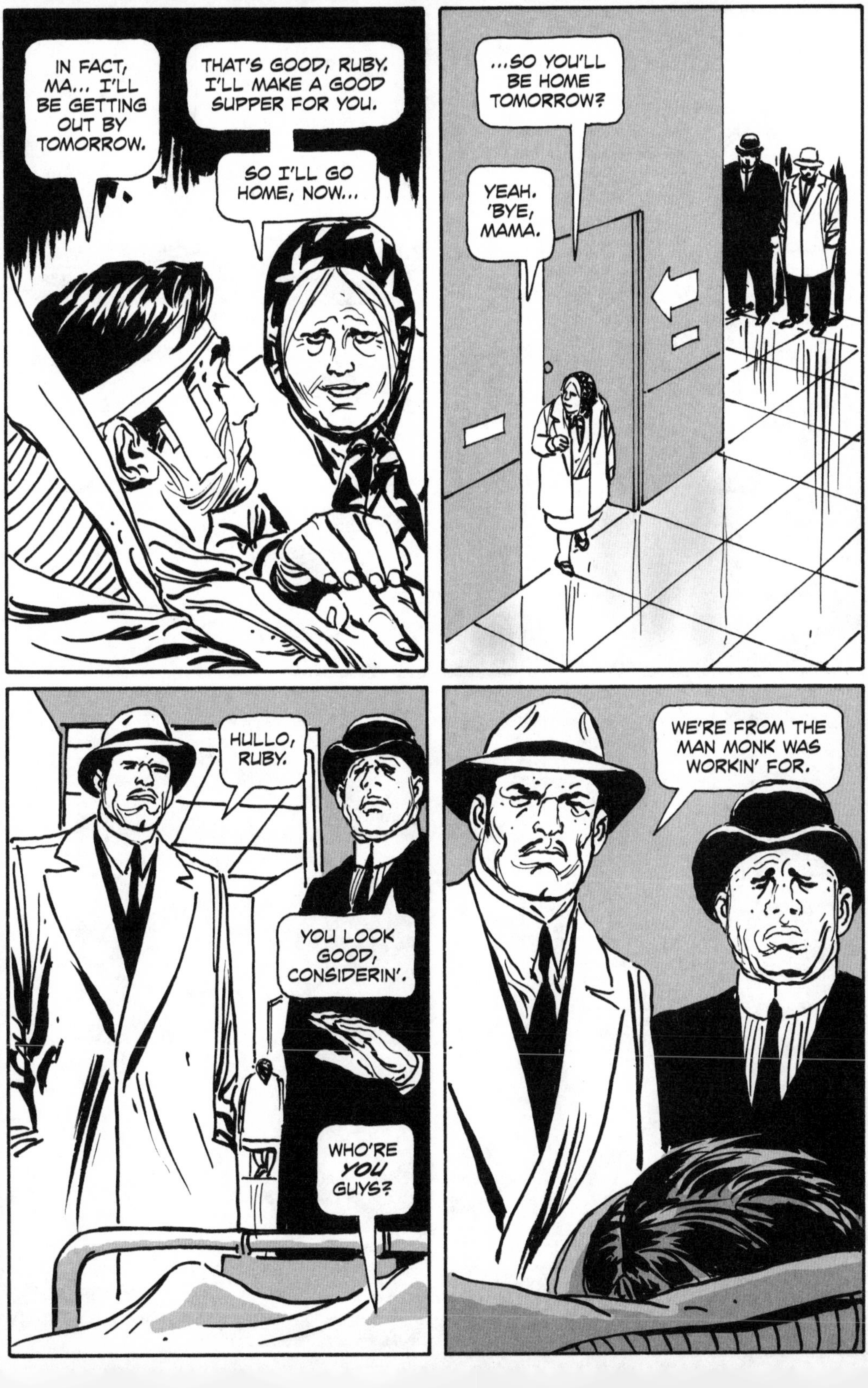
IN FACT, MA... I'LL BE GETTING OUT BY TOMORROW.
THAT'S GOOD, RUBY. I'LL MAKE A GOOD SUPPER FOR YOU.
SO I'LL GO HOME, NOW...
...SO YOU'LL BE HOME TOMORROW?
YEAH. 'BYE, MAMA.
HULLO, RUBY.
YOU LOOK GOOD, CONSIDERIN'.
WHO'RE *YOU* GUYS?
WE'RE FROM THE MAN MONK WAS WORKIN' FOR.

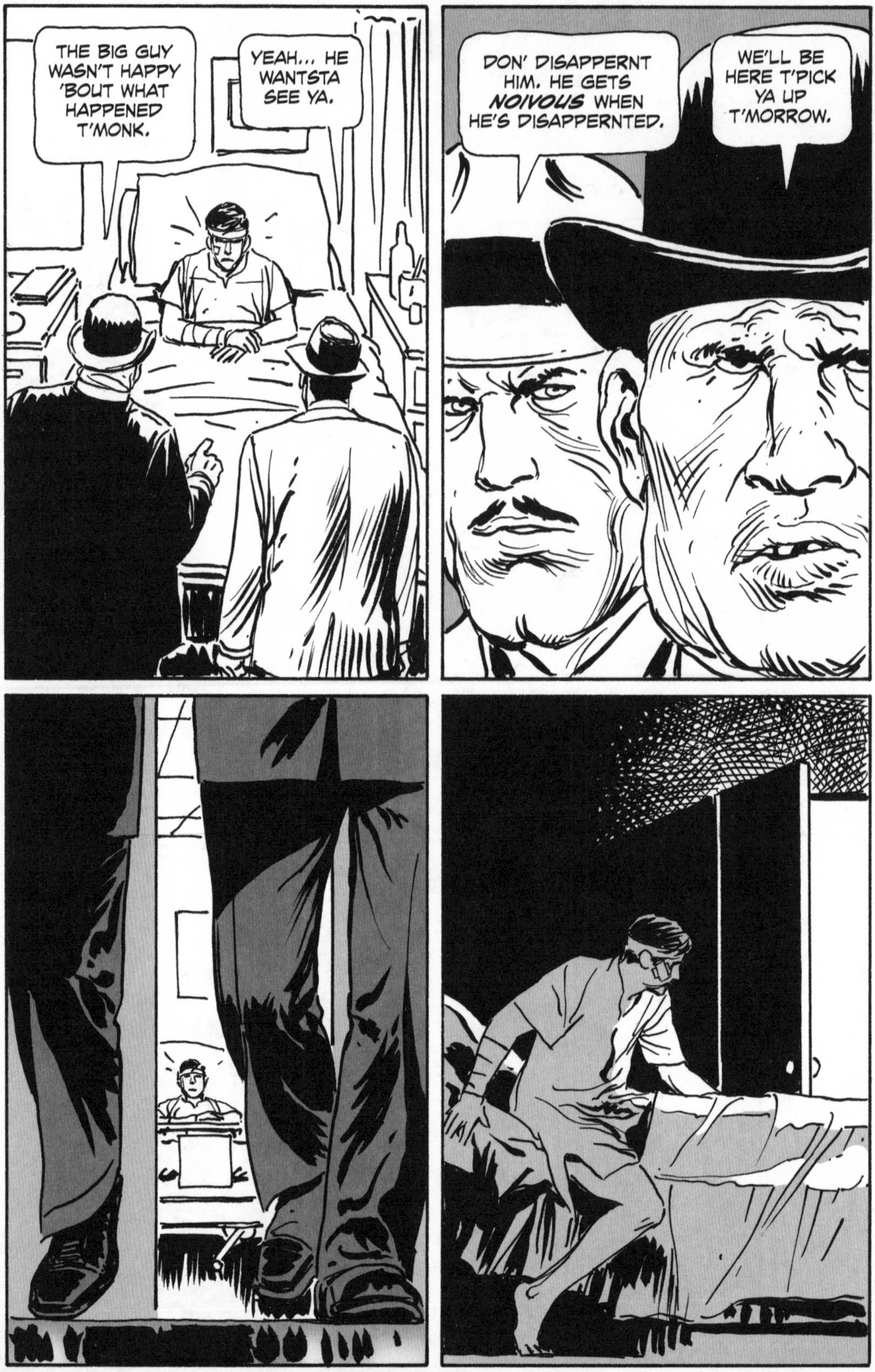
THE BIG GUY WASN'T HAPPY 'BOUT WHAT HAPPENED T'MONK.
YEAH... HE WANTSTA SEE YA.
DON' DISAPPERNT HIM. HE GETS *NOIVOUS* WHEN HE'S DISAPPERNTED.
WE'LL BE HERE T'PICK YA UP T'MORROW.

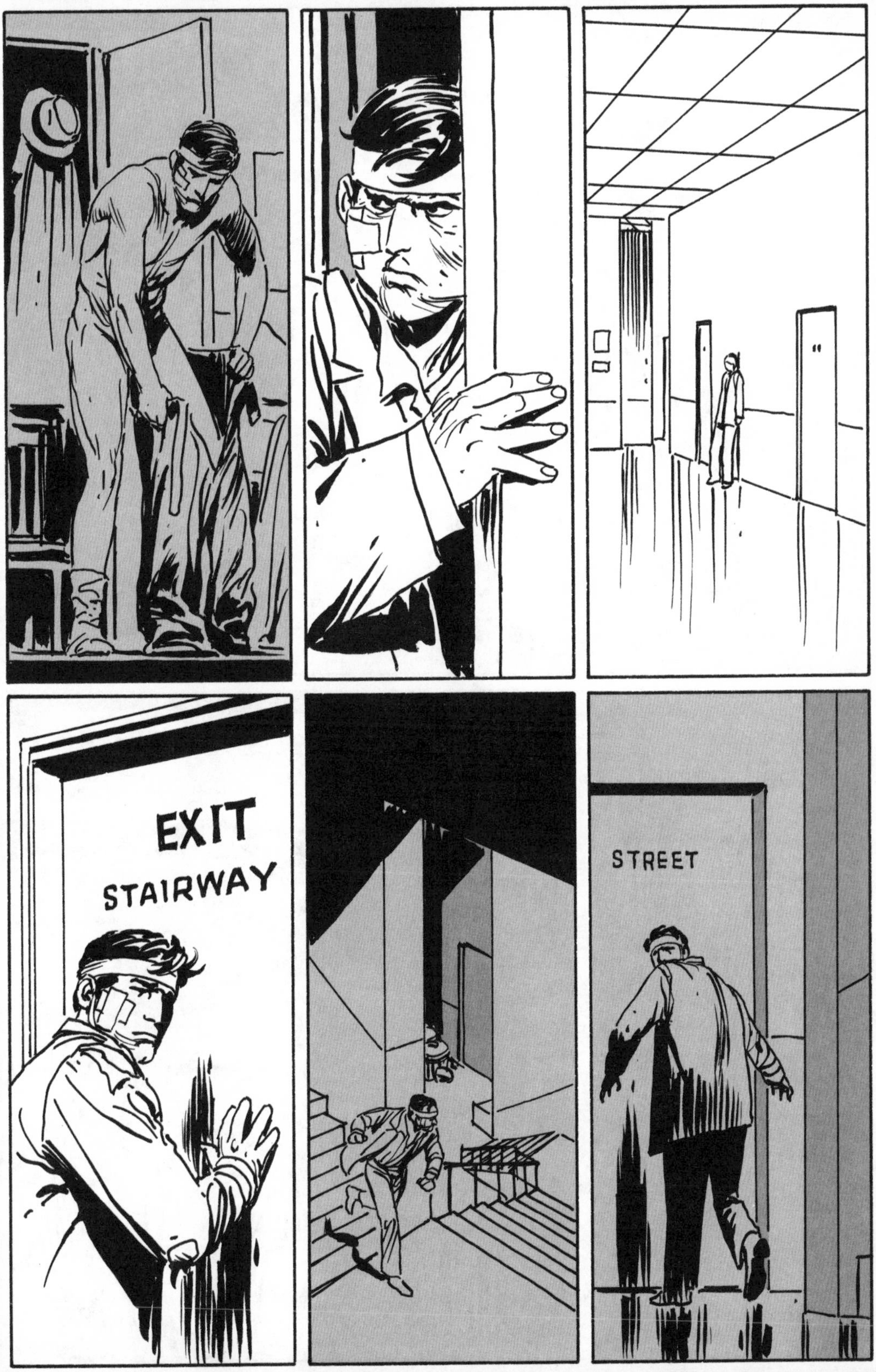
EXIT
STAIRWAY
STREET

NO ENTRY
NO ENTRY
YOU GOT BETTER REAL QUICK, DI'N'CHA?
GUESS YOU WAS JUST IN A RUSH T'SEE THE BIG GUY, RIGHT?
NO ENTRY
WE TOL' YOU THE BIG GUY DON'T LIKE T'BE DISAPPERNTED.
WALK. OUR CAR'S AT THE ENDA THE BLOCK.

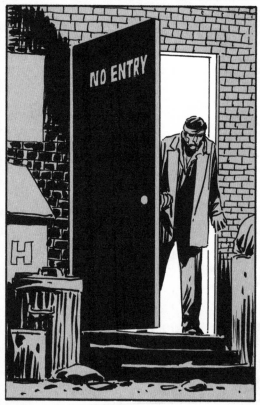

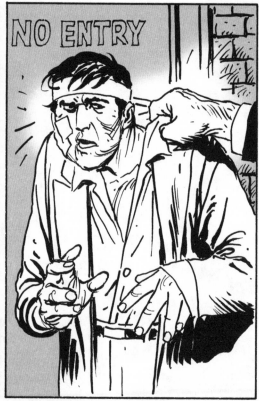

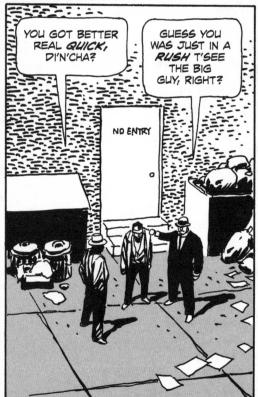

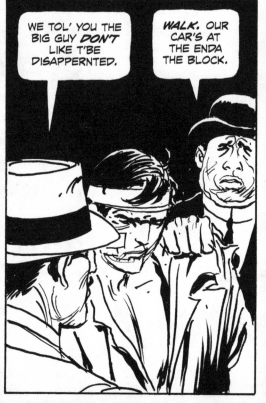

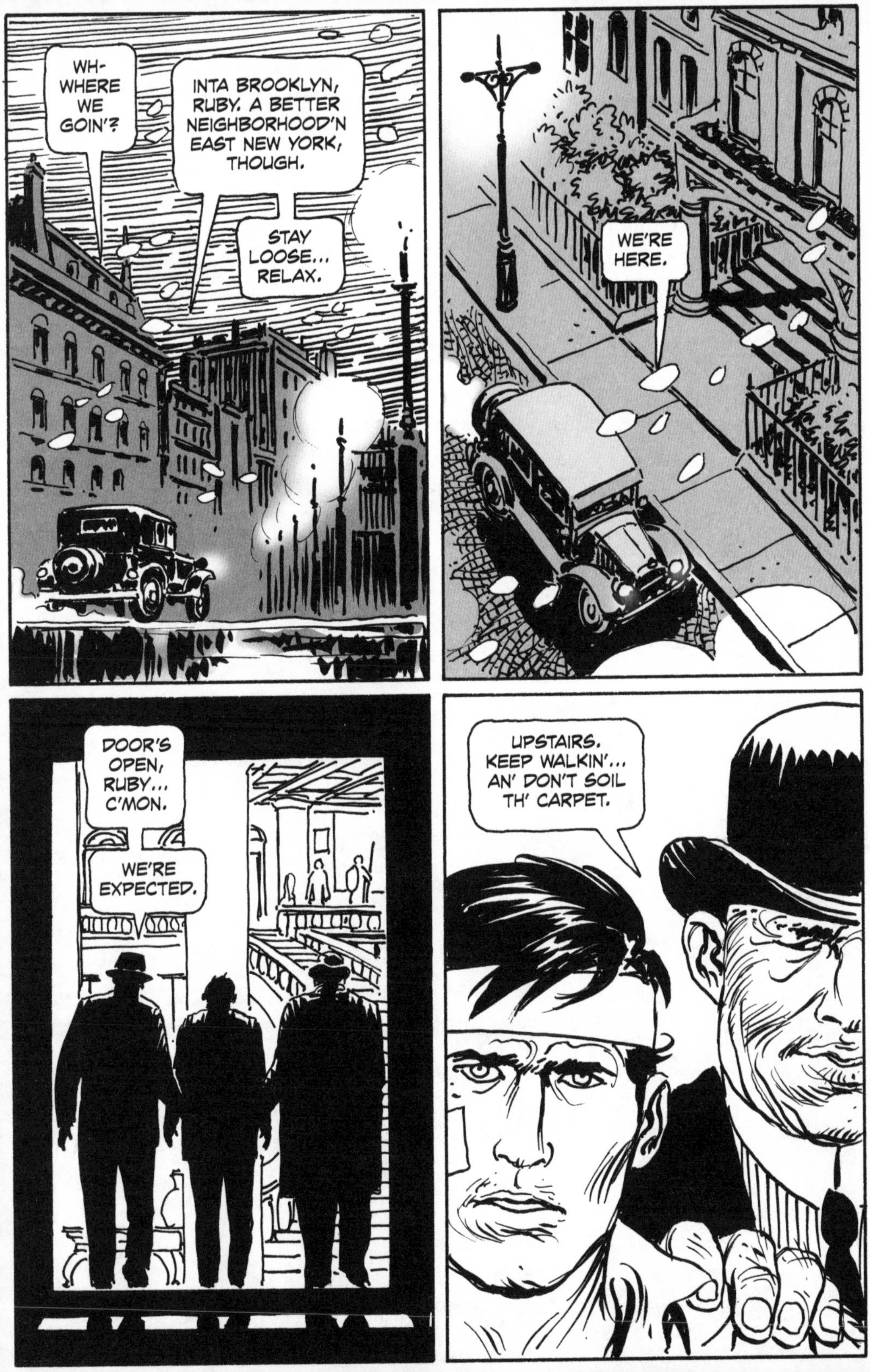
WH-
WHERE
WE
GOIN'?
INTA BROOKLYN,
RUBY. A BETTER
NEIGHBORHOOD'N
EAST NEW YORK,
THOUGH.
STAY
LOOSE...
RELAX.
WE'RE
HERE.
DOOR'S
OPEN,
RUBY...
C'MON.
WE'RE
EXPECTED.
UPSTAIRS.
KEEP WALKIN'...
AN' DON'T SOIL
TH' CARPET.

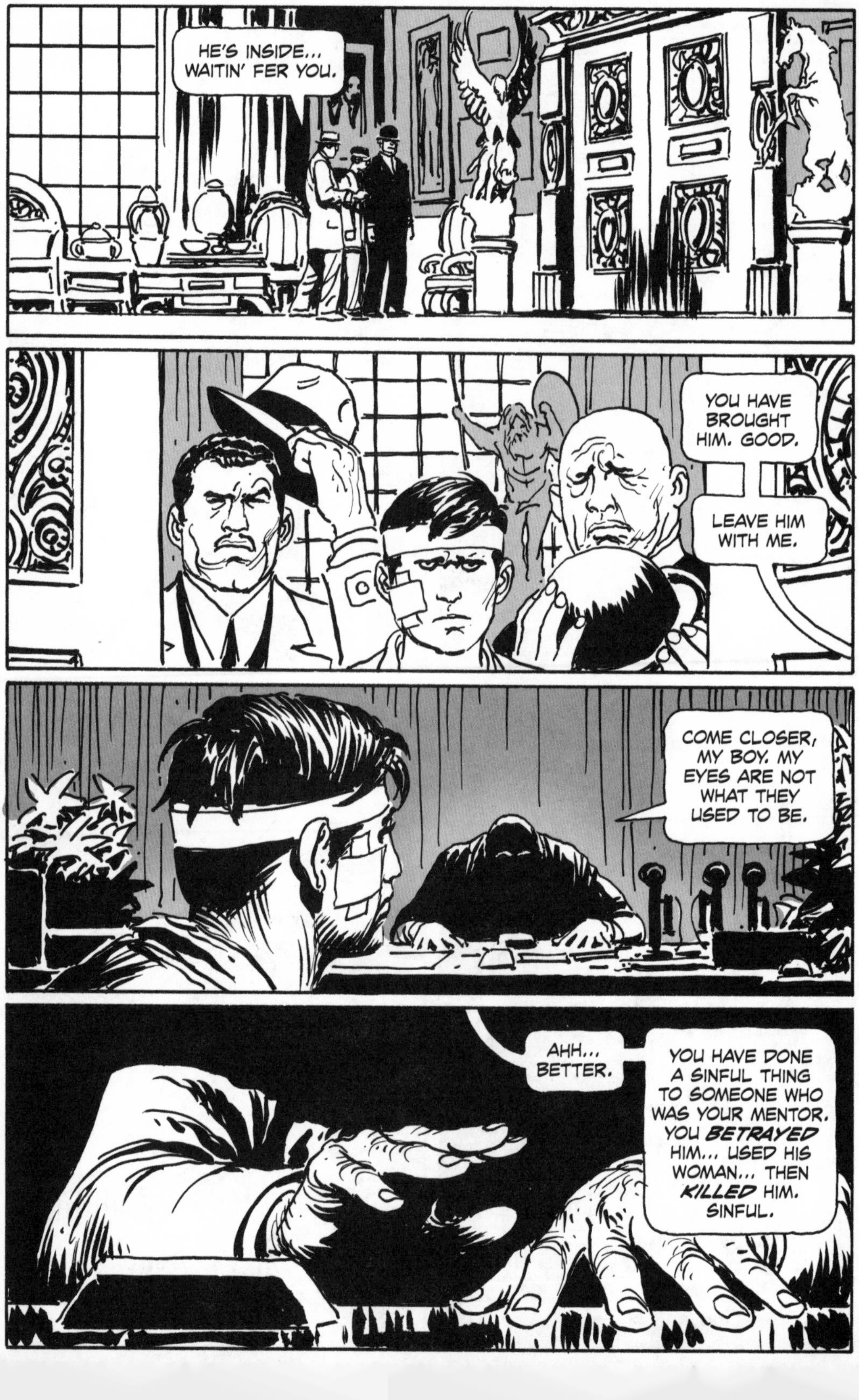
HE'S INSIDE... WAITIN' FER YOU.
YOU HAVE BROUGHT HIM. GOOD.
LEAVE HIM WITH ME.
COME CLOSER, MY BOY. MY EYES ARE NOT WHAT THEY USED TO BE.
AHH... BETTER.
YOU HAVE DONE A SINFUL THING TO SOMEONE WHO WAS YOUR MENTOR. YOU BETRAYED HIM... USED HIS WOMAN... THEN KILLED HIM. SINFUL.

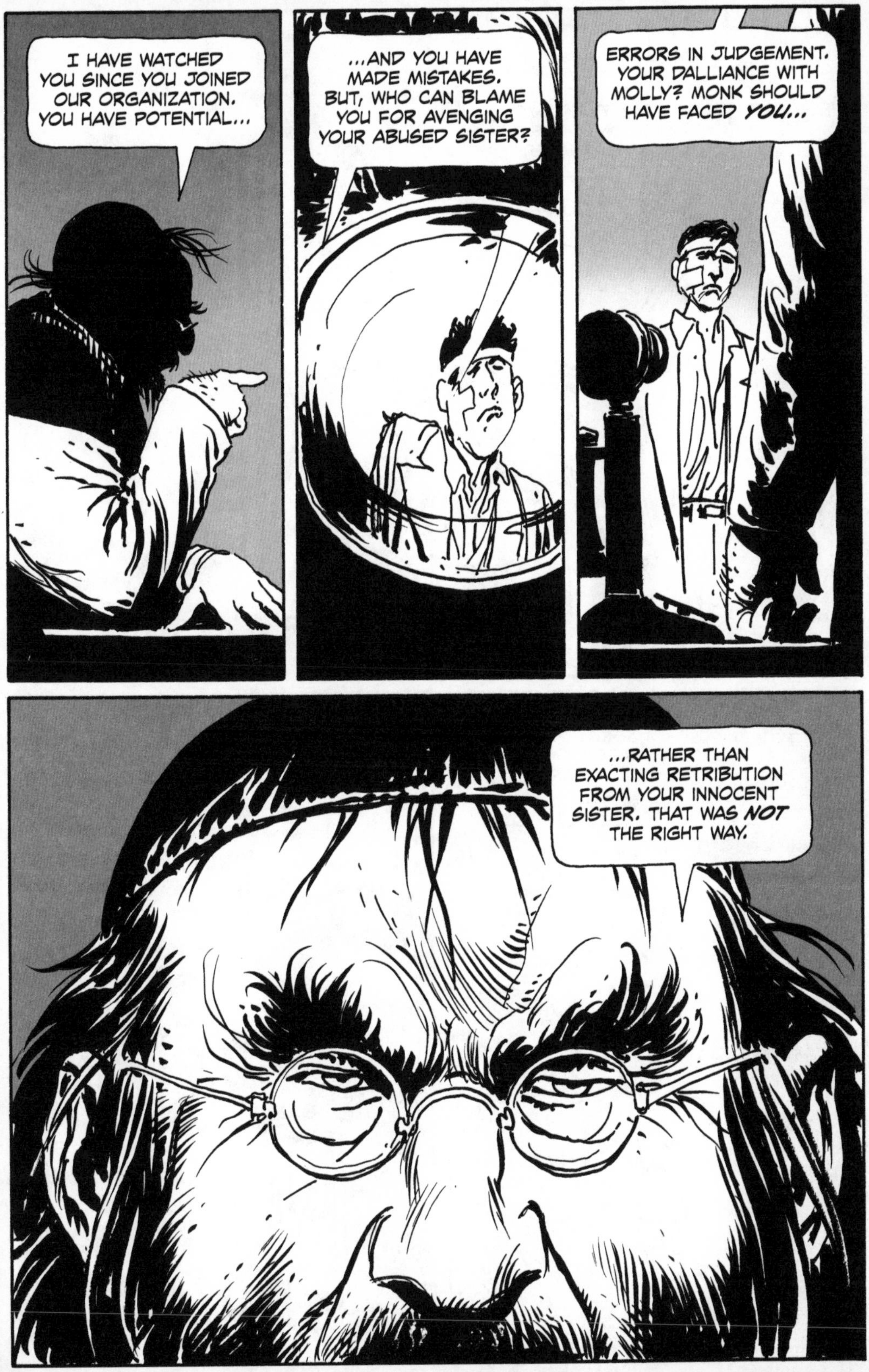
I HAVE WATCHED YOU SINCE YOU JOINED OUR ORGANIZATION. YOU HAVE POTENTIAL...
...AND YOU HAVE MADE MISTAKES. BUT, WHO CAN BLAME YOU FOR AVENGING YOUR ABUSED SISTER?
ERRORS IN JUDGEMENT. YOUR DALLIANCE WITH MOLLY? MONK SHOULD HAVE FACED *YOU...*
...RATHER THAN EXACTING RETRIBUTION FROM YOUR INNOCENT SISTER. THAT WAS *NOT* THE RIGHT WAY.

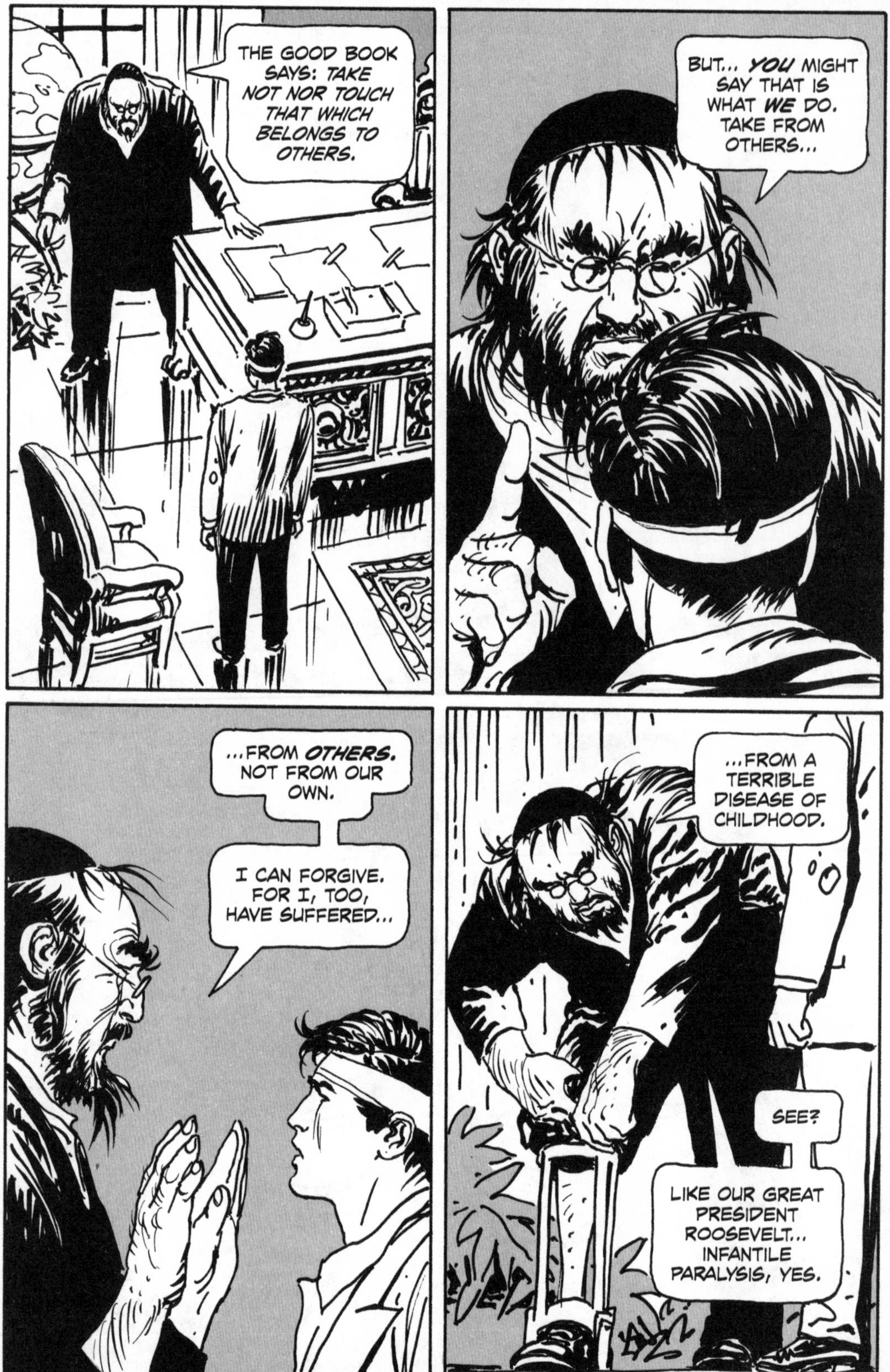
THE GOOD BOOK SAYS: TAKE NOT NOR TOUCH THAT WHICH BELONGS TO OTHERS.
BUT... YOU MIGHT SAY THAT IS WHAT WE DO. TAKE FROM OTHERS...
...FROM OTHERS. NOT FROM OUR OWN.
I CAN FORGIVE. FOR I, TOO, HAVE SUFFERED...
...FROM A TERRIBLE DISEASE OF CHILDHOOD.
SEE?
LIKE OUR GREAT PRESIDENT ROOSEVELT... INFANTILE PARALYSIS, YES.

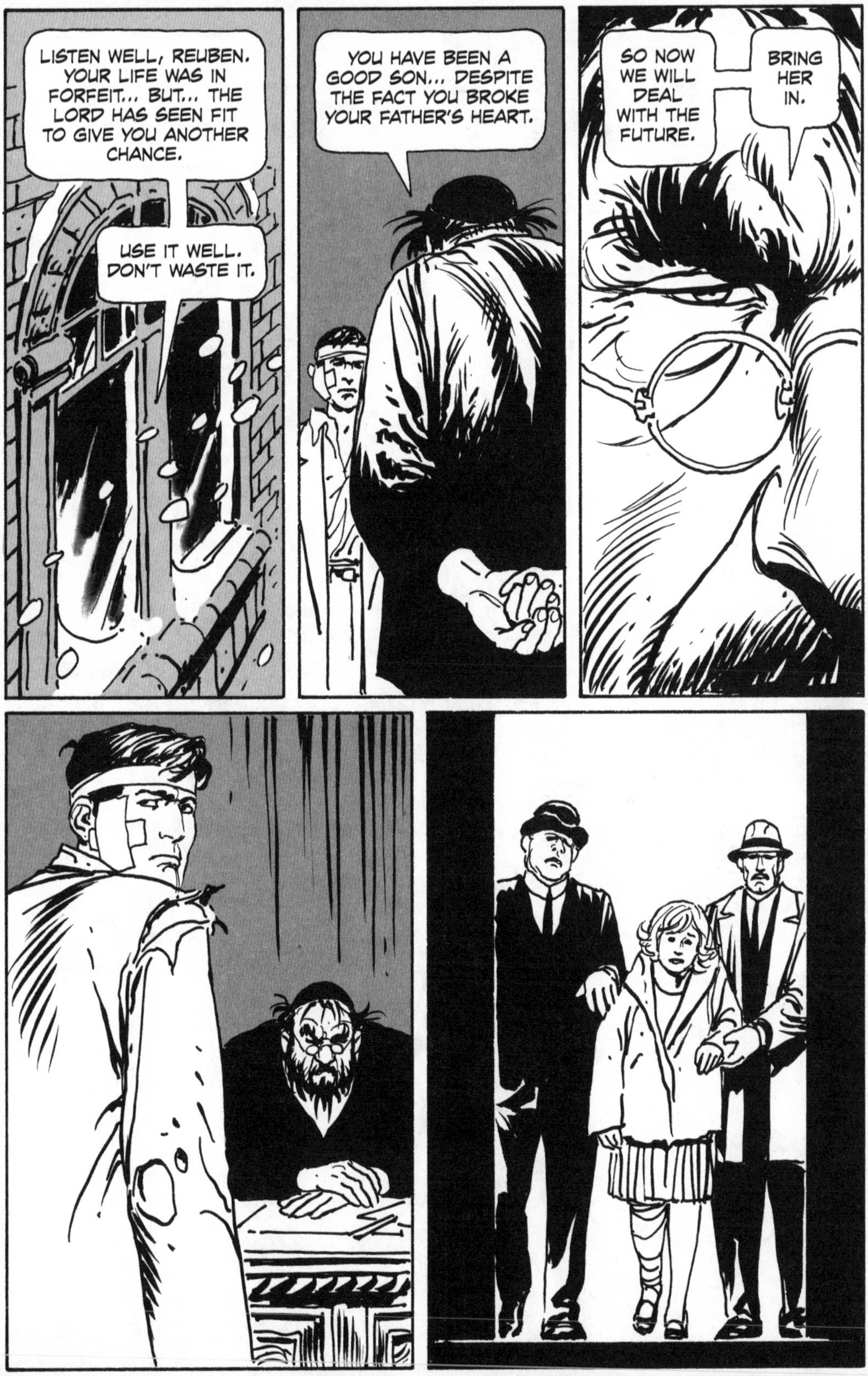
LISTEN WELL, REUBEN. YOUR LIFE WAS IN FORFEIT... BUT... THE LORD HAS SEEN FIT TO GIVE YOU ANOTHER CHANCE.
USE IT WELL. DON'T WASTE IT.
YOU HAVE BEEN A GOOD SON... DESPITE THE FACT YOU BROKE YOUR FATHER'S HEART.
SO NOW WE WILL DEAL WITH THE FUTURE.
BRING HER IN.

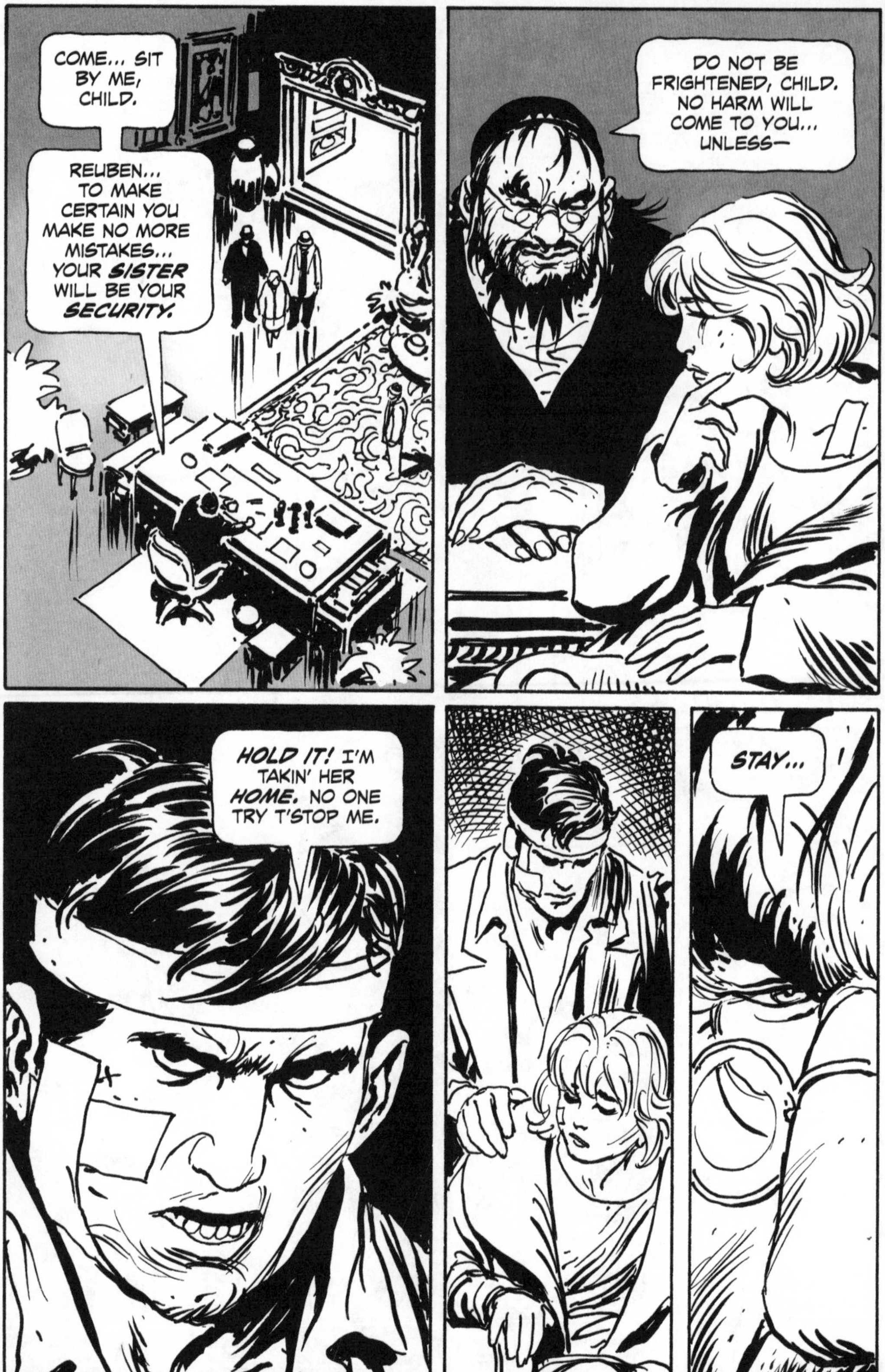
COME... SIT BY ME, CHILD.
REUBEN... TO MAKE CERTAIN YOU MAKE NO MORE MISTAKES... YOUR SISTER WILL BE YOUR SECURITY.
DO NOT BE FRIGHTENED, CHILD. NO HARM WILL COME TO YOU... UNLESS—
HOLD IT! I'M TAKIN' HER HOME. NO ONE TRY T'STOP ME.
STAY...

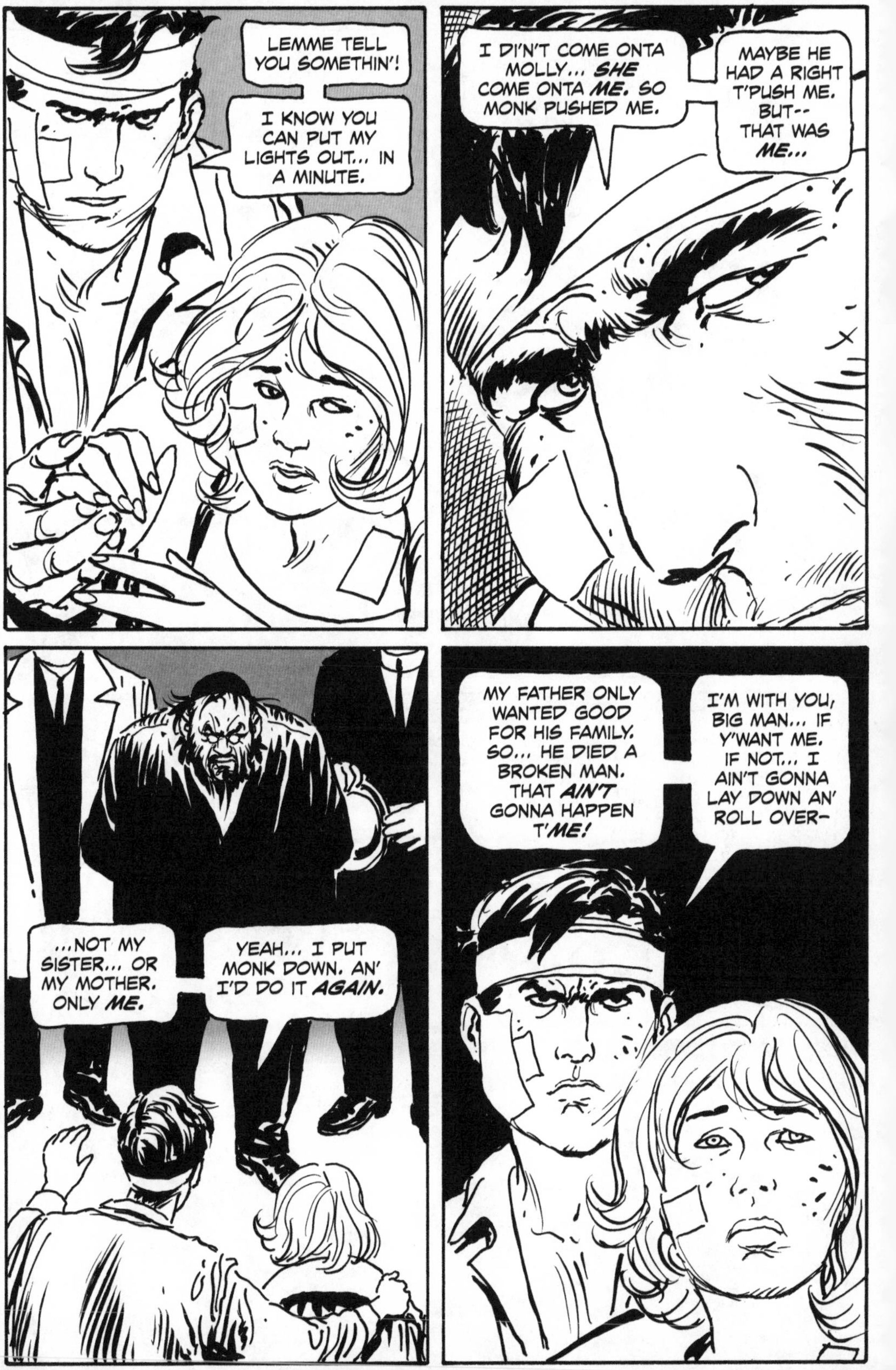
LEMME TELL YOU SOMETHIN'!
I KNOW YOU CAN PUT MY LIGHTS OUT... IN A MINUTE.
I DI'N'T COME ONTA MOLLY... SHE COME ONTA ME. SO MONK PUSHED ME.
MAYBE HE HAD A RIGHT T'PUSH ME. BUT-- THAT WAS ME...
...NOT MY SISTER... OR MY MOTHER. ONLY ME.
YEAH... I PUT MONK DOWN. AN' I'D DO IT AGAIN.
MY FATHER ONLY WANTED GOOD FOR HIS FAMILY. SO... HE DIED A BROKEN MAN. THAT AIN'T GONNA HAPPEN T'ME!
I'M WITH YOU, BIG MAN... IF Y'WANT ME. IF NOT... I AIN'T GONNA LAY DOWN AN' ROLL OVER-

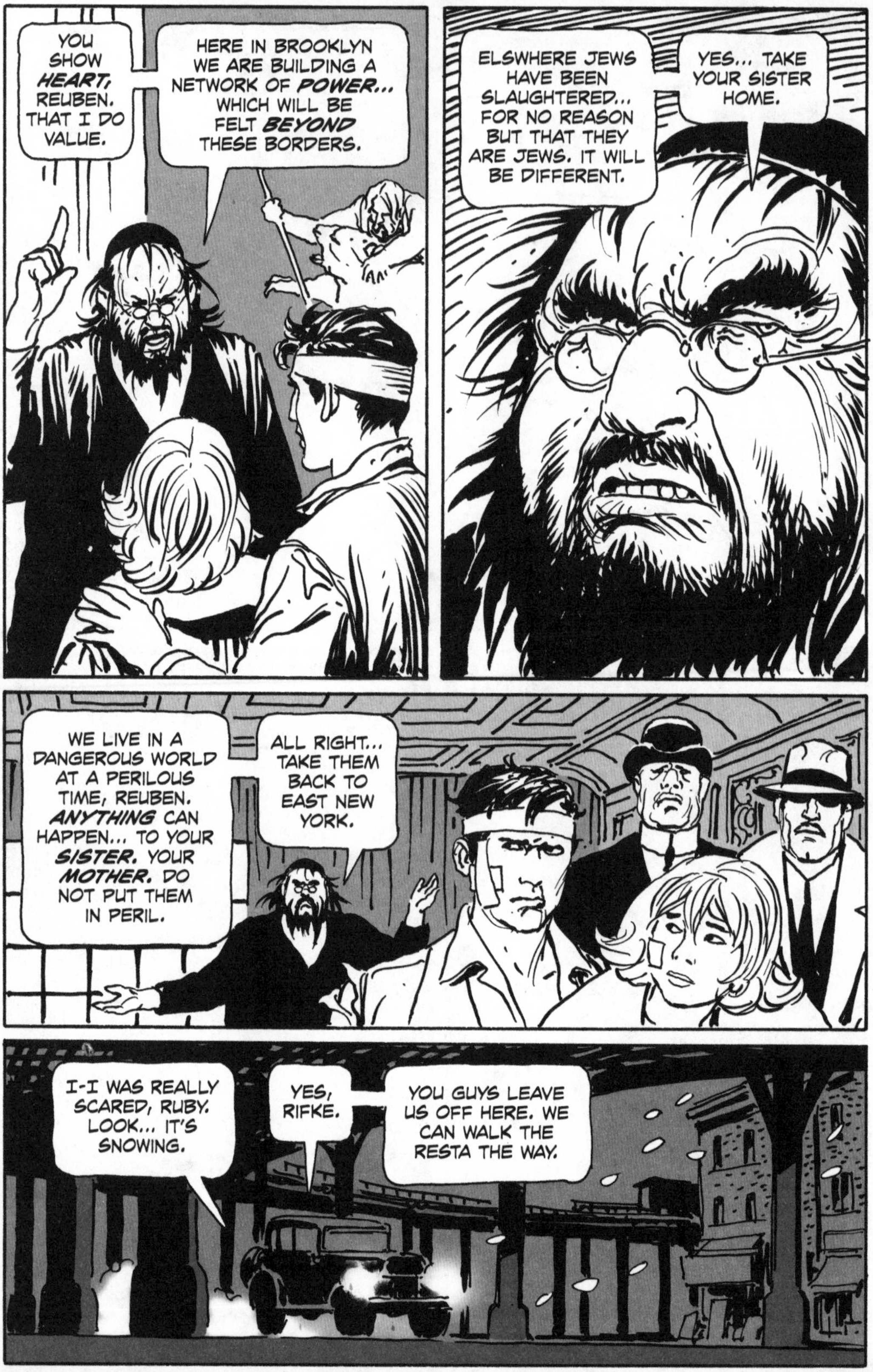
YOU SHOW HEART, REUBEN. THAT I DO VALUE.
HERE IN BROOKLYN WE ARE BUILDING A NETWORK OF POWER... WHICH WILL BE FELT BEYOND THESE BORDERS.
ELSWHERE JEWS HAVE BEEN SLAUGHTERED... FOR NO REASON BUT THAT THEY ARE JEWS. IT WILL BE DIFFERENT.
YES... TAKE YOUR SISTER HOME.
WE LIVE IN A DANGEROUS WORLD AT A PERILOUS TIME, REUBEN. ANYTHING CAN HAPPEN... TO YOUR SISTER. YOUR MOTHER. DO NOT PUT THEM IN PERIL.
ALL RIGHT... TAKE THEM BACK TO EAST NEW YORK.
I-I WAS REALLY SCARED, RUBY. LOOK... IT'S SNOWING.
YES, RIFKE.
YOU GUYS LEAVE US OFF HERE. WE CAN WALK THE RESTA THE WAY.

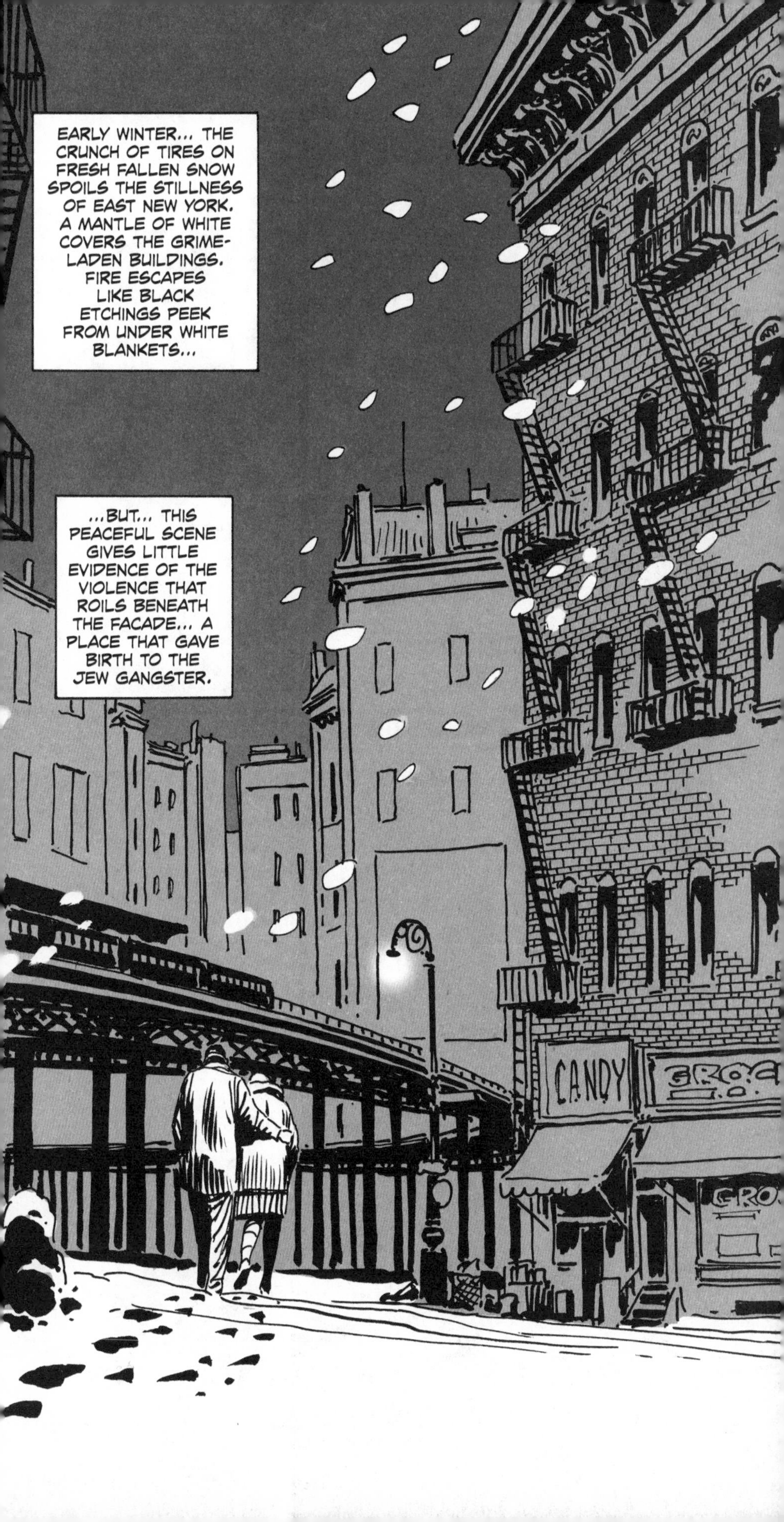
EARLY WINTER... THE CRUNCH OF TIRES ON FRESH FALLEN SNOW SPOILS THE STILLNESS OF EAST NEW YORK. A MANTLE OF WHITE COVERS THE GRIME-LADEN BUILDINGS. FIRE ESCAPES LIKE BLACK ETCHINGS PEEK FROM UNDER WHITE BLANKETS...
...BUT... THIS PEACEFUL SCENE GIVES LITTLE EVIDENCE OF THE VIOLENCE THAT ROILS BENEATH THE FACADE... A PLACE THAT GAVE BIRTH TO THE JEW GANGSTER.
CANDY

MORE TITLES IN THE

JOE KUBERT

LIBRARY

DONG XOAI, VIETNAM 1965

SGT ROCK: THE PROPHECY

TOR: A PREHISTORIC ODYSSEY

TOR ARCHIVES VOL 1-3

VIKING PRINCE

YOSSEL